THE BASIC TEACHINGS OF THE
Great Economists

EVERYDAY HANDBOOK SERIES

BASIC TEACHINGS OF THE
GREAT ECONOMISTS

by JOHN W. McCONNELL

BARNES & NOBLE, Inc.

New York

PUBLISHERS • BOOKSELLERS • SINCE 1874

Printed in the United States of America

Contents

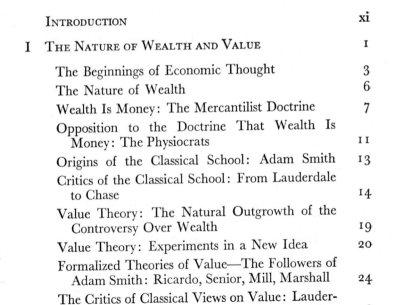

Introduction

THE BASIC TEACHINGS OF THE GREAT ECONOMISTS is a straightforward discussion of economic ideas for the general reader with an interest in economics. Today, more than in any other period in human history everyone needs to know how our economic system works and why. We live in a world dominated by economic forces and economic ideas. To live in such a world intelligently men and women need to know something about it. The events of the past few decades have borne home to us two important facts: first, that most of the world's real difficulties are essentially economic difficulties; and, second, that the economic well-being of one person or nation is inextricably bound up with that of every other person or nation. The workman, the farmer, the businessman, the housewife, in fact all who produce, exchange, or consume goods, are active members of a vast, inter-related economic society. An enlightened citizenry such as America boasts can ill afford to be without some definite knowledge of the underlying principles upon which that society rests.

The basic principles of modern economic society are not new.

They are truly the product of the past. For that reason, in this book the views of economists of the past are included, as well as those of the present. We often delude ourselves into thinking that our problems are unique; but there are few features of modern economy which the great economists of earlier days did not face in their own times. Many of these outstanding scholars were practical men of affairs, businessmen and political leaders, as well as students, consequently their ideas and programs are pertinent to modern life. I do not mean to suggest that all modern economic issues can be clarified by a study of the past. Nevertheless, the confusion and complexity of our problems makes it more necessary than ever to seek whatever insight and understanding the teachings of the great economists can give us.

In organizing the material of the book I have assigned to each of the eleven chapters a topic which is an answer to the question, "What are the most important economic ideas that concern men and women today?" There seemed to be no doubt that chapters should be devoted to such topics as wealth, capital, wages, profit, labor and labor organization, money, credit, taxes, foreign trade, and planning. Each chapter presents the thoughts of economists of the past and present on one of these major topics. The result is a picture of the growth of ideas, in different centuries, under different circumstances, in the minds of different men up to and including the time when they appear as powerful forces shaping the activities of people everywhere.

In any one part of the book the focus of attention is upon a problem, an idea, an institution, a practice, considered in terms of the thought of individual economists. For example, in the discussion of wealth, I have tried to summarize briefly how different economists defined wealth, how they thought it was obtained most effectively, how they thought it should be used, and what the government ought to do about wealth getting, if anything.

The book may also be read in such a way as to make the economists, rather than the problems, occupy the center of the stage. Thus the reader may obtain a complete picture of the economic views of Adam Smith, for example, by turning to the section devoted to his thought in each of the chapters—the index has been planned with this use in mind. What a man thinks is a consequence in part of the environment in which he lives; therefore, in the course of the discussion I have taken occasion to mention the important facts associated with the life and times of many of the economists. In addition, a brief biographical sketch of each of them with dates appears in the Biographical Notes at the end of the book.

The great need today is not alone for more adequate information, but also for a more intelligent use by more people of our present knowledge. The aim of this book, therefore, is the enlightenment of the layman, not the contribution of new data or new ideas to the history of economic thought—a field in which the works of Professors Haney, Whittaker, Roll, Cannan, Spann, Gide and Rist, and Viner are already landmarks. I hope that men and women who want to have an acquaintance with economics as part of their general background will find here an open door to one of the most challenging subjects of modern society.

JOHN W. McCONNELL

THE BASIC TEACHINGS OF THE
Great Economists

CHAPTER I

The Nature of Wealth and Value

PLATO   ARISTOTLE   AQUINAS
QUESNAY   TURGOT   MUN   CANTILLON
ADAM SMITH   LAUDERDALE   RAE   LIST   SAY
RICARDO   SENIOR   JEVONS   VON BÖHM—BAWERK
KARL MARX   WALRAS   MARSHALL

*Economics is sometimes called the science of wealth; but
what is wealth? What gives things value? Are things valuable because they are useful? Because they are scarce? Because they require labor to produce them? Because someone
is willing to pay money for them? What conceptions of
wealth exist under a system of intense nationalism? Do religious or ethical principles influence our ideas of wealth
and the methods by which it is obtained?*

As far back as research into the life and habits of mankind
can take us, there is ample evidence that every society has spent
much of its time and not a little of its thought upon securing
those material things which support life and increase its satisfac-
tions. To describe this activity and to define the general principles underlying and controlling it is the subject matter of
economics.

To be sure, the lines of separation between what is economic
behavior and what is not are often blurred and indistinct. In one

direction economics fades off into the field of philosophy and psychology. What do men really want in life? What are the basic needs which men feel compelled to satisfy? How do men in general arrive at evaluations of the objects surrounding them? What is the highest good for which men should strive? Plato, Aristotle, Xenophon, Augustine, and Thomas Aquinas were concerned with an investigation of economic matters only as they were important to—and shed light upon—such basic questions as these, or as economic activity needed to be brought into line with a general principle of life already established.

In another direction we find economics influencing and being influenced by social institutions. The activities of the family, the state, the church, the systems of law, all are inextricably interwoven with the processes of production, exchange, and consumption of material goods. Any attempt therefore, either now or in the past, to describe economic matters as though they were confined to a separate and distinct area of life results in an exceedingly artificial discussion.

Economic problems are paramount in our age. Indeed, few people are satisfied unless they can find an economic explanation for everything that occurs. But other ages were different. Concern with the material was frequently subordinated to more important and more respectable pursuits. At the very utmost, economic activity was considered as a means to an end. It remained for our modern industrial civilization to turn things around so that those actions which directly or indirectly result in economic gain are considered as the most worth while.

The subordination of economic activity to other interests is responsible in part for the paucity of systematically developed economic doctrines in early civilizations. To be sure, most of the great writers of the past at times dwelt upon economic questions, and many of them were far in advance of their age in the understanding of certain economic principles. But such space as they gave to economics in their writings tended to subordinate it to discussions of the state, of ethics, or of justice. Further, the absence of economic literature in the past may be due in part to the fact that production and exchange were carried on by the less respected members of the community. In the highly stratified societies of ancient Greece and Rome or the Middle Ages only those of inferior status engaged directly in manufacture and trade, and most writers accordingly considered the affairs of such people beneath their dignity. To write about them would have been unwarranted effort. And then again, knowledge of economic matters was scant. Aside from those facts of common observation, little was known of the basic characteristics of production, exchange, and consumption. It would have been impossible in the absence of such knowledge to treat economics systematically. Thus an intensive investigation into the fundamentals awaited the opening of the commercial era of the later Middle Ages and the appearance of the great mercantile states upon the world scene in the 15th century.

The Beginnings of Economic Thought

A few of the greatest men of early times gave consideration to economic problems, and sought principles which might explain them. Of all the ancients the early Greek thinkers contributed most to economic theory. Confined as their ideas were to a superficial treatment of domestic management, the revenue of the city state, and the regulation of occupations, they nevertheless dealt with the basic concepts of modern economic knowledge. PLATO (427–347 B. C.) made his chief contributions in his discussions of the division of labor. He noted the variety of men's needs and the variation in men's abilities and came to the logical conclusion that if everyone did the thing most natural to him greater production would result with a smaller expenditure of effort. Furthermore, specialization presupposed merchants to carry on exchange and a system of currency to facilitate the process.

Plato's ideal state as described in the *Republic* is a strange mixture of the real and the imaginary, of current practises interwoven with what ought to be. It would be difficult to look upon these general outlines of the ideal state as basic economic concepts; although such proposals as the subordination of the individual to the state, the specialization of labor, the rule of the wise, communism in wives and property, rules for the family, inheritance, limitation of population—all these certainly presuppose an acquaintance with economic matters. The *Laws* written some years later is a more realistic appraisal of the practical methods necessary to hold a city state together.

ARISTOTLE (384–322 B. C.) probed deeper into the character of economic activity and expressed himself more directly on these matters. Wealth, he believed, was of two kinds; true or genuine wealth which was limited in supply, and wealth gained through unnatural acquisition which was unlimited. The former was derived from specialized productive activity such as agriculture and mining, in which labor was applied to raw materials. The latter was acquired through the exchange of things having different values. This emphasis upon natural wealth forecasts the thought of the school of French economists of later years known as the Physiocrats. The tendency of modern economists to consider productive activity as only that which produces wealth in a material sense, would find little kinship with Aristotle, for he is emphatic in saying that pursuits which produce non-material values are far more important since the essence of a man, as of a city, is non-material.

Of all the forms of unnatural wealth, that acquired through usury was looked upon as the most objectionable. Aristotle could not conceive of money having a productive use, consequently usury was really appropriating unjustly the natural wealth earned by another. Money was merely an arbitrary, not a natural, form of wealth. Its value was, as he saw it, determined by man for his own convenience. The need for money was great, however, since it was the means whereby values were made comparable in the process of exchange; it performed a certain service also in enabling persons to defer the consumption of goods for a time, since the value of money tended to remain constant. In determining values, Aristotle emphasized the usefulness of the article as fundamental. His acknowledgment of the distinction between value in exchange and value in use placed him into the company of any one of the most modern schools of economic thought. Although he did not formulate anything which remotely resembled a system of economic thought, the relatively few comments which Aristotle did make summarized the current ideas of his time and laid foundation stones for the future schools of thought.

Centuries passed before another figure of the stature of Aristotle paid any attention to economic ideas. Then came THOMAS AQUINAS, a southern Italian cleric who lived from approximately 1225 to 1274. As with Plato and Aristotle, for whom economic matters were incidental to the conduct of the state and the development of certain abstract ideas, so with Aquinas. The society in which he lived was largely dominated by the Church and Christian philosophy on the one hand, and the philosophical ideas of Aristotle on the other. Economic activity of course went on. Since Aquinas was a native of southern Italy he certainly knew the importance of trade to the Italian cities. His contribution, as his work adequately demonstrates, was in making the Christian teachings practical for his time, and in finding a common ground upon which ethical and moral principles might exist side by side with buying and selling.

Early Christian doctrine had looked askance at wealth, and the character of the early Christian communities led many followers to think of Christianity as a type of communism although no direct admonition in that vein can be found. Aquinas took the attitude that wealth and private property were not in themselves either good or bad; it was the use to which they were put which determined their moral status. Property was a trust, placed in private hands to be used for social good. He believed it just as possible for wealth to serve as a means of greater virtue to the individual as to accomplish his moral degradation.

The other economic issues with which Thomas Aquinas concerned himself were the just price and the prohibition of usury. Both were practical applications of the principle of justice which was considered the abiding rule of human relationship in medieval Christian communities. The theories of Thomas Aquinas, which will be discussed more appropriately in later chapters, were essentially revelations of the mental uncertainties occurring under the stress of economic change which went with the growing commercialization of the 13th century. To harmonize both religious and secular knowledge with the practises of the time and with each other was no small task. The completeness with which the work was done gives Aquinas a permanent place among the great intellects of history in spite of the fact that of all the writers on economics, his ideas seem farthest from the trends of current thought. It is not unlikely, however, that some of his theories will again receive prominence as automatic processes in competition give place to forms of public regulation.

The Nature of Wealth

The search for those things which support life and give it meaning has ever been the quest of mankind. Not every age has considered the same things important in this respect, however. Consequently, each age may differ as to the focus of its greatest efforts and the center of its attention. Yet, in spite of the differences, wealth in one form or another has held a more or less prominent place in the history of every civilization. It has brought ease of life, prestige among one's fellows, and power. Naturally it has been much sought after, and such an important factor in social life has received great attention from philosophers, religious leaders, and rulers of the people, as well as economists.

However, our concern is primarily with the views of the economists.

The systematic treatment of wealth as an economic matter begins in the great age of discovery and exploration, roughly during the 15th century. Whatever may have been the incentive, the period was marked by voyages of discovery to the new world of the west by men whose chief interest was the search for silver and gold. Thus was started a chain of events which led to the formation of an economic theory called Mercantilism.

Europe, during the period known as the Middle Ages, was a loose conglomeration of cities and feudal estates with vague lines of authority binding together the dukes, barons, freemen, and serfs of the same language or the same area. Central government as we know it today did not exist. Whatever unifying force existed was exercised by the Church. As commerce and trade increased in scope, political units expanded in size and the heads of states acquired more power, usually at the expense of lesser nobles and the Church. This process was not a simple one, for it was accompanied by such complex movements in history as the Reformation, the Commercial Revolution, and the birth of new political philosophies. The end result, however, was the rise of the great states with absolute monarchs whose courts were the most extravagant in the Christian era. The demands of the latter were the prods of necessity which played no little part in stimulating the more comprehensive study of economic life made by the Mercantilists. They were concerned with the ways and means by which nations could become wealthy.

Wealth Is Money: The Mercantilist Doctrine

The Mercantilists thought of wealth primarily as gold and silver, or—to use a term common at that time—treasure. Most followers of this doctrine acknowledged, perhaps indirectly, that consumable goods were ultimately more important than money; yet since most people wanted money it was always possible to buy what was needed, whether it be goods for domestic consumption or materials of war—including mercenary soldiers. Consequently an abundance of money was more desirable than an abundance of goods. In the absence of a natural supply of silver and gold a favorable balance of exports over imports, which would be paid for in "treasure," was the broad way to wealth.

THOMAS MUN (1571–1641) gave the clearest exposition of the Mercantile theory. He was an Englishman with an active interest in trade. As a merchant he had amassed a large fortune and he subsequently became a member of the Committee of the East India Company and of the parliamentary standing commission on trade. The statement of Mercantilist principles is found in his book bearing the enlightening title *England's Treasure by Forraign Trade, or, The Balance of Our Forraign Trade Is the Rule of Our Treasure.* His main contention was that to increase the wealth of the nation, England must sell to other countries more than she bought from them. In a series of clear admonitions he advised his people to cultivate unused lands; reduce the consumption of foreign wares and avoid frivolous changes in fashion; be clever in selling to foreign nations, holding the prices high on necessities which they must buy and cutting prices on goods having strong competitors; carry English goods to foreign nations in English bottoms, thus getting the price of the goods and the fees of the transporter; be frugal in the use of natural resources, saving them as much as possible for export; develop industries at home to supply necessities; make England a center for exchange between other nations, thus increasing the trade in and out of England; trade as close to the primary producer as possible, thus eliminating or acquiring for England the fees of the trader; place no embargo on the export of money because it is necessary to foster trade between other nations from which England can earn a profit by acting as middleman; place no taxes on articles made primarily for export. These are the tenets of the thrifty business man extended to apply to the nation. They imply the close co-operation of the government and the business interests. Indeed, during the financial administrations of Colbert in France and Cromwell in England, these principles were given fuller application than most economic principles have ever had the opportunity to enjoy. Mercantilism was above all a practical working philosophy of wealth-getting.

Italy was the home of the earliest and most positive exponent of the Mercantilist doctrine. Antonio Serra admitted no quibbling over what constituted wealth—it was gold and silver. In his pamphlet, *A Brief Treatise on the Causes Which Can Make Gold and Silver Abound in Kingdoms Where There Are No Mines,* he set forth certain rules for the production of an abundant supply of the precious metals aside from a natural supply. He advised emphasis upon manufactures; an abundant population; an extensive foreign trade with a favorable balance; and positive government regulations fostering and protecting such trade. These principles were illustrated by a comparison of the favorable economic position of Venice as contrasted with the poverty of Naples.

A more nationalistic twist was given to Mercantilism by ANTOINE DE MONTCHRETIEN (1576–1621). In his *Traicté de l'Œconomie Politique,* published in 1615, this French theorist berated his country not alone for the importation of goods which by a little effort the people could produce for themselves but also for throwing their country open to foreign traders who drained off the natural wealth of the country, and for the importation of foreign books which undermined the strength and vitality of French culture. Montchretien deviated from the line of pure Mercantilist thought, if there can be said to be such, in the emphasis he placed upon domestic trade to the exclusion of foreign trade. His point was simply that France could, if all would labor industriously, be self-sufficient and maintain a high level of material existence. He also acknowledged that wealth was constituted not alone of money but of the abundance of commodities maintaining life. To make sure that sufficient quantities of such commodities were available for all was the chief business of the state. It was this obligation of the state for the economic well-being of the people which led to his coining the term by which economics was so long known, *political economy*.

The last of the Mercantilists was SIR JAMES STEUART (1712–1780). His *Inquiry into the Principles of Political Economy* (with an extremely long secondary title), published in 1867, was the most systematic and comprehensive survey of the Mercantile theory up to that time. Unfortunately for Steuart, the labor and penetrating insight he brought to bear upon the subject yielded him no recognition; for Mercantilism had fallen into disrepute, and Adam Smith gave it the coup de grâce only nine years later with a keen analysis of both the practical and logical shortcomings of Mercantilist doctrine. Steuart's viewpoint was a strange mixture. He believed that a favorable balance of foreign trade was necessary to keep up the wealth of the nation in terms of money, yet he realized that an excess of specie might be detrimental. His discourse on such topics as population, value, agriculture, interest, credit, and taxation was sound and in line with the best thinking of his time; but throughout the work there is the constant emphasis upon the paternal responsibility of the state to regulate, control, and direct economic activity in the interest of national advantage. It was this aspect of his treatise which prevented his rightful recognition in England, yet made him respected above Adam Smith in Germany.

In the works of Philipp W. von Hornick, Johann Joachim Becker, and J. H. Justi (Austrian and German economists of the 18th and 19th centuries) a particular brand of Mercantilism known as Kameralism (*Kameralwissenschaft*) was expounded. Their ideas on wealth were similar to those of the true Mercantilists except that while in their theory money was important to the wealth and power of the state, economic self-sufficiency was likewise important. Hence all kinds of produce, agricultural and industrial, was wealth as long as it was produced at home. The same articles produced abroad and imported actually represented a loss of wealth. These writers were predecessors of the more modern economic nationalists.

Opposition to the Doctrine That Wealth Is Money: The Physiocrats

The reaction to the strictly shopkeeper's appraisal of wealth held by the Mercantilists came first in France where the theories of the Physiocrats became prominent. The name Physiocrats was first applied by one of this school's early members, Dupont de Nemours, and later changed by the members themselves to *Economistes.* Then when the latter term became a general designation for persons of all shades of thought who dealt with the subject of political economy, scholars again referred to this early school as the Physiocrats. The father of the school and the best exponent of its doctrines was FRANÇOIS QUESNAY (1694–1774) a physician, who delved into the problems of economics as an avocation toward the end of his life. Wealth, he said, does not consist in the quantity of money a nation can store up but in the quantity of raw materials available for the purposes of man, or, to put it differently, the increase in wealth of a community consists in the surplus of agricultural and mineral products over their cost of production. This excess is called the *produit net* and upon it depends the well-being of the nation. Manufacturing gives new form to raw materials, but their increase in value is only the quantity of other materials used and consumed in the elaboration. Commerce merely transfers wealth from person to person. What the traders gain is acquired at the cost of the nation and should be as small as possible. The professions are useful but "sterile," that is, they draw income not from what they create but from the surplus created by the producers of raw materials.

The Physiocratic ideas on political economy did not develop from an appraisal of that phase of life alone, but rather as an integral part of the school's comprehensive view of the world in all its aspects. Dupont de Nemours defined Physiocracy as the science of the natural order. The system of thought assumed that there were natural laws which governed man and the universe. To attain true satisfaction in life it was but necessary to discover these laws and conform to them. Since the basis of satisfactory human existence was believed to be in nature, the Physiocrats made the logical deduction that nature was the only true source of wealth, manufacturing and trade were *sterile* or at best creators of artificial wealth. The presentation of these ideas was made in Quesnay's first publications on economics, two articles in the *Encyclopedie,* entitled respectively "Farmers" and "Grains." More detailed explanation of his thesis appeared in 1758 in the *Tableau economique.* The *Tableau* explained how wealth originated in agriculture, and how it was subsequently distributed to both the sterile and the productive classes in the population. Known as the Bible of the Physiocrats, the *Tableau* has aroused great controversies in the nearly two centuries since it was written as to its exact meaning and significance.

Quesnay's belief in the existence of a natural order of things which would serve man's purpose better than the existing order led to certain other ideas of a very modern hue. He believed that every individual should seek the greatest amount of pleasure for the least effort, as this would insure rather than endanger the natural order. Physiocracy gave birth to the famous doctrine of *laissez-faire, laissez-passer* (that is, let things proceed without interference). The work of the legislator was to aid in the discovery of natural laws, and not to interfere with their operation by artificial control. Everyone should have the right to enjoy the fruits of his own labor—hence private property became to the Physiocrats a cornerstone of the natural state. Trade should be free. As Quesnay took great pains to show, the arguments for a favorable balance of trade were logically and practically unsound. But although all trade was essentially unproductive, it was necessary to keep it free in order that the natural forces of competition might exert themselves and control the economic activity of the nations.

The followers of Quesnay were numerous; their ideas follow closely Quesnay's pattern. We have already mentioned Dupont de Nemours. A. R. J. TURGOT will be considered in later chapters. The Abbé Baudeau also contributed to the abundant literature describing Physiocracy. Of these three men, De Nemours was the most ardent disciple; Turgot, the most philosophically inclined; Abbé Baudeau, the keenest mind.

Origins of the Classical School: Adam Smith

The question of what constituted wealth and how nations might acquire it continued to be the most important economic problem of the time during which ADAM SMITH (1725–1790) lived and wrote in England and Scotland. One needs no further proof of this than the title of his world-famous book, *An Inquiry into the Nature and the Causes of the Wealth of Nations,* which was published in 1776. Smith realized that goods had both value in use and value in exchange, but he was convinced that the only objective and measurable value, and hence the only reasonable basis for a systematic analysis of economic principles was exchange value. With this in mind, wealth could have one meaning only for Smith; it was the sum total of all exchange values which an individual or a nation possessed. The central theme running through *The Wealth of Nations* is the importance of the division of labor as a means of adding to the store of wealth. This does not mean, as some writers maintain, that Smith was the formulator of the theory of industrialism. It does mean, however, that many of Smith's economic theories were rooted in his contention that the division of labor was the chief means of increasing wealth. It is labor of all types which produces wealth; not nature nor the labor of agriculturalists only, as the Physiocrats contended. From this premise Adam Smith derived his labor theory of value; this is, that the value of an object is equal to the quantity of labor it can demand in exchange for itself. From it also arose his emphasis upon exchange as the focus of economic activity, for obviously if there is division of labor and no one makes for himself all he needs, exchange becomes the only way whereby everyone can acquire what he needs to sustain life.

There has always been lively controversy as to the sources of Smith's ideas. The passing of time has shown that he must be considered as the founder of Economics as a social discipline in its own right; but that there were important forerunners to Smith who made contributions to his thinking is to be expected. First, there was Francis Hutcheson (1694–1746) who was Adam Smith's teacher and his predecessor as Professor of Moral Philosophy at the University of Glasgow. Hutcheson intimated the importance of the division of labor, and the possible use of labor as a basis of value. Moreover, the general outline of *The Wealth of Nations* seems to have been drawn from Hutcheson's *System of Moral Philosophy,* published after his death. Although better known as a philosopher than as an economist, David Hume also contributed much to Smith. His essays on economic subjects laid the basis for Smith's appraisal of Mercantilism and the opposing justification of free trade. Lastly, while Smith takes some pains to dispute many of the theories of the Physiocrats, he unquestionably owes much to his acquaintance with Quesnay and Turgot, especially in the development of his ideas on the distribution of income. There is such a close resemblance between some of the ideas expressed in *The Wealth of Nations* and those of the Physiocrats that one might justifiably raise the question as to whether Smith was not himself in part a Physiocrat. Smith's treatment of the ideas of the French school, however, surpass even their best presentations in clarity and practicality.

Critics of the Classical School: From Lauderdale to Chase

The first and most important of Smith's critics was a Scottish peer, James Maitland, eighth Earl of Lauderdale. In his book entitled, *Inquiry into the Nature and Origin of Public Wealth and into the Nature and Causes of Its Increase,* published in 1804, Lauderdale said that individual wealth was determined to a large extent by the scarcity of the objects possessed. He reasoned that since exchange value is a basic consideration in estimating wealth, and since exchange value may be determined in part by the scarcity of the object, one is led to a conclusion at which common sense revolts, that wealth can be increased by making things scarce. When the riches of an individual are increased by the augmentation in the value of their possessions, he argued, the wealth of the community must have been decreased, and a conflict in public and private interest is therefore inevitable. Lauderdale further criticised Smith for the latter's belief that the nation's store of capital might—like an individual's—be increased by saving. He apparently was fearful of a condition of an oversupply of capital goods and underconsumption of consumers' goods. In this he anticipated certain modern economists by well over 125 years.

JOHN RAE (1786–1873) was another critic of Adam Smith taking much the same line of attack as Lauderdale. In his chief work, *A Statement of Some New Principles on the Subject of Political Economy,* published in 1834, he said that while individuals grow rich by securing ownership of a larger proportion of the wealth already in existence, nations grow wealthy by the creation of new wealth. For this reason he assigned to invention a place of primary importance in the nation's life. Rae wrote on other economic topics with an insight far beyond his time. His arguments for protection of infant industries were used by John Stuart Mill; his objection to the lavish consumption of wealth, purely for the sake of show or to excite envy in one's fellows, was later elaborated by Veblen in *The Theory of the Leisure Class.* Rae's keen psychological analysis of time as an explanation of interest and the accumulation of wealth were exceptional not only for his time but for ours.

As one goes from the English-speaking economists of the early 19th century to those of central Europe, the criticisms of Smith and his views upon wealth become more comprehensive. Whereas Smith assumed that economic life could be treated systematically without reference to other phases of life, and its operation controlled by natural laws inherent within itself, the early German and Austrian economists began with the opposite assumption. Economic life, they believed, was bound up with all the rest of life; and since the welfare of the state was so dependent upon it, economic activity had to be subordinated to and guided by the government. ADAM MÜLLER (1779–1829) was one of the first European critics of Adam Smith who followed this reasoning. In *Die Elemente der Staatskunst,* published in 1810, he pointed out that the importance which things have to the state must be considered in calculating value, and the question of what is wealth must be discussed in the light of what produces wealth and what conserves and maintains it, by which he meant, of course, the state. In one respect his theories reflected those of Lauderdale. He believed that, contrary to Smith, consumption, not abstinence, was the way to increase wealth. Müller's career as administrative officer and finally as councillor in the state chancellery of Austria gave to his works an air of practicality which survives in spite of the vague world philosophy which underlies his main principles of economics.

FRIEDRICH LIST (1789–1846) who was a contemporary of Müller's—he held the positions of Professor of Economics at Tübingen, administrative official, member of his state legislature, and political reformer—wrote in very much the same line of thought as Müller though in a more popular style. He believed Smith was wrong in confining his work to an analysis of wealth defined in terms of exchange value to the neglect of the productive forces which underlie these values. The well-being of a nation is assured by the development of productive powers rather than by the accumulation of wealth, he argued. In one respect

List went far beyond Müller. He conceived of productive forces as the entire institutional life of the state—its science, law, government, religion, and arts. Teachers, physicians, judges, and administrators do not produce wealth directly, but they develop what is more important, the productive powers of the nation. Something of the Mercantilist outlook clings to List. He believed in national self-sufficiency and in national wealth as distinct from individual wealth; he advocated protection as against free trade; and he emphasized manufacturing. Some of his views and those of other economists of his group seem to be working out historically with uncanny precision. List's major work, *Das Nationale System der Politischen Œkonomie,* published in 1841, was a popular exposition of the theories held by both himself and Müller. It was repetitious and poorly organized but its popular style got it wide circulation and consideration.

Two other aspects of the nature of wealth as described by Adam Smith were criticised by scholars who in most things were his close followers. The great French teacher and popularizer of the theories of Smith, JEAN BAPTISTE SAY (1767–1832), objected strenuously to the way in which Smith restricted wealth to material things bearing a value capable of being preserved. In Say's opinion the "immaterial products," such as physicians' and musicians' services, were wealth even though the value of their actions was consumed in the moment of production. He could see no reason, for example, why the work of a painter should be wealth (that is, bearing a value capable of being preserved) and the work of a musician be not reckoned as such. The argument has been carried even further. Why should not talent itself be considered as wealth although possessing none of the characteristics of wealth as defined by Smith?

John Stuart Mill (1806–1873), prominent in many fields of thought in England, did little toward originating any new facets to the existing views on wealth. His chief contribution was, as a follower of the classical school originated by Smith, the systematization in English of the views held by this school with such reasonable modifications as he saw fit to make. In this respect he and Say followed similar lines. Indeed, their views on wealth are almost identical. Mill said that wealth consisted of all useful or agreeable things which possessed value in exchange; they must be material and susceptible to accumulation. Like Say, also, he included the talents and skills.

Then there is a final criticism of wealth when defined as the sum total of all material objects having value in exchange. It is a criticism from a purely ethical point of view. Implicit in the writings of both Müller and List, it was first advanced directly by the essayist John Ruskin and more recently by Stuart Chase in his *Tragedy of Waste*. Things which possess value in exchange may include a great deal that is personally harmful and socially undesirable. Narcotics have value in exchange. In the field of medicine they make an important contribution to social well-being; but used as a habit they are distinctly bad. As Chase saw it, our society is burdened by the production of useless and harmful objects, frequently pushed onto an undesiring public by high-pressure advertising. Yet these things have value in exchange. Ruskin met the problem by coining the word illth to be applied to those objects which in his opinion were undesirable.

At most points the early socialists were critical of ideas advanced by the followers of Adam Smith, but on a definition of wealth they seemed to be in agreement. As a matter of fact, the socialists were not as much concerned over what constituted wealth as they were over how it was distributed and who owned it. KARL MARX (1818–1883) conceded that wealth in its economic sense consisted of an accumulation of commodities. Material possessions were not the only things of value, but they were the necessary prerequisites for achieving non-material values. Hence it was necessary to provide everyone with abundance of the material means of existence in order that all might enjoy the non-material advantages of society.

Value Theory: The Natural Outgrowth of the Controversy Over Wealth

As economic theory bordered on maturity, economists began to realize that definitions of wealth implied preliminary conceptions of utility and value. Early economists assumed an understanding of these terms or ignored their existence; those coming later felt that they needed to be more precise. Utility is defined as the power to satisfy a want or serve a purpose. If, as some writers claim, wealth includes all things which have utility, fresh air and sunshine are wealth. Yet that seems too broad an interpretation. To restrict the all-inclusive nature of this definition, the idea of scarcity was introduced. That had its fallacies too, for— as has been pointed out above—it is not common sense to hold that if items have become less plentiful, wealth has increased. And it is just as absurd to hold that if the quantity of goods in the country has increased—which may result in a decline in the value of each unit—the nation is thereby impoverished. A third way of analyzing wealth was to consider only those things which can be procured with difficulty. Thus the pain involved in the production was the essential factor in differentiating between things which were wealth and those which were not. Difficulties here are obvious. Is all labor of the same importance, the same quality, the same speed? If not, who is to determine the relationship between some labor and other labor? How could various kinds of wealth be evaluated for purposes of exchange? Thus—between the extremes of utility, scarcity, and labor—has the theory of value been evolved over the last two hundred years. Not that we have arrived at any acceptable statement as yet; for the specific problem of increasing farm income by creating scarcity of farm products without at the same time reducing the wealth of the nation has in recent years brought this issue once more to the fore.

If one were to look at the definition of value as a philosophical problem, it would resolve itself into the age-old conflict of the ideal versus the material. Value in the former sense is a subjective matter; it is an estimate of the power of an object to give satisfaction. In the latter sense there is a striving for objectivity: it is the quantity of an object which another object can command in exchange for itself. Attempts have been made to set a quantitative measure upon the utility possessed by an article in order to make the subjective aspect of value as concrete and exact as the objective. To most economists this is artificial. It is doubtful whether the gap between these two estimates of value can ever be bridged satisfactorily.

There has been and there still exists great confusion in economic thought upon the subject of the value and the market equivalent of value (which is *price*). Some writers think of these terms as interchangeable; others hold value to express all the underlying factors contributing to an ideal estimate of importance while price is but the reflection of unstable market conditions at a specific time. There is no solution to this difficulty save a more precise use of terms and adequate statement as to how they are being used.

Value Theory: Experiments in a New Idea

The volume of literature which was written on value, even before economics took form as a definite discipline, was considerable. Naturally the ideas were somewhat vague, but many of them hint at later ideas of great consequence. With the decline of the self-sufficient feudal manor and the rise of the town and appearance of commerce, the religious control over estimates of value disappeared. As Aquinas pointed out, the utility of an object might vary considerably depending upon the need which an individual felt; but this had little bearing upon the objective estimate of value (except in unusual circumstances), because the idea of the just price tied value inseparably to the value of the labor of the craftsman as judged by the standards of custom and status. What Aquinas was saying was reiterated centuries later. The value of an article, in the long run, is determined by the quantity of labor necessary to produce it.

Following Aquinas the emphasis tended to swing away from labor toward utility as the essential basis of value, though for some time the two ideas existed side by side. Buridan and Biel, writers of the 13th and 14th centuries, said that the ability to satisfy human needs was the basis of value, and was the cause of fluctuation in value as reflected in price. This view was shared at a later date by Nicholas Barbon (1640–1698) one of the early English writers who elaborated his ideas in a very modern form. Things derive their value, he believed, from their capacity to serve the needs of men's bodies and minds. However, he recognized that the supply of articles available for use influenced their "present value" or price. Ultimately the market was the best judge of value; therefore, price and value were essentially the same.

Sir William Petty (1623–1687), a British writer on economic statistics, added land as a value-producing factor. "While labor is the father and active principle of wealth, earth is the mother," is an often quoted expression to which he subscribed. He believed that land as well as labor should be considered in any system of evaluation. He apparently was searching for some method to express labor and land in terms of each other. At another point in his works he said that the cost of a day's food for an average adult man is a better measure of his value than the day's labor.

John Locke (1632–1704), a contemporary of Petty's, took the opposite position. Labor determined value; land as such was valueless and it was only by the application of labor that it yielded any value at all. Capital was labor stored up in tools and equipment. This theory, incidentally, reappeared in Ricardo and in socialist thought nearly two hundred years later. Locke was quite aware of the short-term effects of supply and demand upon price, or market value. Over short periods, and in a superficial sense, supply and demand affect value, he said, but in the long run labor alone (which is the principal cost of production) determines value. It is interesting too that he should have understood the principle of elastic and inelastic demand. He said, "Things absolutely necessary for life must be had at any rate; but things convenient will be had only as they stand in preference with other conveniences . . ." The idea of competition of substitutes was also known to him.

Though Adam Smith usually gets the credit, it was JOHN LAW (1671–1729) who first used the diamond-water example to illustrate his exchange theory of value. Water which is useful is plentiful and has no value in exchange, while diamonds which are useless command high prices. In his *Money and Trade Considered,* he said:

Goods have a value from the uses they are applied to; and their value is greater or lesser, not so much from their more or less valuable or necessary uses, as from the greater or lesser quantity of them in proportion to the demand for them. (pp. 4–5, 2nd ed.)

A return to emphasis on utility as a criterion of value is noted in the writings of TURGOT (1727–1781). In fact the systematic formulation of this concept is sometimes credited to him. He was aware that value was created by several factors, but the most important was the need of the individual, or, in other words, the utility which an object possessed to the individual. There was, of course, great variation in utility from individual to individual, from time to time, and from place to place. Future need and difficulty of attainment also influenced evaluation. As far as market price was concerned, Turgot understood the importance of supply and demand, and believed that midway between the various offers and demands a price would be set.

RICHARD CANTILLON (1680–1734) was a French banker who laid the foundation for the classical theory of value in his *Essay upon the Nature of Commerce in General* which was published in 1755. (Adam Smith acknowledged his dependency upon the work of Cantillon from time to time.) The intrinsic value of a commodity is the measure of the quantity and quality of land and labor entering into its production. Market prices are set by supply and demand and do not always reflect intrinsic value, although for commodities that are in constant demand and general use the market price is stable and remains close to the intrinsic worth. Other prices vary greatly, being in general determined by supply and demand, but also fluctuating according to the whims and fancies of bargainers and the aggressiveness of sellers.

Twenty years after Cantillon's *Essay* came *The Wealth of Nations*. At the outset Smith distinguished between the two types of value—value in use, and value in exchange. These two values are seldom equal, for things which have value in use may be plentiful and have no value in exchange, and vice versa. It is at this point in his explanation that he uses the previously mentioned diamond-water illustration employed earlier by John Law.

Although not a thoroughgoing advocate of the labor theory of value, Smith nevertheless indicated that value in exchange was rooted in the labor necessary to acquire it. In fact labor was the original purchase price paid for all things. While gold and silver vary in the amount of labor they may purchase, the quantity of labor necessary to produce a commodity varies but little from time to time, thought Smith. The latter is the real estimate of value, however much prices may change. The labor value is the real price; the money value is the nominal price.

But it was only in the simplest societies that commodities were really exchanged on, or in consideration of, their labor value. When land became scarce, and capital important, the owners of such could exact a fee for their use which had to be met out of the market price of the commodity; consequently labor costs no longer were the only costs which established real price. It is not clear whether Smith believed that rent and interest came out of value created by labor or whether additional value was added from a different source to provide for their share.

Smith recognized the difficulties inherent in applying the labor theory of value. Since he had already intimated that it could apply only in relatively simple communities, he did not worry about such problems as how various degrees of skill and speed were to be equated, or how persons in entirely different occupations would balance their effort. Nevertheless, he indicated that labor never could be evaluated on a purely quantitative basis, for esteem and prestige modified the evaluation of different kinds of work.

Market values fluctuated above and below the normal values set by the cost of production (costs of labor, land, and capital). Prices could not continue long at variance with normal value, for a kind of magnetism made up of forces in the economic order itself tended to draw them together. However, monopolies and "natural causes" might temporarily or permanently sustain market values above the normal value level.

Formalized Theories of Value—The Followers of Adam Smith: Ricardo, Senior, Mill, Marshall

For more than twenty-five years no serious criticism was raised against Adam Smith's analysis of value. Then a great economist arose, who, although associated with the classical tradition, in some respects took issue with and overshadowed the founder of the school himself. DAVID RICARDO (1772–1823) was the son of a London stockbroker, who at an early age made a fortune in the stock exchange and then retired to study and write in the field of economics. In analyzing the process of evaluation Ricardo assumed that competitive conditions existed. He ruled out the short-term market value as non-essential, and dealt exclusively with the long-term or normal value. Both scarcity and the quantity of labor required to produce articles influenced their value. Certain objects which could not be reproduced at all had their value set by scarcity alone, he believed. There were really so few of these that they did not need to be considered in the development of value theory. The economic life of the nation was carried on with commodities which could be produced in infinite quantity if sufficient labor were expended in their production. For these, labor costs set the basis of value. Since rent was paid on land only in terms of its superiority over the poorest land under cultivation, and capital was merely stored-up labor, logic indicated that only labor contributed to value. Qualitative differences in labor, as, for example, between skilled and unskilled, between the professional man and the common laborer, were of no moment since the market had long ago adjusted the differences and these were subject to little variation because of the power of custom.

In spite of the tenacity with which Ricardo held to the pure labor theory of value, changes of titles to chapters in successive editions of his *Principles of Political Economy and Taxation,* published in London in 1817, indicate his dissatisfaction with the labor theory. The new titles forecast a clear modification of the power of labor alone to determine value. His efforts to discount the influence of profits and rents on value appear to most economists either as outright failures or as the exercise of arbitrary power to define terms in such a way as to reinforce his theory of value.

The next of the great economists in the classical tradition was NASSAU SENIOR (1790–1864), a man trained in the legal profession but who spent the greater part of his life as a teacher of economics. Senior built upon the foundations laid by Smith and Ricardo, but he was closer to the former than to the latter in his conception of value. He disapproved of Ricardo's labor theory of value and tried to show that it was a misplaced emphasis which led people to confuse the fact that labor was necessary, with a limited supply, and thus with value. It was Senior's belief that scarcity was a fundamental aspect of value whether the scarcity arose because of the difficulty in applying labor or because of natural causes. But he added that the costs of production, which include expenses of capital as well as labor cost, also influence value. Of the expenses of capital—he said that these were but the necessary payments for the sacrifice of present enjoyment which made possible the accumulation of capital. Senior thus provided the ingredients for the commonly accepted theory of value developed later by Alfred Marshall and the so-called neo-classical school.

Before describing the views of the neo-classical economists on the subject of value a mention of the position of JOHN STUART MILL is in order. His contention was that two factors were responsible for value, utility and difficulty of attainment. Actually, however, this could be demonstrated only by reference to specific things. Drawing heavily upon the analysis made by Samuel Bailey (1791–1870) who first attacked the Ricardian labor theory of value, Mill said that commodities fall naturally into three categories: those absolutely limited in supply; those which can be increased indefinitely by the application of labor; and those whose quantity can be increased but only at increasing costs. Of the first he said value depends solely on supply and demand. With the second class of commodities the law of supply and demand still operates, but value is determined by the cost of production which includes wages, usual profits, and—in exceptional cases—rent. Market prices might vary from true value, but competition would tend to make prices gravitate toward the cost of production—since supply would tend to increase or decrease to the point of lowest possible profitable production. In the third class of commodities it was indicated that cost of production again determines value, and price tends to rise to highest costs incurred in producing the necessary supply.

It remained for ALFRED MARSHALL (1842–1924) to rework the old classical theory of value into something which would stand the test of modern industrialism and large-scale business enterprise. He was Professor of Economics at Cambridge University, England, from 1885 to 1908. Schooled in the classics and well trained in mathematics, he was well fitted to do the work of synthesizing and revitalizing economic theory. Marshall made value problems the center of his system of economics. His chief contribution lay in bringing together and harmonizing the utility and the cost of production theories of value. Not so much in England, but on the Continent and in America, theorists had revolted against the cost of production theory in favor of utility. To these writers it was essentially the power of a good to satisfy human wants which gave it value, not what was spent in producing it. A homely illustration provided Marshall with his insight into value theory. A pair of scissors did not cut with either the upper blade or the lower blade alone, but with both together. However, value theory is not quite so simple, he commented; and proceeded to show why. Value is almost entirely influenced by demand when a short-run point of view is taken, for once goods are on the market the consumers' willingness to purchase determines the price. In the long run, said Marshall, supply is important—the price of a commodity cannot vary greatly from the expenses incurred in producing it.

This exposition of Marshall's brought to the classical theory of value new life and a sense of reasonableness. Yet there existed, and probably still exist, economists who take exception to the classical doctrine, and who because of their differences of viewpoint have strongly advocated a revision of classical theories. The principal objection was that in attempting to be objective and scientific, the classical theories dealt only with the external aspects of economic phenomena. Specifically, in emphasizing exchange values, utility or use value was neglected, when actually utility was more important in understanding value than any of the more obvious characteristics of exchange.

Another deviation from the classical doctrine is found in the work of Karl Marx and other socialists. The socialists extended the labor theory of value to further limits, using it as a tool both in an economic and an ethical sense to prove their contention that rent, interest, and profits were unjustifiable charges upon the true values created by labor alone.

The Critics of Classical Views on Value: Lauderdale

Let us review the theories of some of those who guided these critical currents of economic thought. One of the earliest writers to explain the relation of utility to value was that Scottish critic of Adam Smith, Lord Lauderdale. He pointed out that it was the persistence of men's desires in relation to the quantity of a good available which actually created value. In this regard, however, he noted that the demand for necessities persisted as supply decreased; but the demand for luxuries was more likely to rise and fall. Lauderdale made a very clear statement of what we now call elasticity of demand.

The first use of the concepts of diminishing and marginal utility, and their first formulation were in the work of W. F. Lloyd (1794–1853). First he pointed out that specific wants were satiable, and that value disappeared at the moment of satisfaction. His use of the example of the hungry man getting successive ounces of food, showing that the desire for food diminishes with each additional ounce, has become commonplace in economic text-books dealing with utility and value. Value, said Lloyd, really meant a state of mind which showed itself at the point of separation between satisfied and unsatisfied wants.

The Marginal Utility School and Further Criticism of Classical Doctrine

The work of HERMANN HEINRICH GOSSEN (1810–1858) anticipated the work of W. S. Jevons in England and the later Austrian school of thought. Gossen claimed that the value of things is proportional to the ability to provide enjoyments, but as the quantity available increases, the satisfaction of each succeeding unit decreases. The satisfaction that each unit gives is modified by the cost of production of that unit; hence value is represented by an equation of two unknowns—satisfaction in consumption and the cost of production—and value is established at that point where marginal utility and marginal disutility balance one another. The methods used by Gossen were statistical and graphic. He hoped that through quantitative methods economics might be lifted to the plane of an exact science.

The English-speaking world is better acquainted with those theories of value, very similar to Gossen's, presented in the works of W. S. JEVONS (1835–1882). He had a varied career as assayer of the mint in Sidney, Australia, and later as lecturer and professor at Owens College and at University College, London. The unique contribution of Jevons to economic theory lies in his insistence upon the need for understanding consumption. Actually he stated little that was new in the theory of utility. The earlier works of Gossen set forth most of the theories developed by Jevons; but Jevons himself stated that he had no knowledge of Gossen's work until years after his own *Theory of Political Economy* was published in 1871. Jevons further emphasized both the infinite variety of human wants, as Lloyd had done earlier, and the idea of marginal utility which ultimately determined exchange value. As he explained it, the exchange value of two commodities could be determined by comparing the degree of utility possessed by the relative quantities available after exchange had been completed. For example: a man, A, has ten units of an article, while a man, B, has three units of another; A might be willing to give five units of his article for one of B's; but if he wished a second unit of B's article it is hardly likely he would part with five more units of his article, because that would leave him with none. Although B might be willing to make the second exchange at the ratio of 5 to 1, he would be less willing to do so at 3 to 1. Nevertheless a compromise might be reached where exchange could take place at some other ratio, say 4 to 1. It is obvious that value (or the exchange ratio) is determined by the degree of utility of the supply on hand at a given time. All of this and other manifestations of the value theory and utility, Jevons presented in the form of graphs, using artificial incidents and quantities to illustrate the application of his theory. Indeed, it is on this score that the most telling criticism of the whole marginal utility school of thought can be levelled. The school seeks mathematical certainty for its theories but has no adequate measure for utility which in the last analysis is largely an individual matter. The appearance of exactitude is entirely misleading. To Jevons' credit it must be said that he recognized the difficulty of finding quantitative expression for his utilities, but he claimed that he overcame this by dealing with people in the mass, and with the relationship of many utilities rather than with the utility of one commodity alone. In a detailed analysis of utility, Jevons noted several different types. For example, the sum of the utility of all the available units of supply is total utility, that of the last unit consumed is final or marginal utility.

The work of the Marginal Utility School was carried on in Switzerland by Léon Walras, a Frenchman who spent much of his life as professor at the University of Lausanne. In 1874 he published his *Elements d'Economie politique pure*. Value, he said, is the total utility of a given commodity, but its value in exchange is not judged merely on its own relation to supply but rather in a relationship to all other desirable things. The value of one object in terms of another will be judged by a comparison of the marginal utility of each. This, of course, is similar to Jevons' analysis. To some extent Walras tried to harmonize cost of production and utility theories of value, for he considered supply as well as utility, but formal connection is never made and his treatment rests essentially, as does Jevons', upon subjective matters given quantitative expression.

The Philosophical Approach to Value: The Austrian School

While Jevons was working on his utility theory of value in England a similar line of thought was developed by CARL MENGER (1840–1921) in Austria. Menger is looked upon as the spiritual father of the Austrian School which presses the subjective analysis of economic causation to the extreme, and carries forward the original German criticism of the exchange theory of value. To Menger, value is really the utility which goods possess; exchange and disposal is merely the external evidence of what is inherent in the mind and in the nature of the good. Obviously value can be nothing more than a subjective phenomenon, so Menger completely ignored objective evaluations.

FRIEDRICH VON WIESER (1851–1926), one of the best known of Menger's followers, made all of economic theory the problem of value. He even went so far as to suggest that the purpose of economic investigation and the function of the state is the maximizing of values. Value, he believed, arose only from utility. Far from dismissing the cost of production as a factor in the value of any commodity, he acknowledged its importance but demonstrated—to his satisfaction, at least—that costs of production were in reality matters of utility. Cost of production was more than the payment necessary to attract productive forces into operation on a certain article; it was the payment necessary to make this use of available productive forces more desirable than some other alternative use. This did not mean that cost value superseded use value. The latter was still primary and it alone set the limits to cost value—and in so doing limited the supply of a commodity which would be produced. The proposition might be stated this way: Assuming that use value of article A equals a sum of money X for Y units, it is first necessary to assure the producers of A a return better than they would receive by using their powers to produce another article B; but under no circumstances can they be assured a return greater than X which is the sum of money representing the value of Y units.

The best known of the members of the Austrian School, at least among English-speaking peoples, is EUGEN VON BÖHM-BAWERK (1851–1914), a university teacher and three times minister of finance of the Austro-Hungarian Empire. It was not alone in the field of value theory that Böhm-Bawerk made great contributions to economics. He subscribed to the marginal utility theory of value; that is, he believed value to be determined by the power of the least important want satisfied by the supply of goods available. He recognized and subscribed to the theory that the power of one good to satisfy wants influences its power to acquire other goods in exchange for itself. In a sense this was a substitution of a subjective exchange value for the older subjective use value and in a sense it drew closer to the value theory of the neo-classical thought of Alfred Marshall.

The Extension of Classical Ideas of Value: The Socialists

Another growth which branched off from the original classical root was the socialist development of the labor theory of value. Accepting the original contentions of Ricardo that labor was responsible for all value, the early socialists, WILLIAM THOMPSON (1783–1833), J. F. BRAY (1809–1895), and JOHN GRAY (1799–1850) were ardent supporters of the labor theory as applied to value. In their socialistic doctrine, the term property is frequently, if not always, substituted for material goods. Making this allowance, we find their writings filled with declarative statements that labor is the source of all value, and that if people secure property (material goods) without labor they are defrauding the worker of what is rightfully his. Thompson believed that machinery was stored-up labor in the first instance, and that management was a form of labor; hence both had the right to a return. Bray said that labor created all value, and in exchange equal value should be exchanged for equal value; any deviation from this practice was unjust. Gray said, "It is labor alone which bestows value." The work of these men is not so much an economic analysis of values as an ethical assumption.

Implicit in the writings of socialists is the theory of surplus value as well as the labor theory of value. Marx endeavored to find a reasonable economic explanation of these ideas. In this respect he is similar to Thompson who also felt the necessity of a reasonable and not just a moral foundation for his economic beliefs. KARL MARX (1818–1883) had prepared himself to be a university teacher, but he became absorbed in the social reforms of his time and took up the writing of political pamphlets and tracts instead. Exiled from Germany, he spent the remainder of his life in England except for short excursions to the Continent. His interest in reform never flagged, and while his work was chiefly academic it was designed to establish the scientific validity and the historical necessity of his reformist views. Marx conceived of value in the Ricardian sense as the labor necessary to produce an article under average conditions, "with average degree of skill and intensity prevalent at the time." Such a modification thus accounted for the variation in market value from the time of production until sale. While differences in quality of skill may produce variations in value, the variations in skill are themselves accounted for by the variations in the cost of the worker's training. These differences are established by custom much after the fashion described by Ricardo.

The disagreement with Marx's labor theory of value is far overshadowed by the controversy stirred up by his theory of surplus value. This, too, was presaged in Ricardo's writings but never stated clearly or explained. It may be briefly stated in this way: Labor is paid on the basis of its physical reproduction and maintenance costs; but the laborer is required to work hours over and above the hours necessary to meet these costs. Thus every additional hour that he works above the point necessary to produce sufficient articles to supply the laborer's reproduction and maintenance costs (his wages), he is producing value which is appropriated by the employer. This value above his reproduction and maintenance cost is *surplus value*. Marx accepted the thesis of Locke and Ricardo that capital was stored-up labor. The value of raw materials was the labor necessary to produce them. Thus costs of capital and raw materials were justifiably incorporated in the final sale price which approximated the cost of production at all times. It was not in the sale price of each unit that the employer received surplus value but only on additional units produced in the extra hours of labor exacted by him.

Attempts to put the labor theory of value into practise on numerous occasions, especially in the Utopian communities founded through the inspiration of ROBERT OWEN, proved the theory's impracticability. No one was able to solve the problem of how to equate the labor time expended by one man on one article against that expended by a second man on a second article.

Looking back across the several hundred years of economic thought on the subject of wealth and value, several issues seem to stand out clearly, not alone for the questions they raised in times past but for their pertinence to the contemporary scene. The very nature of the economic world in which we live makes money of great importance. A nation or a person accumulates money because of its intrinsic qualities—durability, ease in exchange, and relative stability in value. This was the opinion presented by the advocates of Mercantilism. It was not in the quality of their reasoning that the Mercantilists were unsound; it was that they failed to take the long-run effect of their policies into account. Mercantilism as a working principle never died. Until the Second World War it was followed assiduously, concerning itself with a short-sighted policy of amassing a store of money while neglecting the inevitable consequences of such a general thesis of selling more than one buys.

Not the least important of our modern issues is the unconscious tug-of-war between the advocates of individual wealth, in the form of exchange values, on the one hand, and the proponents of socially held wealth on the other. Is a country wealthier with a vast number of individually owned fortunes to be used at the discretion of their owners, or with state owned or controlled natural resources, public utilities, and extensive social services such as low-cost housing, health centers, play grounds, and schools? The present trend seems to favor the method of state control, not necessarily because it is more desirable as an abstract proposition but because of necessity. An extension of this question merely raises another. A stock of money or goods on hand has been considered from the economic angle as wealth; but in a larger conception a healthy, well educated, talented, and morally upright citizenry may be, in a much truer sense, considered as a store of wealth.

As the problems of wealth shade into those of value, other difficulties arise to plague the economist. No solution has been found to the question of whether subjective factors as well as objectively measurable ones should be considered in defining value. To include the former means giving up for a time at least all hope of exactness. Dealing only with the latter seems to reduce the data of economics to superficial things of questionable validity. There has been a tendency, noted frequently in the past, to describe value in terms of what ought to be rather than in terms of what is; or in terms of what is socially desirable rather than what is indifferent to social consequences.

It is hardly possible to expect to find one sole controlling factor in such a complex phenomenon as value. With our present knowledge we cannot determine with any assurance the relative importance of the several factors which influence it. Much of the economic theory of the past assumed an economic world of a particular character. Differences in theory between English and Continental economists usually can be traced to the different economic worlds in which they lived. Just so, it is entirely possible that questions of wealth and value will be decided in an altogether different fashion by the economists of tomorrow.

CHAPTER II

Land, Private Property, and Rent

MORE GROTIUS PETTY TURGOT ROUSSEAU
BENTHAM HUTCHESON SMITH SAY
MALTHUS RICARDO MILL
PROUDHON MARX ENGELS SAINT–SIMON
HENRY GEORGE VON THÜNEN CAREY BASTIAT

How did land become the property of individuals? Is land most useful and productive when individuals own it or when it is owned by the community as a whole? Why and how do forms of land ownership change? What is rent? What determines how much rent should be paid for a given piece of property? Does land become more valuable or less valuable, more productive or less productive as civilization advances? Should land be taxed more heavily than other forms of property? Does the fact that no one created land make rent an unjust source of income?

LAND HAS EVER BEEN a center of mankind's interest and a constant source of his disputes. It is perhaps trite to say that the primary demand for land is for space in which to live. Except for the most primitive peoples, land in some form has been essential to maintain life. Historians are loathe to estimate the time during which civilization has been supported by agriculture alone, but even the layman knows that for seemingly endless centuries man has lived under the spell cast by God on Adam:

Cursed is the ground for thy sake, in sorrow shalt thou eat of it all the days of thy life. Thorns also and thistles shall it bring forth to thee . . . In the sweat of thy face shalt thou eat bread, till thou return unto the ground.

In spite of its meagre rewards and the sweat and toil which the working of a piece of land exacts, wars have been fought and governments overturned as a result of controversies over land.

The Rise of Private Property in Land

The lush years of the age of commerce and industry have helped to dull man's mind to the importance of land because so few members of the modern industrial state are concerned directly with it. With the extensive use of rubber, iron, coal, oil, and water power, land has taken on added significance until today the affairs of the world are frequently described in terms of land use and land control. The term "Geopolitics" is just a new way of expressing an old truth which somehow in the rush of getting and spending got pushed into a dark corner, to be rediscovered by people to whom living space and raw materials for industry had become a problem.

The value of land itself has been generally assumed; and, except for eulogies by poets and philosophers, literature on the subject has been scant until recently. It is the property relations which surround land with which men have been concerned. Among primitive tribes when the gathering of berries, roots, and herbs, or hunting and fishing was the means of existence no one worried about ownership. The mobility of these tribesmen rendered private ownership of land a matter of indifference. The temporary use of it was all that was desired. Tribal wars, of course, were fought to retain use privileges of a hunting ground, but no individual sought title to a particular area. Confusion has resulted innumerable times when primitive tribesmen have sold a use title to land which the civilized recipient accepted as an individual property right. In the pastoral stages of economic development land continued as communal holdings, since extensive rather than intensive use was required. Circumstances did not demand individual land holdings on this level of existence. Although some 19th century economists held out for private property rights against communalism among primitive people, the facts accumulated by anthropologists have pretty well repudiated their neatly built arguments.

The introduction of agriculture as the principal source of food brought a radical change in the idea of land tenure. Interest now centered in a particular plot of land for the planting and growing season. Property in land really begins with the idea of use and ownership of the produce of the land. Actually, at first, the land itself was parcelled out to the members of the tribe; for a time ownership still resided in the tribe. From here on the evolution of private property in land is a rapidly moving story. Ownership by the chief, family holdings, and serfdom and vassalage are intermediary stages to private ownership of land.

Of chief importance to this description is the transition from the feudal estates to private land tenure. No one held land absolutely in his own right under feudal law. Each person held it by the grace of a superior, the king being legally the only true landholder. In return for the use of the land, serfs and vassals rendered such service, and paid in produce, whatever the law at the time required. The decline in feudal holdings came as a result of the following extremely complex social developments; the increase in trade, the rise of towns, the extension of the use of money, and the emergence of new social groups such as merchant-employers and wage-workers. Those who retained their land holdings in time came to pay dues or fines in money. These were legally set amounts charged in money values; and even these payments were soon reduced to a mere form so that the holder of the land obtained practically a free title, although vestiges of feudal tenure were still retained. Where serfs or vassals left the land, as many did in the migration to the cities, or where they were resolutely pushed off the land by the application of some law favoring the nobility, title to land reverted to the lord of the manor, who might then lease the land or use it for his own purposes. The Inclosure Acts of 18th and 19th century England did away with common lands in the interest of increasing the land under cultivation. Parcels of such common land were granted to individuals with a clear title. This, of course, merely illustrates the universal principle that when land comes under cultivation, communal property passes into private ownership.

Why the private title to land should become a characteristic of some societies is difficult to explain. However, one cannot go far astray in citing some of the most plausible explanations. Of most importance is the demand by individuals themselves that once they have cleared land, improved it, or planted crops which need long periods of care or which produce perennially, they should be guaranteed possession. The increase in population which creates a scarcity in land, leads to a demand for more cultivated land, and to an effort to preserve for oneself and one's children the right to living space and maintenance area. This factor is likewise responsible in no small measure for the payment of rent. Ethical considerations are frequently raised in connection with the private ownership of land and the rent which owners exact for its use. These arrangements have evolved as a process of adjustment to existing conditions. That someone thinks they are good or bad is apparently of little consequence. Only when such social devices prove inadequate or harmful to community purposes will they tend to disappear.

The Views of Plato and Aristotle

The first writers on economics of whom we have record were concerned with land. They assumed the importance of land as a factor in production, and devoted their attention principally to the question of ownership. PLATO in the *Republic* called for communism in land among the rulers of the State, as a means of removing sources of discontent. But sometime later in the *Laws* he advocated private property in land and houses because the people were not capable of managing their affairs in common. Private ownership was in a sense a trusteeship held from the city, and enlargement of land holdings was distinctly forbidden. ARISTOTLE did not favor communism. To him private ownership, through which an individual was assured the result of his labor, seemed more likely to elicit the best efforts and the most conscientious attention to obligations. He did advocate restrictions on the accumulation of property, mainly through limitations on inheritance.

Writings of the early Christians give no clear picture of what the Church held as a policy on private property in land. Some favored the communal ownership of property, others upheld communal ownership as an ideal but recognize the inability of the members generally to follow such a practice. AQUINAS, the spokesman for the religious viewpoint of the Middle Ages, presented able arguments in favor of private property. It was advantageous because of the greater care an individual owner would take, because of the greater industry that would be exercised, and because it reduced friction among members of the community. Individual owners should consider their property a trust from God and be ever willing to share with others in need.

Protests Against Medieval Land Tenure

With the breakup of Feudalism, two conflicting strains of thought were born. Out of the misery of the common people and the extravagance of the court came a protest against private property, especially private property in land. But because of the continued dabbling of the kings into the financial affairs of their subjects, and the hampering effect of feudal bonds, a movement to free private property from all restrictions also arose and ultimately carried the day.

Perhaps the most important of the protests was written by SIR THOMAS MORE (1478–1535). He lived at a time when the land problem in England was acute. To gain adequate land for sheep raising—which was more lucrative than tenants' fees—the tenants were excluded from the lands. His *Utopia* (1516) described a society in which lands would be held in common and production and distribution would proceed on a basis of equality.

The Digger movement of the late 1640's of which Gerrard Winstanley was the intellectual and political leader was essentially a protest against private property. In 1649 the members of the group took possession of some untilled land outside of London to cultivate; but the leaders were soon arrested and, although Winstanley wrote in later years advocating the abolition of private property and proposed an advanced type of communal society, the movement never became active again.

Quite in contrast to these reformers were the ardent advocates of individually owned property free from external control. HUGO GROTIUS (1583–1645), THOMAS HOBBES (1588–1679), and JOHN LOCKE (1632–1704) originated this policy which has since become one of the dominant aspects and most important issues of modern society. Grotius discussed the evolution of society and showed how private property was an inherent feature of the first contracts made by men to give order to social living. Any interference with private property by the sovereign power must be justly paid for, he believed. Hobbes, while emphasizing the necessity for individual rights in property, made them conditional upon the power of the king to change or alter them at his will without restriction or compensation. Locke, however, raised serious objection to any control by the king, saying that labor was responsible for the first private ownership. Private property should only arise where there was enough left in common for others, and where the owners could adequately put such property to use. Thus Locke claimed that private property was a condition of the earliest existence (which, as later research has shown, is quite unfounded) and became a matter of contract when societies were formed.

Strong support of Locke's theories came from the Physiocrats, the school of economists in France, headed by Quesnay. Their theories were posited on the existence of a natural order which was not necessarily the early state of man described by Grotius and Locke; but it was an order, based upon inherent laws of nature which man could understand. Property and authority seemed to them to be the very foundation of the natural order. Property especially, because it stimulated the production and accumulation of wealth. Quesnay thought of private property as the real basis of the economic order of society, and other Physiocrats looked upon it as the tree out of which grew all other social institutions. In a violent reaction to the Mercantilists, Quesnay and Turgot claimed that all value was derived from land. Labor on land produced a surplus (*produit net*); labor applied in other areas created nothing, but shared in the surplus derived from land. This emphasis upon land, coupled with a firm conviction of the sanctity of private property and the rejection of royal interference as an economic principle, fostered profound changes in the economic and political life of France which reached their climax in the French Revolution.

ROUSSEAU (1712–1778) looked upon property as a violation of natural rights to which most of the ills of mankind could be traced. By means of acquiring property, certain individuals were able to increase their wealth and gain control over their fellows. To Rousseau the established order of society was an evil which perpetuated unnatural and man-made injustices and inequalities.

*Theories of Land Reform: Godwin, Proudhon and
the Socialists*

Although Rousseau died before the French Revolution had
begun, many of the theories concerning property which he set
forth in his work *Sur l'Origine de l'Inégalité Parmi les Hommes,*
published in 1755, were elaborated by the anarchists and socialists of the century and a half which followed. Among the first
of these was WILLIAM GODWIN (1756–1836) in England. Godwin was the son of an austere and conservative dissenting minister. Although trained for the ministry he found his beliefs
shaken by the writings of the French philosophers. He found that
he possessed a gift for writing and consequently followed that as
a career. In his *An Inquiry Concerning Political Justice and Its
Influence on General Virtue and Happiness,* published in 1793,
he analyzed the problem of private property and presented a
thesis which has earned him the classification as an anarchist. In
his opinion, property not only distorted judgments and values
but was intimately tied up with the system of coercion and pun-
ishment which marked the modern state. He clearly saw that
private property in land prevented the access of some persons to
sources of food, clothing, and shelter to which all had a right,
since the good things of the world were a common stock. The
rights of private property, he says, are of three types: first, those
granted to an individual because they are more useful to this
person than to any other; second, those representing objects
which have resulted from the person's own labor; and third,
those created by law and passed on through inheritance. The
second and the third are obviously in conflict with the first, which
was the most natural and fundamental right of the three. Consequently, the second and third types of property should be abolished and a state of equality should be introduced where natural
rights would be secure against usurpation.

As later events indicated, it was the second of Godwin's types

of property which received the greatest support both from theoretical economists and social reformers; human labor became the
source of value as well as the justification of private property.
However, there was one who took up Godwin's viewpoint. This
was PIERRE-JOSEPH PROUDHON (1809–1865). Proudhon was
the brilliant son of working-class parents. His education was good
but achieved at great parental sacrifice. In later years he obtained a higher education while earning his living as a printer.
The winning of several prizes for essays on contemporary subjects fostered his literary career, but marked him as one of radical
and revolutionary opinions. There is no indication in Proudhon's
writings that he was at all dependent upon Godwin, but spiritually at least he is closely identified not only with Godwin's analysis of property but with Godwin's plans for social reform. He
believed that every man had a right to the materials necessary
to produce his means of existence, but since population never
remained constant, continuous redistribution of property would
be necessary. Hence it could never become a private possession.
Furthermore, property must be used in conformity with general
utility, but this also undermined the very foundation of private
property, which was the unrestricted right to its disposal. He believed that for the reasons cited society itself could be the only
property holder. This was such an obvious principle of social life
in his mind that the debates on the question sickened him.

The popular economic arguments that private property could
be justified because of the labor expended to produce it, seemed
to Proudhon disproved by the social conditions existing at that
time. Men labored on lands and in factories but received no title
to the goods they produced. Value in land was not finally created
by the single act of clearing and improving; its value was re-cre-
ated and increased each year by the careful attention of the
tenant. Yet the tenant received no property right in the land.
Even if labor were rewarded with the totality of what it produced,
injustice would still continue. Here Proudhon used the Ricardian

theories of wages and value to prove his point. Wages are the cost of maintaining and reproducing labor; since talents are natural endowments and not created by man himself, and since society supplies the materials and training for the skilled workman, why should one man receive more than another as a result of his labor? Absolute equality was the only just principle to apply. Since labor was responsible for value, anything taken by the owners of property was theft.

The most objectionable feature of property to Proudhon was not the simple fact of ownership, but that ownership gave the proprietor a right to any increase in value which the property might acquire. Since owners were few and laborers many, the drain of interest, land- and house-rent, and profit was enormous, and was responsible—in Proudhon's opinion—for economic crises.

The most numerous critics of private property were the Socialists. For the most part their criticism rested upon two assumptions. First, that all value was created by labor; and, second, that the labor necessary to produce a thing was the only justification for private property. Adam Smith and Ricardo had already accepted the first of these tenets but never bothered to explain the justification for rent, interest, and profit. It remained for the Anarchists and Socialists to point out the ethical implications of this theory.

JOHN GRAY gave a clear statement of this point of view in his *A Lecture on Human Happiness* (1825). He said that labor is the foundation of all property. But land cannot be created, and those who claim rights to property through conquest, or merely taking possession, or inheritance are not citing adequate evidence to hold title to property. That perhaps ownership might arise from clearing and draining land Gray readily admitted, but confined ownership to as much land as the amount of labor in obtaining it might justify. He claimed that if the possession of land itself was unjust the charges made for its use by another were also unjust. Consequently owners accepted the result of another's labor and gave no equivalent in return for it.

J. F. BRAY followed much the same line of reasoning in his *Labour's Wrongs and Labour's Remedy,* except that perhaps he was more absolute in his denial of the right of anyone to own private property in land, since this would interfere with the right of another to use the land for productive purposes.

The theories of COMTE DE SAINT-SIMON (1760–1825) who was himself a possessor of great wealth (gained, it is believed, through speculation) were not nearly so absolute as the early English Socialists. His main criticism was not directly of private property itself but of the system of inheritance which made it impossible for members of new generations to begin life with equality of opportunity. Although his followers wanted the complete destruction of private property in the instruments of production, Saint-Simon himself believed there was some justification not only for private property but also for paying the owners of capital a return. Rewards, however, were not to be apportioned in society on the basis of ownership but rather on the basis of ability and social contribution.

The socialist analysis and criticism of the institution of private property was most completely propounded in the comprehensive works of KARL MARX and FRIEDRICH ENGELS. As long as production was a matter of an individual's labor with his own tools upon raw materials which he owned, no dissatisfaction arose when the individual owner appropriated the product. In modern civilization, however, where tools were concentrated in large factories, the owner continued to appropriate the product, paying the laborer a wage equivalent to mere subsistence. This, according to Marx and Engels, was unjust, for it was the appropriation of values created by the labor of others. In planning to do away with private property they contended that nine-tenths of the people no longer owned property anyway. The essential means of production would not be destroyed; in fact, they would be employed for social interests rather than for individual interests. Only the power to derive earnings from ownership would be eliminated.

It is difficult to discuss the question of land and private property without running into philosophical literature. One might dwell at length with profit upon the writings of Bentham, Kant, Hegel, and Fichte, who defended private property as an expression of individuality, as the rightful return for one's labor, as the natural result of inequalities, and as the spur necessary to secure production. Only in a mild manner did these writers restrict the use of property so as to conform with the best interests of the state, and on the whole private property was accepted as a good and inevitable aspect of life. Our interest, however, is with the economists rather than the philosophers. One fact that stands out clearly is that only those economists with a philosophical or reformist turn of mind pay much attention to the function of private property. The more objective of the economists, shall we say, accepted the fact of private property and endeavored to describe its effect upon distribution of income, and to state the general principles which governed the relation of property to economic activity. To this point we will turn in a moment, but first a word about the economists who tried to see the relation of property to the total operation of society.

FRANCIS HUTCHESON (1694–1746) followed closely the teachings of Aristotle in believing that private ownership of the fruits of labor was an incentive, and that mankind as a whole would enjoy greater happiness if this law of nature were followed. However, land should not be owned unless it were used for productive purposes.

We have already mentioned the philosopher JEREMY BENTHAM (1748–1832). His formula of "the greatest good for the greatest number" did much to serve as a justification for the institution of private property. Bentham agreed that ideally greater happiness would result if a measure of equality existed in the distribution of property, but this he claimed could not be. Equality could not last. Furthermore, if people could not keep all that their labor produced they would not work. He did advocate the regulation of inheritances to prevent too great an accumulation in the hands of a few.

The discussion of private property which one finds in the work of JOHN STUART MILL shows clearly its dependence upon the theories of Bentham. Mill argued that production followed certain fundamental laws that were as unchanging as laws of the physical world. This was not true of the distribution of wealth. Mankind established its own principles in this matter, and they could be changed "if mankind so chose." He showed that while the present results of the system of private property were intolerable, a better organization of the laws of property might be worked out which would still retain the institution of private property which he believed to be, on the whole, desirable. He condemned that aspect of private property which guaranteed to some persons the fruits of labor and denied it to others. He defended payments made to the organizers of business activity, for he believed the provision of machinery and raw materials was accomplished only by labor and abstinence and that these had a reasonable claim upon the final product. On the question of inheritance he had strong views. Within the limits of reason and practice, inheritance should be curtailed; but he cautioned all to understand that, while those who did not inherit suffered a disadvantage, it was not nearly as great as the disadvantage which would have been felt had no saving and inheritance been possible. Only by saving is capital acquired and only with capital does man's labor improve its productivity. With land rent more than with any other aspect of the property relationship, Mill took the greatest exception. The most uneconomic feature of it was its tendency to increase as population increased without any effort on the part of the owner. To remedy this fault he advocated taxation of the surplus.

Because of the nature in which rights in land were originally acquired—violence, fraud, force, and superior cunning—and because of the far reaching implication of the power land owners held over non-land owners, HERBERT SPENCER (1820–1903) believed private property in land to be socially undesirable, although later he modified his position considerably. He argued for the right of the community to dispossess owners and put land to use whenever that seemed a desirable procedure. The only restriction was that just compensation should be paid. As for private property in movable wealth, Spencer chose to accept the probability of its permanent existence; but property in land he felt would eventually prove an impossible basis of social organization.

Henry George and the Single Tax

One of the most important figures in the conflict of ideas on the subject of private land holding was HENRY GEORGE (1839–1897). The son of a publisher of religious books in Philadelphia, he gained wide experience through travel. A brief adventure in politics brought home to him the power of vested interests. This experience along with his observation of land booms following early railroad construction in California, plus the obvious poverty surrounding him, and his own firsthand acquaintance with it as a young man, gradually produced the ingredients for his famous work *Progress and Poverty,* published in 1879. The last part of George's life was spent as a lecturer and journalist popularizing his ideas. It was the theory of Henry George that poverty tended to increase and wages were forced down even though productive capacity and wealth increased, "because land, which is the source of all wealth and the field of all labor, is monopolized." Private property is justified only by the labor expended to produce it, hence labor provides the only right to property— what a man makes is his own; the process of exchange does not change this fact. To George this had the aspect of a natural law.

He drew from this proposition the obvious conclusion that no man had a right to anything which he did not produce. Nevertheless, said he, men exact rent for the use of land which they did not create, and reap the increase in value for which society alone is responsible. It is this toll exacted by the land owner that fosters poverty and stifles progress.

To remedy this condition George offered one solution. It was not necessary to confiscate property; "it was only necessary to confiscate rent." This would be done by abolishing all other taxes and introducing a *single tax* on land. In theory the scheme appears sound: Merely tax the surplus or unearned increment above necessary expenses of land use. But practical difficulties arose and the proposal has remained a theory save for a small number of modified local experiments.

What Is Rent? The Theories Before Ricardo

The justice and injustice of private property in land has been for ages a point for philosophical speculation. Accepting the realities of private ownership as they exist at the present time, the fact of practical importance is that some payment is necessary to bring privately owned land into productive use. The professional economists have concerned themselves with questions emerging from this condition of our economic life. What is *rent?* From what conditions in the nature of society and the economic process does it arise? Where do the surpluses out of which rent is paid come from? Why are some lands more valuable and capable of exacting more rent than others? To be sure, a great deal of idle speculation and fine theorizing has accompanied the efforts to answer these questions, and not a few of the modern economists have dropped all discussion of rent as a separate subject from their works, merging it with treatments of capital and interest. However, the theory of land value and rent is of significance not only for its influence upon economic theory generally throughout the decades, but also because of the relationship it has had to historical movements.

The origin of rent in the modern sense is lost in the confusion associated with the decline of Feudalism and the rise in individual rights, responsibilities, and enterprise in modern times. Suffice it to say that strong as custom was in determining the relationship between the lord of the manor and those who worked on his land, certain aspects of the rent relationship existed in the form of socage, quit rents, and customary dues paid in money rather than service. To what extent competition influenced the amounts paid, or whether there was any variation at all, is at this moment unknown. We face rent as a more or less modern phenomenon which became an important item in the economic literature of the 19th century.

The earliest known modern discussions of rent came from SIR WILLIAM PETTY, the English economist of the 17th century. In his treatment, rent is the surplus over and above the maintenance cost of the workman and the production costs of the crop. The value of land is really determined by the number of persons for whom it can provide a livelihood. To secure a money value of rent Petty offered a unique formula. He said the surplus of corn on the land after maintenance costs and expenses were paid should be equated with the surplus of silver mined by a man in the same length of time as the farmer labored, after all his expenses were paid. However fanciful this formula may sound, Petty was exceedingly farsighted in some matters. He saw that values of land and amounts of rent tended to increase directly with the population; and he was conscious that an increase in production could be secured either by cultivating more land farther from the center of population or by adding labor or fertilizer to the present land. In both cases an increase in price of the food-stuff was warranted by the additional costs either of transportation or cultivation.

The origin of rent as visualized by the Physiocrats and especially TURGOT is the same as that of any value. It arises from the land itself. After taking from the produce of the land the subsistence cost of labor and materials needed for cultivation, and taking out a new supply of seeds, the remainder is the *produit net* which apparently is the equivalent of rent, for it goes to the land owner. In a competitive society the rental on land is determined by consideration of the probable produce, the price at which it will sell, and the prices offered by others desiring to use the land. If competition is keen, rent will be the total amount of the surplus; if not so keen, the renter may be able to retain some of the surplus himself.

The work of ADAM SMITH does not contain any conclusive statement on the nature or origin of rent. Actually, it is possible to draw three different conclusions as to what Smith thought rent to be. In the first place he shared the Physiocratic doctrine that land produces a surplus over and above the expenses of the labor and capital applied to it. This might be considered rent. Secondly, it may be a fee paid to entice the owner to use his land, and the investment it represents, for productive purposes rather than withdrawing it for some other use. And thirdly, it is the result of monopoly in land and an unjust exaction from the value created by labor. That is, under natural conditions when land was plentiful, the man who applied himself to the land received the total produce as his own. But when all land is occupied, the owner can exact a portion of the produce of the soil merely because of a legal relationship he holds to the soil, and not because of any value-creating labor he has performed. There is little difference actually in the last two ideas. Essentially they represent the same fact, in one instance from the owner's viewpoint, in the second instance from that of the renter.

J. B. SAY, who in most cases was the great exponent of Smith's theories, discussed rent from a different point entirely. Rent, he claimed, was in the first place produced by the supply and demand for the products of the land which set a price providing a surplus over and above all costs of production; and, in the second place, it was an interest payment on improvements necessary to bring the land into a state ready for cultivation. These theories were not elaborated by Say, but they were taken up and given prominence by other authorities. It should be noted, however, that Say engaged in heated controversy with Ricardo over the latter's analysis of rent, always insisting—as later economists have insisted—that where the demand is greater than the supply, a price will be paid which will give a surplus over costs of production. This is the real basis of rent.

The Formulation of the Modern Theory of Rent: The Pessimists, Malthus and Ricardo

The problem of rent came full force upon England in the early 19th century when the increase in population caused such concern over the food supply that the Corn Laws which set duties on the importation of grain were abolished. Popular debates on the subject were numerous. It is probably due to this historical circumstance that the theory of rent figures so largely in the writings of English economists. THOMAS R. MALTHUS (1766–1834) and DAVID RICARDO (1772–1823) were the principal contributors to the literature on the subject during this period, although many of the ideas met in theories of Malthus and Ricardo had been set forth fifty years earlier by James Anderson. Apparently his writings never came to the attention of Ricardo or of any of the prominent economists of the time.

MALTHUS was one of a large family. He was educated as a clergyman but his theological training broadened rather than narrowed his field of interests. Continued study, after his formal education was complete, centered his attention on economics and population. Later in life he was appointed Professor of History and Political Economy at the East India Company's training college. His writing upon the subject of rent began with two pamphlets written during the Corn Law disturbances in 1814–1815.

The second, *An Inquiry into the Nature and Progress of Rent,* is the most important. Malthus agreed with the Physiocrats that land produced more than enough to maintain those who tilled it. He added to this his own observation that population tended to increase faster than the food supply, resulting in an ever increasing demand for agricultural products. It was also true that land differed in fertility, and the labor and capital applied to different areas yielded different results. The difference in productivity of the best land over the poorer constituted a surplus which went to the landlord as rent.

RICARDO's statement is not greatly different from that of Malthus, a little more systematic and a little more detailed perhaps, but in assumptions and principle it is similar. The reason that Ricardo receives credit for these theories is perhaps due to his more comprehensive work in economic theory in which rent is given a prominent place. "Rent," says Ricardo, "is that portion of the produce of the earth which is paid to the landlord for the use of the original and indestructible powers of the soil." There is no rent when land of nearly equal fertility is present in sufficient abundance to supply human needs. When an increase in population causes land of inferior quality and less advantageous situation to be called into cultivation, then rent is paid. Assuming the presence of land of three degrees of quality, let us suppose an increase in population creates a demand for food, making it necessary to call into cultivation the land of the second quality. The greater costs of production, either in labor or transportation, will cause the price to rise. Obviously the smaller costs of production on the first quality land in relation to the price paid for each unit of the product will yield a surplus to the first land over the second. This, says Ricardo, is rent. If further increase in population brings land of the third quality into production, rent on both first and second quality lands will rise. The price of natural products will be determined by the higher labor costs necessary to produce the additional quantities needed under the least favorable circumstances. As Ricardo says, "Corn is not high because rent is paid, but a rent is paid because corn is high." The laws of supply and demand and the cost of production on the least favorable land fix the price of corn.

An alternative analysis of rent is frequently presented, calling into discussion the law of diminishing returns as applied to agriculture. Instead of seeking the less fertile lands, additional expenditure for labor and fertilizer may be used. But beyond a certain point application of additional capital and labor to the land produces proportionately less return. This principle had been carefully described by Sir Edward West (1783–1828) in his *An Essay on the Application of Capital to Land,* published in 1815. Therefore one might analyze rent from the point of view of the diminishing returns, either as less fertile soil is brought into cultivation to meet increased demands, or as additional applications of capital and labor are made to the land originally under cultivation.

It is important to note that however clear Ricardo's theory may be as an economic concept there are endless complicating factors when one attempts to put it into practical use. Numerous writers, beginning with John Stuart Mill, an admiring follower of Ricardo, became quite involved when they attempted to find real situations to illustrate the theory. The theory assumes that rent is the difference in the produce of two similar areas worked with the same expenditure for labor and capital. The biggest stumbling block lies in equating the conditions under which two different areas are cultivated.

Modifications to Rent Theory from the Continent

A theory of rent similar to that of Ricardo was developed about the same time in Germany by an agricultural economist, J. H. von Thünen. He was the son of a landed proprietor, and himself, after a brief period of study at Göttingen, bought an estate and spent the remainder of his life developing economic theories applying to agriculture. His work, *Der Isolierte Staat* (The Isolated State), is important because of its method. The basis of the analysis is, as its title indicates, a hypothetical community entirely free from external contacts. To develop his theories, von Thünen introduced new elements, as for example, increments to the population, while holding all other factors constant. Then by a logical-analytical method he evolved the principles governing the observed effects. Artificial as his setting was, the facts and figures analyzed were real enough since they were drawn from the practical management of his own estate. It was by this method that his theory of rent was deduced. Arranging the tillable area surrounding the community into concentric circles, and assuming for the most part equal productivity, he showed that, at a given price for grain, the costs of transportation made production beyond a certain distance from the town unprofitable. This leads directly to his theory of rent. He maintained that some capital is always expended on farm land. After deducting interest on capital and other costs of production and transportation the remainder of the earnings is rent. Thus the price of grain is an important element in rent. In order to get the necessary amount of corn, the price the community is willing to pay must cover the costs of production and transportation from the most distant source necessary to provide the required quantity. Since the price paid for grain to the nearest and the farthest producers will be the same, the surplus going to the nearest producer is rent. Extending his analysis to cover not only the disadvantages of distance but of fertility as well, he said that rent arose from the advantages which a piece of land possessed over the worst farms. It is quite obvious that von Thünen interpreted value in terms of marginal qualities. This is apparent in his discussion of interest and wages as well as rent.

Critics of Ricardo: The Optimists, Carey and Bastiat

The critics of the Ricardian theory of rent have been numerous. Most have been concerned more with the impracticality of the theory; others have questioned the assumptions upon which it rests. Of the latter critics the two most important are Carey and Bastiat, representatives of the so-called "optimistic school" of economics as opposed to the so-called "pessimistic school" identified with Malthus and Ricardo. The reasons for the distinctive names will become obvious as we proceed. HENRY CAREY, an American economist (1793–1879), was led to discard two of the foundation stones upon which Ricardo erected his theory of rent. He, and Anderson before him, denied that the law of diminishing returns applied to agriculture, and he protested the Malthusian doctrine of population increasing more rapidly than the food supply. As for the first, by a vast collection of data on the original settlements of communities, Carey was able to show that the most fertile land is not settled first. In fact, the reverse is true. Settlers tend to congregate on bare spaces, hill tops, and hill sides, whereas the fertile land requires clearing of forests and underbrush, and draining of valleys, all of which require capital and years of toil. Consequently, the price of grain is likely to decline instead of rise as new lands are brought into cultivation. Obviously, Carey was writing of a recently opened country where free land was to be had for the clearing. Ricardo was writing of an old established country which had long since placed every bit of available land under the plough. Moreover, in criticising Ricardo, Carey seems to have misinterpreted the significant points of the theory. Its validity does not depend upon the chronological order in which the land was first tilled but on the manifest differences in fertility which later show themselves at any given time.

Although not very clearly described, Carey's other point is this: Instead of diminishing returns, land, when properly cared for, will yield a constantly increasing rate of return for the capital and labor expended. Moreover, an increasing number of births should be considered not only as an increase in the number of mouths to be fed but as an increase in the number of producers. If land increases its rate of return with each new application of labor and capital, it is obvious that no fear need exist. All these arguments taken together allowed Carey to reverse the order of Malthus and Ricardo, so that the future instead of being plagued by wars, disease, and famine, because of overpopulation, might well be a period of greater satisfaction for more people. But what is rent, if this is the case? It comes only as a payment for the past expenditure of labor in draining, clearing, and maintaining fertility.

The argument advanced by Bastiat is not so logical as that of Carey, although it carries many of the same optimistic hypotheses, such as, the increasing productivity of the soil and labor, and the decreasing costs of production. FRÉDÉRIC BASTIAT (1801–1850) remained an obscure farmer until late in life when the free trade-protection controversy gave him opportunity to exercise his latent journalistic powers, and to participate in local politics. His *Harmonies économiques,* published in 1850, the year of his death, is the vehicle for his optimistic analysis of economic principles. His basic contention is that commodities possess utility contributed by two agencies, nature and labor. The first is free; the second requires payment. But the essence of progress is, that the expenses of nature decline, and man ultimately enjoys more of nature's free gifts with less toil and expense. Agricultural products should be sold at a price which covers the cost of the labor necessary to produce them. Rent, then, to Bastiat is payment for the labor and capital expense involved in rendering the land suitable for cultivation. The land owner is simply an intermediary between natural resources and the consumer, who through toil puts land into a condition so that its produce can be utilized.

While there is more hope than logic in the ideas of Bastiat and

Carey, both in a measure foresaw the modifications which ultimately were applied to the ideas of Ricardo and Malthus. In the
case of the rent theory of the former, a long line of economists
beginning with Nassau Senior and including among others Jean
Baptiste Say, John Stuart Mill, F. A. Walker, Karl Menger, and
Alfred Marshall, saw no reason for confining the idea of rent to
the surplus over and above what could be earned by the least
fertile unit of land. The same phenomenon appears in the case of
all forms of capital, and indeed, of labor. Certainly the principle
must apply to mines, fisheries, and land for building purposes.
The tendency was then to extend the idea of rent to cover any
differential surplus regardless of source. Senior actually defined
rent as "all revenue earned without sacrifice," or "revenue earned
after sacrifice had been compensated." Furthermore, as Say very
early pointed out, it was not the higher costs on the less fertile
land which produced rent on the more fertile, but the fact that
demand for the commodity had so raised the price that after all
costs of production had been met, a surplus remained. But this
was true of the product of a machine as well as of land. Finally,
these later writers held that it was impossible to separate the
return due the land itself and the return on the capital investment made on the land in order to put it in cultivation. Consequently, as a practical measure, and perhaps well in line with
sound theory, rent could be discussed just as the return upon an
investment of any other type. Old ideas of the limited amount
of land and its indestructibility which at first were considered
sufficient reason for discussing rents as a separate and unique
economic factor have been proved untenable. Land is no more
limited than machinery, since both are derived from the substance of the earth; and the fertility of the soil as well as the soil
itself can be destroyed. The present-day search is for a more
practicable theory of rent; and the line of reasoning seems to be
in the direction of minimizing the distinction between land and
capital in so far as payment for its use is concerned. Modifica-

tions of Malthus come mainly from those writers on population who see that increases in population can be supported if an improved technique of production is introduced. For example, the change from handicraft to machine technology enabled the economic system to produce additional food to support a phenomenal increase in the population of western Europe and America during the last two centuries. The more radical of economists have pointed out that the ultimate capacity of the productive system of the world has never been taxed; if the distribution of our national income were more equitable, they maintain, there would be enough and more than enough to support large increases in population. In short, they say, the changes in the economic system have ushered in an economy of abundance, supplanting the Malthusian economy of scarcity. The problem remaining is not one of production but one of distribution.

Practical Measures of Land Reform

The most tantalizing facts about land have always been that owners of it receive a return on its use without doing work; and that as population increases, land increases in value, again accruing to the owner without labor on his part. The English economists—beginning with Adam Smith and greatly reinforced by Ricardo—did not quiet the ever present discontent with land distribution. In fact it was Ricardo's theories which served as "scientific" justification for modern efforts to make land common property. The seeming injustice of "reaping where he has not sown," has led social reformers to give a prominent place to measures eliminating private ownership in land. John Stuart Mill, believing that rent and the increase in the value of land represented unearned increment, advocated a tax which would take from the land owner all future rents. A periodic evaluation would be made to see whether any increase in value had occurred as a result of society's action. If so, a general tax would be levied upon the increase. Mill was not opposed to immediate appropriation of land in principle, but he felt that more efficient administration would be forthcoming if the community acquired title to the land slowly. This he felt would eventuate as the profit was removed from ownership in land.

GOSSEN (1810–1858) presented a plan about the middle of the 19th century which bears a resemblance to Mill's and forecasts the program of Henry George which was to come some time later. Gossen believed that industrial progress was hindered by lack of capital and by the obstruction caused by private property in land. He therefore advocated a government bank to take care of the first need, and a system of taxation which would absorb all rents and ultimately lead to government ownership, to deal with the second. Expenses of the government would then be entirely paid by the rents or rent taxes which it received. However, owners of property should be paid not only for present values but for anticipated values in any transference of ownership to the state. Indeed, Walras (1834–1910), in advancing his own theory of land reform in 1867, advocated outright purchase of land by the issuance of government bonds providing not only for present value but anticipated income. The rents of the property would be received by the state and used to pay off the bonds.

The scheme which has had the longest period of popularity and which is frequently advocated as a practical measure for systems of local taxation in America today is Henry George's single tax program. The tax would be levied upon that portion of the rent which remained after the expenses of maintenance and the return of capital invested in improvements had been deducted. The apparent simplicity of the proposal is misleading and the practical difficulties of the plan have prevented potential advocates of the reform from obtaining active support.

Land reforms of a more practical and less theoretical and radical nature have been devised from time to time throughout human history as necessity demanded them. Such programs have seldom been the work of scholarly economists, but usually that of professional politicians and statesmen. There were the reforms of the Gracchi in ancient Rome whose purpose it was to preserve the small farmer from extermination at the hands of the great land owners. Then there was the program of land reclamation by the Cistercian order of monks which helped to re-establish individual freedom by opening up new lands to free tenants. Later the Inclosure Acts of 18th and 19th century England broke up the village commons in order to provide additional areas for tillage. More modern programs (the United States government's free land policy of the last half of the 19th century, and its more recent attempts to safeguard the farmer through mortgage moratoria, aid in soil erosion, and crop reduction payments) have sought to adjust land use and land ownership, not only to economic, but also to social needs. The Hitler government in Germany, finding itself faced with a persistent agricultural problem existing for decades, likewise evolved a program creating a new nobility of farm proprietors and guaranteeing the maintenance of a family estate through new laws of inheritance. Thus in theory and in practice the problems of the land challenge the thought of man. Yet in the age of industrialization the concern of most people is directed to the machine and its products. It is the machine and the market which bring ease of life and personal wealth. How different is the outlook today from that of the economists of yesterday!

CHAPTER III

The Productivity of Labor and the Theory of Wages

PLATO   ARISTOTLE   AQUINAS   CALVIN
THE MERCANTILISTS   THE PHYSIOCRATS   SMITH
MALTHUS   RICARDO   MILL   MARX
BAKUNIN   SOREL   VEBLEN   WALKER   TAYLOR
THE WEBBS   CLARK   TAWNEY   COLE

Why do men work? Does man have greater dignity when he works, or when he is wealthy enough to spend his time in leisure? Why do some occupations demean an individual and others make a man or woman more respectable? What determines how much a man receives for his labor? What effect does increase in population have upon wages? Does it pay a workman to increase his output? Are wages paid out of capital? What is the relative bargaining power of labor and employers? Do trade unions increase wages?

NOT EVEN THE MOST ROMANTIC among us ever conceived of a world where all men might live without work. The exploration of this possibility has been left for the makers of dreams. Even the writers of utopias have considered work as an essential part of their cities in the sun, if only for the moral benefit of the citizens. For all who live on earth, work sooner or later becomes an unescapable reality. But the fact that man must work for what he gets is rather a blessing than a curse. If it were not that nature is reluctant to yield her wealth, the thing we call civilization would never have arisen. It is only when nature challenges man's ingenuity that he is spurred on to productive achievement. However, it is not with the sweat and toil of the individual that the economist has been concerned, but with labor as a general factor in economic activity. Where does the supply of labor come from? How is labor organized as a factor in production? What effect do changes in the population have on the labor supply and upon labor's willingness to work? What are wages, and how are they determined? Why does labor organize? Can the antagonisms between the employer and employee be removed? These and similar questions demand an explanation if not an answer.

Incentives to Labor

The discussion of the question of why men work may lie more in the literature of psychology than in that of economics, but the fact is that economists have felt it necessary to make some assumptions on the question even though they have little scientifically established data. Many of the early economists wrote before psychology as a science was born and, in the absence of its present day findings, they made the best observations they could. The systems of economy, either real or fanciful, as proposed by Plato and Aristotle, take for granted that man will respond in certain ways when faced with certain conditions. PLATO expressed an ideal conception of man—almost a selfless ideal—when he asked man to merge himself with the state and accept his place in it according to some judgment outside himself. The communism of the *Republic* assumes such a perfect adjustment to life that each man in doing what he is best fitted to do ceases to be stimulated by personal ambitions. Plato was well aware of the selfish interests, not to say greed, which marked the ordinary life of Athens. Indeed, it is the disgust which he felt for such behavior that caused him to write the *Republic*.

ARISTOTLE was more realistic, although, like Plato, he assumed the willingness upon the part of the ordinary man to become subordinated to the will of the state. He nevertheless opposed Plato's communistic state on the grounds that self-interest was more dependable than interest in the common good as an incentive to industry and care of property. He was sure that man would work more diligently to care for his own family than he would for persons whom he did not know. On one point Plato and Aristotle agreed. Certain economic pursuits, they claimed, were worthy, while others were unbecoming to a citizen. As of old, agriculture was a highly honored calling—not the actual tilling of the soil but the management of an estate. The occupations of merchant, craftsman, and common laborer were only for foreigners, the poor, and slaves. In the organization of the ideal state each was to follow that for which he was best fitted, although it was not clear who was to do the selecting or how. Aristotle's defense of slavery is even more critical of the inherent abilities of individuals, for in his opinion some persons were born with a slave temperament. It was obvious that to work for one's living could never be respected in a society where the culture and education of its citizens were made possible by the toil of others.

Religion Dignifies Work: Aquinas and Calvin

THOMAS AQUINAS, writing much later, with a vast store of Christian doctrine behind him, nevertheless agreed with Aristotle in the principle that by guaranteeing to a man the fruits of his labor, he would be more industrious and conscientious in his work. Work indeed was a Christian duty. In his veneration of labor, Aquinas departed radically from the Greek philosophers, to whom menial work and the affairs of the market place were undignified. Even the work of buying and selling was acceptable to Aquinas, provided the merchant recognized the fact that, in his occupation, opportunities for the unrighteous accumulation of wealth were numerous and to be guarded against.

It was in the theological writings of JOHN CALVIN (1509–1564) that the religious incentive to labor reached its most compelling form. Recognized as a necessity by almost everyone, and dignified in the Christian tradition because almost all of the religious leaders had themselves worked, it remained for Calvin to give work its moral force. Labor became a Christian obligation. Calvin was a Swiss religious reformer who became the intellectual leader of the Reformation. To labor industriously in a calling was God's command to man. Men should not choose a calling because of the riches to be obtained; but once in a calling, they should not be unmindful of the wealth to be obtained by a close application to duty, since an increase in wealth could be used for Christian purposes. Men were admonished to shun luxury and be thrifty. Finally, while salvation came only to those who were predestined, success was accepted as a mark of God's favor. It therefore followed that, since no one knew beforehand who was predestined, such success was a confirmation that one had already been called by God. What stronger incentive could be exerted in a religious way than this combination of Christian teachings? One can readily understand why several authors, especially Max Weber, have described Calvinism as a powerful stimulus to the evolution of modern capitalism, if not its cause. The writings of R. H. Tawney in England and Werner Sombart in Germany have turned this thesis around however; making the rise of modern capitalism, in the countries of northern Europe, the cause of the Reformation and the reason for its ready acceptance.

The strong individualistic doctrine of the Reformation was taken over by the less religious philosophers and economists of the following centuries. Accepting individualism as a fact of the world in which they lived, they needed some other justification for it than the favor of God or the salvation of the soul. They founded their doctrine on the premise that it was instinctive for man to seek his own self-interest. This had been affirmed by philosophers as far back as Plato and Aristotle. Where they fell short, however, was in failing to understand that the powerful drive of self-interest had to have a sense of direction other than the individual's own happiness. Plato and Aristotle subordinated the individual to the state; Aquinas deferred to custom; Calvinism implied control in its moral admonitions and its doctrine of salvation; but the utilitarians found no such control save the sensitivity of man himself.

Work and the Pursuit of Self-Interest

There is little need to investigate at any length the doctrine of individual happiness and self-interest as advanced by Hobbes, Locke, Hume, Hutcheson, and Bentham. They believed in general that the criteria of human action were pleasure and pain; that human wants were insatiable; that for the most part everyone sought his own happiness above everything else; that work was not pleasurable; and that no one would work except as a necessity. They questioned the ability of material wealth to bring happiness but they presented no clear statement on this point. They recognized that men in general sought wealth, but criticized most wealth-getting as short-sighted.

The Physiocrats accepted the principle of individual self-interest as the basis of their economic system. The emphasis upon the right of the individual to determine his own course of action without government interference was the outgrowth of their belief in natural law. Quesnay, the leader of the Physiocrats, recognized that the rights of one person limited the rights of another, but he argued that an individual knew his own interests best and could be depended upon to carry out the laws of nature. Economic conduct, specifically, was to seek the greatest pleasure with the least effort.

ADAM SMITH in his *The Theory of Moral Sentiments* (1759)

and his *An Inquiry into the Nature and Causes of the Wealth of Nations* (1776) appears to have two views of labor's incentives. This may be due to the fact that in one book he was speaking as a philosopher and in the other as an economist. Smith, in his earlier writings, emphasized the force of vanity in motivating human action. Men strive for more than they need and for more than brings satisfaction, simply to secure the approval of their fellows. The riches themselves are not only useless but harmful to the individual, and usually the rich man finds that the happiness he anticipated from them is an illusion. Nevertheless nature uses these characteristics of man to inspire him to labor. In the end man produces useful things for the benefit of others. At the time of writing *The Wealth of Nations* Smith had no criticism to offer against the pursuit of wealth. He apparently assumed that wealth had happiness value or utility-creating power in no small measure. Furthermore, it was the individual search for wealth, and not vanity, which spurred men to labor. Smith was consistent throughout in sponsoring the principle that nature can and will direct the selfish actions of men toward the social good. An all-pervading force somehow correlates all the individual pursuits of self-interest into patterns that are socially beneficial.

Smith, rightly or wrongly, is given credit for the creation of the *economic man*. This is merely a short way of saying that the average man seeks his own economic self-interest, that to secure wealth with the least effort is his chief motivating force and because of this he seeks the cheapest market in which to buy and the dearest in which to sell. The followers of Smith accepted the psychological theories of *The Wealth of Nations* and completely overlooked the teachings of *The Theory of Moral Sentiments*. They expanded the identification of wealth with happiness which Smith's earlier book had denied.

The chief innovations of the classical writers were: the recognition of differences in intensity of desire; the law of diminishing utility; the importance of custom in determining the nature of the expression of self-interest; and the necessity of balancing wealth getting with the pain of so doing. All of these, in one way or another, were modifications of certain characteristics of the *economic man*. However, they continued to believe that man's self-interest led him to seek wealth.

It was because they refused to accept the definition of wealth proposed by Smith that men like Lauderdale, Rae, and those of the Austrian school broke with the classical tradition. They agreed that man's self-interest and his search for wealth were axiomatic, but they wanted the definition of wealth to include more than mere material goods, or objects with value in exchange.

The Psychological Approach to Labor: Veblen

Not until late in the 19th century did an economist appear who shared Smith's idea as set forth in *The Theory of Moral Sentiments*. It was an American, THORSTEIN VEBLEN, who hit upon the same idea—that of vanity as the motivating force behind labor. With this interpretation, Veblen gave new life to the search for the psychological basis of human action, and at the same time undermined the abstract methods of classical and neoclassical economic theory. In defense of the classical position Alfred Marshall and his followers turned from the psychological aspects of economic behavior altogether, contending that their only legitimate interest was in the objective facts of the market place. Such a retreat was unsatisfactory to Veblen and the growing school of institutional economists. The underlying theory of their school was that by research into the economic behavior of people, throughout the ages, valid conclusions might be drawn as to the persistent psychological factors which motivate human behavior. They not only believed it possible to make valid assumptions about these psycho-social drives, but also that it was impossible for economics to exist without making these assumptions. Herein lies the significance of Veblen's work.

By investigations of the behavior of primitive people and moderns, Veblen concluded that in the simple life of early man the basic drive was the production of things which were useful to the common good. Men got social approval and satisfaction through the exercise of their skill. The advancement of civilization brought a division of labor into warlike pursuits and peaceful industrial pursuits. Success in the former gradually made the latter secondary. Prestige and power resulting from personal exploit became wholly desirable. The symbols of success were the trophies of forceful acquisition. Instinctively conscientious labor, even the most skilled, brought little commendation; only through predatory occupations was social approval secured. The change to a commercial, money-making society changed standards of achievement. The predatory behavior was now transferred to the great industrial undertakings; ordinary labor remained undignified; symbols of success were now possession of property, opportunity for leisure, and the ability to consume conspicuously vast quantities of wealth. A characteristic of every age is the spirit of emulation. Those things which bring the respect and approval of one's fellows are sought after with all the energy one can muster. Usually this means imitation of those who are already respected and honored. The positions they hold and the things they do are honorable. The spirit of imitation is not always a pleasant competitive attitude; it becomes in modern society a bitter, envious thing, called by Veblen "invidious comparison." Consequently since wealth and leisure and conspicuous consumption are the marks of success in our commercial-industrial civilization, the pursuit of these things becomes the dominant motive of human behavior. But what has happened to the instinct of workmanship? Temporarily at least it is buried beneath the acquired characteristics of our time. But it shows itself in the dissatisfaction and restlessness which mark even the most successful persons according to the world's present standards.

To the problems raised by this examination of incentives to

labor there are as yet no final answers. One thing seems clear. We know very little about the motivating forces which compel men to work. Although the concept of an *economic man* whose chief aim in life is to acquire the greatest amount of wealth with the least possible effort now seems woefully narrow and inadequate, we have no other concept which permits an analytical approach to economic activity. Perhaps in the future research of psychology and institutional economics, new tools of analysis will be devised.

What Are Wages? The Early Hypotheses

The practical man of affairs has seldom troubled himself about the theory of what makes men work. If he paid his workers enough, he knew they would work. If he paid them enough!— here is a point at which businessmen and economists share a deep interest. Even more than rent, *wages* has been the battle ground of social reform. Laws of wages at various times in history have supplied the slogans for social upheavals and the placid justification for preserving the status quo.

Wage labor is a relatively new development in economic history. In societies of the past, menial and laborious tasks were the work of slaves or serfs. Only the artisan in such societies had the dignity of freedom, and the privilege of selling the product of his labor for a price. Of course, special forms of contractual relationship appeared frequently, but on the whole only a few persons participated in the system. Since the beginning of the 17th century in western Europe most men have been free to sell their labor to whoever would buy, at a price mutually agreeable to themselves. This system, combining freedom and wage labor, has been one of the most prominent characteristics of our economic order.

The use of the wage system is coincidental with that of modern capitalism. In the evolution from the legal and economic semi-bondage of Feudalism, the intellect, labor, business enterprise, and government all were freed from the stifling restriction set by custom, law, theology, and absolute monarchs. The change was not instantaneous. For a long time in England following the Black Death in the 14th century wages were regulated by law. Gradually these controls disappeared, and men assumed responsibility for determining their own wage scales. Under the new freedom where men worked for others with someone else's tools and raw materials, the old wage formula of a just wage according to one's social status, explained by Thomas Aquinas, no longer sufficed. The search for new explanations was on. The result was an array of theories of endless variety.

On most issues the Physiocrats and Mercantilists differed greatly, but they held the same views on wages. Both agreed that wages were set at the subsistence level of the laborer. It is an exaggeration to say that the Mercantilists formulated a definite theory of wages. That they accepted such a theory without question is inferred from their writings on taxation and foreign trade. For example CHARLES DAVENANT (1656–1714), in his discussion of foreign trade, pointed out how a rise in the price of foodstuffs would cause a rise in the wages of workers producing goods for export, thus shifting the advantage to England's competitors.

The Physiocrats stated the theory a little more positively. Quesnay believed the wage earners received only a subsistence wage because the pressure of competition reduced wages to a minimum. Turgot said that in all cases the industrial worker was paid only what was necessary in order for him to secure subsistence, although the worker on the soil was not so restricted. The low level was due, he believed, as Quesnay first had said, to the severe competition among workmen.

The Subsistence Theory: Smith, Ricardo, and the Socialists

Adam Smith appears to have accepted the subsistence theory of wages, but his discussion was more suggestive of alternate theories and possible modifications of the "iron law" (as Lassalle later called it) than it was a definite statement of it. The low standard of living, he declared, was not a cause but an effect of low wages. Fundamentally the subsistence of the workman and his family set the bottom limits to wages. A rise in wages, therefore, did not so much improve the lot of the wage earner as allow him to bring more children to adulthood. Hence high wages increased the number of workers, and low wages reduced the supply. Wages were never absolute in amount at a given time; there was room for bargaining to take place. The discrepancies in the bargaining power of the wage earners and the employers were clearly described. On the one hand, employers were few, no restrictions were set upon their organization, and tacit agreements existed among them as to wage policies. On the other hand, the opposite conditions applied to the wage earners.

Variations in the statement of the subsistence theory of wages continued to arise, even from those who have been regarded as its staunchest advocates. MALTHUS, basing his theory of wages on his theory of population, followed a supply and demand thesis, advocating the restraint of marriages as a means of decreasing the supply of wage earners and thus raising the standard of wages. The subsistence level does set the level of wages, but it is a subsistence level governed by custom. Malthus defined it as "that amount of those necessaries and conveniences, without which they would not consent to keep up their numbers." Therefore wages could not fall below this level for the various classes of people without a fall in the labor supply and a consequent increase in the rate of wages.

RICARDO's contribution to this doctrine was the theory of the natural wage and the market wage, the natural wage being the wage which enabled the laborers to subsist and perpetuate their race without change. But, he added, the subsistence level was determined by custom for the various strata of society. Ricardo, of course, merely transferred his general theory of value to a theory of wages. Since value is the labor cost of production, wages are the cost of reproducing the same quantity of labor. Variations in the supply of laborers or changes in the demand for the product may change market wages, but in the long run they will tend to conform to the natural wage. There is also the admission that market wages might continue for an indefinite period above natural wages. One must draw the logical inference that an increase in market wages raises the customary standard of living. Does the new wage become the natural wage? Ricardo, without being aware of it, anticipated aspects of the wage problem which are still plaguing economists. In an expanding economy, Ricardo was well aware, things may act quite differently than they do in a static period of history.

Still in line with the classical tradition, this theory has had something of a revival in recent years after losing ground in the last half of the 19th century. Alfred Marshall advanced the opinion that wages (Ricardo's natural wage) in the long run would tend to equal maintenance and reproduction costs.

The Socialists have fastened upon Ricardian theories and used them as a justification for the overthrow of the capitalist system. According to Ricardo, labor is the only source of value. He also said that wages tended to be just sufficient to provide for subsistence and reproduction on a given customary standard of life. It takes no imagination to foresee the socialist line of reasoning from this point on. Labor has created ample value for a decent existence; in return labor has received a subsistence wage. Obviously, value has been taken from labor by someone who had no right to it since it was the creation of labor.

In the hands of Marx these ideas were worked out as the theory of surplus value (already explained in Chapter I) and the doctrine of increasing misery of the working class. The last is an embellishment of a process of change first explained by J. K. Rodbertus (1805–1875) but given currency by Marx in the *Communist Manifesto*. Briefly, MARX said that as the productivity of labor increased through division of labor and the use of machines, the variation in wage levels tended to disappear since skilled workers were reduced to unskilled, all wages falling toward the barest minimum of subsistence. Consequently an increasing disproportion appeared between wages paid to the laborer and the value he created.

John Stuart Mill's Wages-Fund Theory

The credit for formulating another theory of wages, complementary to, rather than a substitute for, the subsistence theory, goes to JOHN STUART MILL. The theory known as the wagesfund or wage-fund theory was first suggested by Adam Smith when he intimated that a store of funds was available out of which wages could be paid. J. R. McCulloch, James Mill, Nassau Senior, Malthus, and Ricardo all found the concept of a wagesfund acceptable as an explanation for the level of wages. Wages, according to this theory described by John Stuart Mill, depended upon the relationship which existed between the supply of population and the capital available to employ workers. Mill was forced to add qualifications to the concepts of population and capital. By the former he meant those members of the laboring population who offered their services for hire; and by the latter, the amount of capital to be used for the payment of wages and any amounts incidental to the hire of laborers. Thus the funds available for wages were fixed at any given time, and the only way to increase wages was to reduce the number of wages to be paid or increase the capital funds available. The theory had important bearing upon the relation of trade unions and legislation to wages. At best the effect of either of these would be merely the shifting of a share of wages from one group of wage earners to another, since no absolute increase in the total wages paid was possible. That there was no fundamental contradiction between the subsistence and the wages-fund theories is clearly demonstrated by the fact that the strongest advocates of the subsistence theory also accepted the wages-fund theory without criticism.

Mill had influential supporters for his theory in Henry Fawcett and John Elliot Cairnes. To their credit it must be admitted that a modicum of truth appears in the general idea that wages are paid in part out of capital. This does not validate the general theory, as a glance at some of the fundamental criticisms will show; but it does relieve it of some of the stigma of being a distinct capitalist class doctrine.

Criticism of the wages-fund theory came from a variety of sources. Several decades before the final statement of the wages-fund theory, F. B. von Hermann in Germany had raised objections to it. Later Francis Walker, Francis Longe, and W. T. Thornton pointed out such errors and impracticalities that the theory failed to survive. These writers pointed out that it was the consumers who set the demand for labor, and workers might be provided for out of current income as well as from capital. Also there was no specific fund for wages which was separable from other funds to be used in production. The "fund" then was really a matter of the employer's discretion as to how much he would provide for wages. Mill was aware of the telling effect of these criticisms upon his theory, but he was not prepared to submit another; so his original statements continued to stand though the general acceptance of the theory lost ground.

The Residual Claimant Theory: W. S. Jevons

In countering the wages-fund hypothesis of Mill, an alternate theory known as the residual claimant theory was proposed. Adam Smith and others before him intimated that rent and profits were deductions from the produce of labor. WILLIAM STANLEY JEVONS first stated the theory positively in 1862, but the analysis of FRANCIS WALKER, twenty years later, is usually referred to. The essence of it is that portions of the product are first deducted for rent, interest, and profits. The remainder is the property of labor. The validity of the theory rests upon the independent determination of, and limitations upon, the shares of these three prior claimants. These being assumed, further economies in production or increased production would enlarge the share remaining for wages. The difficulty lies in establishing the independent determination of rent, interest, and profits. That apparently is yet to be done.

The Bargaining Theory—The Modern Idea

Also implied in Smith's *The Wealth of Nations* was the possibility of a bargaining theory of wages. His statement of the employer's advantage in bargaining as against the employee's disadvantage sounds extremely modern. He also noted the great variation in wage rates from community to community and from occupation to occupation. Likewise W. T. Thornton took into account the adverse bargaining condition of wage-earners. John Davidson and Maurice Dobb, American economists writing in 1898 and 1938 respectively, became dissatisfied with previous theories which tried to isolate one single determinant of wages, and they contended that a variety of factors influence wages not at all equally or consistently. Furthermore, there was competition among the various claimants for the larger shares in the total product. The limits within which bargaining can take place are a maximum at the top beyond which the employer cannot stay in business, and a minimum below which the employee will not work. A great many factors will determine the point, within these limits, at which an agreement will be made—not the least of which is the organized bargaining power of the employer and employee.

The chief criticisms of this hypothesis are: First, that the theory really begs the question. For, what really determines the limits of the employer's and employee's power? It might easily be subsistence modified by custom on the one hand and the sum of the claims of rent, interest, and profits on the other. Secondly, the theory seems to have its real application in organized industries, which actually account for a minority of employees and industries.

Neo-Classical Ideas on Wages

The most generally accepted theory of wages today is the marginal productivity theory. Once again, it is to Adam Smith that we turn for the first mention of such a thesis. He stated— without explanation, possibly without much thought—that the produce of labor was the wages of labor. A fuller statement occurred in JOHANN HEINRICH VON THÜNEN'S *Der Isolierte Staat* in 1826. This statement was worked out with mathematical precision; but in spite of the later popularity of the idea itself, this author's work has not been seriously considered. The best exponent was JOHN BATES CLARK (1847–1938), Professor of Economics at Columbia University. As analyzed by Clark the marginal productivity theory is really the explanation for the payment of rent, interest, profit, and price. Essentially the theory is this: the price of labor is determined by its marginal utility to the employer. Each unit of labor hired by the employer contributes to the value of the product, but the amount which each successive unit contributes is less than that of the one preceding; when the point is reached at which the contribution of the worker most recently hired just equals the wages he receives, the employer will no longer hire additional workers. The price of every other worker can be no greater than that of the last hired who stands ready to replace any of the preceding workers. The wages paid, then, are equal to the productivity of the last worker hired, or to the marginal productivity of the labor force.

The assumptions which must be made and the impracticality of the theory have, in recent years, undermined its popularity. It assumes a state of perfect competition which of course does not exist. The lack of knowledge of the market, the immobility of labor, and the presence of trade unions make it unrealistic. Moreover, the difficulty of separating the productivity of labor alone, from that of capital, seems insurmountable. On the whole, while such authorities as Alfred Marshall supported the theory, with reservations, the peak of its popularity has passed. No other theory of consequence has yet appeared to take its place.

The Division of Labor: Adam Smith and F. W. Taylor

In the very first chapter of *The Wealth of Nations* Adam Smith propounded an idea that seems commonplace, yet it is the basic theory of all modern economics. This is the theory of the subdivision of labor. The idea of each man doing the thing he is most capable of doing was not unique with Smith. Plato, in his *Republic,* claimed that the formation of society itself was due to the benefits achieved through specialization. Articles of consumption were produced better, more easily, and more abundantly "when one man does that thing which is natural to him . . ." The Physiocrats, likewise, were aware of the advantages of specialization, but their emphasis was on the unproductiveness of some labor and the productiveness of other. Agricultural labor produced all value from the land; other labor was sterile and drew its reward from the original value created by agriculture.

Smith took a different view of things. Labor was the source of wealth. Not just some types of labor, but all labor. All labor produced value, and in the fact of their cooperation none could be called useless. At great length Smith described the tremendous amount of cooperation which was necessary to provide a nation with the things it desires. The true source of the increase of the wealth of nations lies in the subdivision of labor and the system of automatic exchange which enables specialization to take place. The increase in total production is best exemplified by the pin industry, said Smith, and he then described it, showing that one man working alone could produce from one to twenty straight pins a day, while through specialization and subdivision of labor each workman could make the equivalent of more than one pound per day. The reasons for these great advantages were stated clearly: learning one job well saved the time usually absorbed in changes from job to job, and the close acquaintance with a single job led to the invention of new techniques. In further describing the division of labor he saw only two limits to its gradual increase—the extent of the market and the supply of capital. The former was a limitation because specialization required the presence of a large market in which to exchange the increasing quantities of the product. The latter was a limitation because subdivision required increased investments for space, materials, machinery, and advances for wages. These are not clearly defined by Smith but seem to be implicit in his description.

The other side of specialization Smith believed would be taken care of by man's "propensity to truck, barter, and exchange one thing for another," and the beneficial effects of each person seeking his own self interest. In exchanging that part of one's labor which was a surplus for the surplus of another, both were benefited; and through the participation of all, the total wealth of society increased. That some of Smith's assumptions were naïve, such as a "propensity to truck and barter," is obvious, but these are more than offset by the clarity with which he described the methods and advantages of division of labor and free exchange.

Criticism of the division of labor because of its dehumanizing effects has come from many sources. Smith himself said that concentration upon a few simple operations for long periods of time might cause the laborer to lose the faculty of exercising intelligent thought. WILLIAM GRAHAM SUMNER, an ardent advocate of many of Smith's theories, noted that the subdivision of labor caused the wage earner to lose all sense of responsibility for the conduct of the business and to lose with it his ability to calculate his own advantage and to foresee opportunities to improve his lot. The chief critics of the subdivision of labor are the Socialists. Marx claimed that machinery and the division of labor had taken from the work of wage earners all individual character, leaving only simple, routine, monotonous jobs which reduced the worker to an unimportant cog in a vast system of production, with his wages lowered to the level of the means of subsistence for propagation of his kind.

From the time of Adam Smith until early in the 20th century no real advance was made in the theory of labor's use as a productive agent. Then came the farsighted ideas of FREDERICK WINSLOW TAYLOR. Called scientific management or Taylorism, the plan was the beginning of revolutionary changes in the application of labor to industry. Taylor's aim was to introduce into industry certain "natural laws" which if followed would result in maximum prosperity for employer and worker alike. In general the plan called for the introduction of three new principles of industrial administration: First, to secure greater cooperation of the labor force, the best workmen were hired at wages high enough to guarantee their continued affiliation with the company. Second, to secure greater efficiency, work was standardized and reduced to a routine. Third, to insure the success of larger ventures as well as efficiency in small ones, a system of functional planning was introduced. It was business organized, not by the profit maker but by the engineer.

While the great hopes for prosperity and harmonious industrial relations faded rapidly in the disturbances accompanying World War I, Taylorism set the pattern for the gigantic workshops of today. Labor has opposed scientific management, and employers have abused its programs and purposes; but like Adam Smith's outline of the division of labor it presaged something new in the relationship of labor to production.

One final word on the subject of labor may not be amiss. The economic developments described so clearly by Smith, especially his division of labor, have cut the general population into antagonistic parts, each with its own economic interests, organizations, and political programs. This tendency was described by Marx as the class struggle and elevated to the position of the central factor in human history. In the *Communist Manifesto,* Marx described the process of the class struggle. In modern society this exhibits itself as the struggle between the property-less wage earner and the owners of the means of production; that is, the proletariat and the bourgeoisie. The latter group, not satisfied with its economic control, seeks to perpetuate its privileged position by securing control of the government. The wage earner finds the mechanization of his job the cause of declining wages. Women and children are brought in as competitors to do the simple tasks created by machines. Moreover the working class is constantly being augmented since the lower strata of the middle class is being pushed down into the ranks of the wage earner. Actually, however, the increasing size of business units brings workers together in larger masses, makes them aware of their common problems, and welds them into a strong revolutionary force. Such is Marx's theory of the progress of labor to a position of power.

Even those who do not subscribe to Marx's theories have been inspired to seek a fuller understanding of the problems of the wage earner. THE WEBBS, Sidney and Beatrice, English authorities on labor and social problems, describe the progress of the trade union movement in England, and point out clearly in their book, *Industrial Democracy,* how the organization of labor unions is gradually removing freedom from the labor market, substituting in its place institutional procedures of collective bargaining, wage determination, and control of working conditions, thus reverting to the controlled labor and customary wages and prices of the Middle Ages.

Theories of Trade Union Organization

The extensive literature on the theory of labor organization stresses the principle that a society controlled by organized workers is more desirable than the system of control by property owners.

We have already mentioned the formation of the revolutionary party which Marx believed was essential to the transformation of society into the socialistic state. The Webbs advocated the complete unionization of wage earners and the direct participation of the organized workers in government through the agency of a labor party whose membership would be identical with the membership of the trade unions. This program presupposes a democratic government in which majority rule is cherished. The essential principles of this plan have been achieved in England.

Of quite a different character was the anarchistic theory of MICHAEL BAKUNIN (1814–1876). He believed in the strong economic organization of all wage earners, but he was confident that any attempt to achieve political reforms would only lead to a diluting of the basic philosophy of the working men's movement. Economic equality should come first, principally by the confiscation of capital. The method he proposed was international organization of wage earners for revolutionary purposes.

The Syndicalist movement has had much more extensive growth in Europe than in America. One of its leading exponents was GEORGES SOREL (1847–1922), a one-time Marxist who had lost patience with the Socialist movement and allied himself with the more militant Syndicalists. His program depended upon the organization of wage earners into syndicates (associations of working men), not unions. The aim of the organization was not political, there was no intention of taking over the power of the state. General strikes and violence were looked upon as the chief means of securing control of industry, and domination of political institutions would follow automatically.

A less violent form of Syndicalism has been advocated by the Guild Socialists. R. H. TAWNEY and G. D. H. COLE, famous English economists, are prominent leaders of Guild Socialism. They believe that by gradual evolutionary means, workers organized along industrial lines can assume control of industry without at the same time controlling political institutions.

Perhaps the most conservative of all labor movements is to be found in the development of the American trade unions. As outlined by Samuel Gompers, founder of the American Federation of Labor, union organization should be confined to the skilled trades, which by the very nature of their control of skill could bring pressure upon employers to achieve their aims. The unions should also control the training of new craftsmen through systems of apprenticeship. The labor unions as a whole would not participate directly in political activity, nor would they become affiliated with any political party. In general their policy could be described as "rewarding their friends and punishing their enemies." Their chief weapons were strikes and boycotts. In dissatisfaction with the aristocratic type of union, John L. Lewis, president of the United Mine Workers of America, sponsored a new type of labor union called the industrial union. As described by Lewis, every man in a given industry, regardless of his craft or job, should be united in one union. The strength of such would lie not in the withholding of essential skills but in the complete organization of all workers in an industry. The policy of the industrial unions in politics has been to give direct support to the candidate most favorable to labor, but only as a temporary expedient until a party representing labor can be formed.

The absence of the names of the theoretical economists from this discussion of labor organization may be surprising. One must realize that the great economists of the past believed that the economic system could operate only under free competition. Labor organizations were unborn or in their infancy at the time. The reaction of the economists, therefore, was either to ignore the existence of trade unions or to look upon them, where they were present, as an evil of more or less consequence. That Adam Smith should have been aware of labor organizations and the problems associated with them even in his day is a true measure of his stature. Even Mill, for all his sympathy with the working man, felt that unions were useless. The disappearance of the freely competitive market—if such ever existed save in the minds of economists—has made it easier for later writers to discuss the theory of trade union organization as an important aspect of modern economy.

CHAPTER IV

The Place of Capital in the Economic Process

PLATO   ARISTOTLE   AQUINAS
CANTILLON   TURGOT   SMITH
LAUDERDALE   VON HERMANN   RICARDO   MILL
BASTIAT   VON BÖHM–BAWERK   SAY
SISMONDI   MARX   MARSHALL   KEYNES

What is capital and where does it come from? Is capital productive? What makes it possible to pay interest on capital? At what point does legitimate interest cease and usury begin? Why did early philosophy and religion condemn the taking of interest? What is profit? Is profit the payment for risk; for managerial ability; or is it merely theft from the earnings of labor? Should profitableness or social desirability be the test of whether or not an enterprise should be started or continued?

A s GENERALLY DEFINED, capital is an accumulation of wealth used in production. Land, labor, and capital are looked upon as the three chief elements of production. Of the three, *capital* is the most recent; for less than two hundred years ago it was almost completely ignored in the writings on economic subjects. As a matter of fact, there is no use of the word *capital* in the English language prior to 1600. For the next hundred years or more, it was used only as a term in the keeping of accounts or in signifying an investment of a certain amount in a business venture, such as a commercial voyage of the East India Company. Throughout its early history, the meaning of the term was confined to the idea of money investment, very much as the layman today looks upon it.

Development of Modern Ideas on Capital

The word *stock* was the predecessor of our word capital. Early discussions of economics constantly referred to an accumulation of stock as necessary before production could begin. The word seemed to signify a supply of consumer's goods on which the producer might live while he was in the act of preparing or actually producing the final commodity. Adam Smith's use of the word stock, in *The Wealth of Nations,* showed it to mean a supply of consumable goods, tools, equipment, and money. But his use of the term capital was not very clear. From his most definite statement, capital was that portion of a man's stock on which he expected a revenue. That there was some confusion in the meaning of the term in this period is quite understandable. It was the age of *commercial* enterprise. The principal use of capital was to finance trading companies. Industrialization, with its heavy emphasis upon factories and machinery, was just emerging.

It will be doing the Physiocrats more honor than they deserve to credit to them the first use of the idea of capital. Nevertheless in their writings, especially those of Turgot, the concept of circulating wealth was clearly a step in the direction of recognizing capital as an agent of production. The cultivation of the soil from which all value arose was, they said, made possible by advances for tools and seed and for the maintenance of the workman while crops were growing.

Adam Smith and His Early Critics: The First of the Modern Ideas on Capital

ADAM SMITH was the first to produce an analysis of the place of capital in production. His ideas were vague and indefinite, as later controversy proved; but none the less, he grasped the essentials of the use of capital. Although he believed that labor was the source of all value, he also said that the productivity of the laborer increased with the subdivision of labor, this in turn being dependent upon the quantity of capital available. Furthermore, the number of laborers could not be increased except by the augmentation of capital. In his opinion capital was accumulated by the savings of individuals, not as a social contribution but in the pursuit of self-interest. However, one who saved was a public asset; and a spender was a liability. It is impossible to discover what Smith believed to be the source of capital's productivity or its relative contribution to the value of the total product. As with so many other questions, Smith left his followers to debate the point and find explanations.

Criticisms of Smith as well as alternative explanations of the function of capital came from Lord LAUDERDALE who in 1804 published *An Inquiry into the Nature and Origin of Public Wealth and into the Nature and Causes of Its Increase*. He argued that Smith had not really given capital its due as a factor in production. Then he proceeded to analyze capital as an independent factor, productive in itself. Capital, as he saw it, either supplanted a certain amount of labor, or performed services which labor could not do. In either case capital was productive. Pursuing this point further, it was shown that not only were industry and labor limited by capital but it was also possible for a country to be oversupplied with capital. This resulted in Lauderdale's belief in a potential overproduction of consumer's goods. Parsimony, or saving, as a source of capital was denied in favor of labor itself as a source.

F. B. W. VON HERMANN (1795–1868) must also be rated as a critic of Adam Smith, although he supported many of the master's doctrines. In 1832 he published his *Staatswirtschaftliche Untersuchungen* which criticized Smith's discussion of capital on the two points that it did not go deeply enough into the nature, operation, and interrelations of capital, and that capital was not treated consistently throughout. Such objections did not destroy the original soundness of the idea, however. Hermann defined capital as "all producers of income which have durability and exchange value." Capital was divided into *use capital* and *industrial capital,* the latter being further broken down into loan and productive capital. His unique contribution to the theory of capital was that land, being a durable source of income, was capital. For purposes of the critical analysis, Hermann made capital a separate entity from any of the incorporated forms which it might assume, such as a machine or a tool. The purpose of this was to show that total capital was never destroyed, being replenished out of the income it produced.

RICARDO's point of view on capital was thoroughly in line with his labor theory of value: Capital was stored-up labor. That he was never completely satisfied with such a definition was borne out by his correspondence with McCulloch, and by his belief that value might be increased without labor. Of two objects brought to the market each requiring the same expenditure of labor, the superior price of one which arrived later was due to the longer period for which profits were withheld. This was obviously payment for waiting time. The idea was given more careful treatment by Nassau Senior who is credited with the formation of the abstinence theory of capital accumulation. He believed that land and labor were the primary factors in production, but unless tools were used the productive capacity of a people remained on a low level. In order to provide tools it was necessary to abstain from present consumption (unproductive consumption) in favor of using the resources available to produce more commodities (productive consumption). Abstinence was the term he gave capital; more elaborately defined, capital was wealth produced by labor to be used in the production of more wealth.

JOHN STUART MILL described with facility the ideas of the classical school. His discussions of capital reached back to days before Adam Smith for their basis. He seemed to consider capital as the maintenance for workers advanced during periods of activity until such time as they could get the benefit of their labor. This was not only the essence of the earliest ideas of capital as stock, but also it was a necessary ingredient of Mill's wages-fund exposition of wages. In his more practical sections, his conceptions of capital appear similar to the stored-up-labor theory of Ricardo.

The Continental Writers on Capital

The contributions of the later Continental economists to the understanding of the phenomenon of capital showed marked innovations, most of which have been rejected by the neo-classical school. BASTIAT, writing in the late 1840's, explained capital as stored-up labor, but showed how its value was constantly diminishing. The increasing productivity of labor made it possible to produce the same item of capital a year later at a smaller labor cost. Certain obvious questions arise concerning the gaps in Bastiat's analysis, for example what causes labor's increasing productivity.

VON THÜNEN added to the theory of capital the diminishing productivity concept which he had applied so well to rent and wages. Indeed, starting with his basic definition of capital as stored-up labor, he analyzed the function of capital in much the same fashion as he had dealt with labor and land.

One of the most extensive works on capital is found in the writings of EUGEN VON BÖHM-BAWERK (1851–1914). His *Kapital und Kapitalzins* is a description and critique of the history of theories of capital and interest, and a presentation of his own understanding of these subjects. His theory, depending upon the assumption that future values at the present time are less than present values, is known as the time preference concept. Men, he said, fail to calculate fully their future wants, therefore goods in the present are of more value than the same goods in the future. He also believed, as Bastiat, that present goods had greater value because capital was productive. The addition of more capital, however, had the effect of postponing the enjoyment of benefits for increasingly longer periods. Therefore, the value of capital had to be judged by its ability to make up the loss between the present consumption and future consumption of the goods which were turned into capital. By incorporating into his own theory the ideas of von Thünen on diminishing returns, Böhm-Bawerk provided the basis for much of our current thought on capital.

Keynes and the Modern Revolt Against Classical Doctrine

The recent works of JOHN MAYNARD KEYNES (1883–   ), the great economist of Cambridge, England, have challenged many of the older ideas on capital, although in general he has remained well within the neo-classical tradition. His book on *The General Theory of Employment Interest and Money* published in 1936 is of importance in this connection. In the first place he shared the views of certain of his predecessors that it was possible for the supply of capital to become larger than a community could put to use. This condition would arise because the search on the part of savers for a prospective yield (appreciation in value of an investment) reduced the demand for present goods, and would not, as most economists had contended, create a demand for future goods. Since prospective yield depended upon the demand for goods, the withdrawal of present demands would make even the existing supply of capital too large. According to his own statement he claimed to "sympathise, therefore, with the pre-classical doctrine that everything is produced by labor aided by what used to be called art and is now called technique, by natural resources which are free or cost a rent according to their scarcity or abundance, and by results of past labor, embodied in assets, which also command a price according to their scarcity or abundance." Furthermore, the theory of being paid for waiting, upon which Nassau Senior and von Böhm-Bawerk placed so much emphasis, has no foundation in fact, he felt, since waiting or abstinence cannot in itself produce value.

Theories of capital play an important part in the teachings of the exponents of socialist doctrines. One of the first to complain about the effects of capital was SISMONDI (1773–1840), who in so many instances used the theories of Adam Smith as a starting point in making his analysis of capital. The division of labor was the principal cause of the increased powers of production. This, however, was dependent upon an ever increasing quantity of circulating capital. The machines and the expensive establishments in which they were housed required a first cost which was only returned over long periods of time. This presupposes a quantity of capital which can be spared from present use "in order to establish a permanent kind of rent." Sismondi contended that the introduction of new machinery should serve a social purpose such as creating a new demand for labor or putting goods within the reach of new consumers. If it did not achieve this purpose, it should at least not displace or render useless a certain number of producers whether native or foreign. He saw no way to control inventions at home, much less abroad; and concluded, that economic life was a war of machines against man.

The Socialists

The views of KARL MARX were in the same direction, but better grounded in theoretical economics. Modern capital came into being in the 16th century in the form of money to be used for commercial purposes. Through the process of appropriating the surplus value produced by the worker in the form of goods which were then sold on the market for cash, the employer was able to purchase additional means of production. This process is continued, as Marx says, "by incorporating living labor with their dead substance" and the employer continues to convert a "materialized and dead labor into capital . . . a live monster that is fruitful and multiplies." This new capital is then used to exploit labor further. As additional machinery is added from the surplus value already appropriated by the employer the productivity of labor is increased. The worker does not share in it, as we have noted before, for his wages can never rise above a subsistence level. The net result of this process is the increasing impoverishment of the working class and the increase of capital (the means of production) in the hands of the employer. Marx did not condemn capital as such, only the fact of private ownership which enabled the employer to appropriate for himself surplus value created by labor with the aid of capital. There is no doubt that Marxian capital was the old Ricardian concept of stored-up labor.

The Theories of Interest: From Ethics to Economics

This discussion has from time to time bordered upon the related field of the theory of interest and profit. In fact, no discussion of capital would be complete without an analysis of these two subjects which have proved themselves to be among the most controversial in economic theory. Much of the early literature on interest was concerned with its ethical rather than its economic aspects. PLATO condemned interest as it applied to loans. ARISTOTLE, investigating the various aspects of economic life more deeply than Plato, also condemned it on the ground that money was barren and could not reproduce itself. To require payment over and above the value of the thing itself when it had produced nothing, he believed, was unjust. The early Christian fathers declared that usury was sinful, but they had not only the Greek philosophers but also biblical precedent for their objection. It remained for AQUINAS to modify the earlier Christian doctrine in the face of clearly observed conditions and practices in his own time. He divided material wealth into those articles which were consumed in use and those which were used without consuming. The first could not be loaned but only purchased outright; the second could be leased for use and returned. Money, somewhat illogically it seems to us moderns, was looked upon as of the former variety. Hence Aquinas sided with Aristotle in condemning the dishonest practice of requiring more than its face value as the sale price of money. Nevertheless, interest could be paid to persons who were professional usurers (who were usually not controlled by Christian doctrine) if the borrowers desired the money for good purposes. Two general conditions prevailed during the Middle Ages when payment of interest might be considered legitimate. One, *damnum emergens,* occurred when the owner realized a loss because of having loaned the money. The second, *lucrum cessans,* was the occasion of the owner losing an opportunity for profit while his money was loaned to another. Christian doctrine approved the first but raised doubts against the second. The general trend was to increase the number of exceptions to the prohibition against interest. Purchases on credit might carry a higher price; bills of exchange were discounted; money invested in partnerships was allowed to earn interest; city debts carried interest and lending societies were able to set a rate. The periodic decline of the prohibition against usury corresponded closely to the rise of opportunities to invest money in productive enterprise. The final break in religious objections came when Calvin took a positive view on the legitimacy of interest, with only minor reservations. For a time following the Reformation, usury laws setting a maximum rate of interest existed. Then, finally, under the attacks of men like Bentham the laws were abolished. BENTHAM'S point of view was that the usury laws made it easy for the old settled business enterprises to get money, but new industries which involved risk but which also were the origins of progress could not borrow because no lender would assume so great a risk at such a low rate of interest. At last, during the 20th century, usury laws returned in the form of small loan acts regulating the amount of interest allowable on loans of less than a certain small sum, commonly $300.

Interest and the Productivity of Capital

Concern for the economic aspects of interest dates from the latter part of the 17th century when a pamphlet debate engaged in by Sir Josiah Child brought forth the theory that the wealth of a country was a cause and not an effect of a low interest rate. Locke proposed that the interest rate could be determined by the ratio of ready money to the "whole trade of the kingdom," by which he probably meant business transactions. John Law also took the position that if the quantity of available money increased the interest rate would fall. Sir William Petty in opposing attempts to restrict the rate of interest protested that such a course was impossible since interest rates were set by the quantity of money, which was beyond Parliament's control.

DAVID HUME writing in 1752 subscribed to the quantity of money theory in the sense of a temporary cause of interest. Using Spain as an illustration, he showed how the influx of gold and silver from the New World caused prices and interest to rise temporarily, only to subside again to normal levels. This theory, he believed, was not the true cause of variation in interest rates. Very realistically he claimed that the interest rate was set by supply and demand. If society was composed mainly of poor persons who were always wanting to borrow, interest rates would be high; should society have an abundance of wealthy men seeking profitable places to lend money, the competition among them would tend to drive down interest rates. He added a significant factor, that interest rates were also influenced by the profit to be secured from commerce. High profits meant less money to lend, therefore high interest rates, and vice versa.

CANTILLON, in a book published in 1755, although written much earlier, objected along with Hume to the quantity of money theory of interest. Though an increase of money might raise prices it would not necessarily raise interest rates. He believed that a change in the class status of borrowers and lenders also influenced the rate. For example, in the Middle Ages when borrowing was by persons in dire need, interest hinged upon the degree of necessity of the borrower and the unscrupulous nature of the lender. In the time during which Cantillon was writing, borrowing was for business enterprise, and the interest rate rose in direct relation to the number of such enterprises. He claimed that the prodigality of nobles and war also caused a rise in interest rates by increasing the activity of business enterprises. In addition to this he made a unique contribution to interest theory by describing the importance of a person's social class upon the rate of interest.

Upon the simple foundations laid by Hume and Cantillon, TURGOT built a more elaborate concept of interest. He accepted the supply and demand theory. To this he added the new idea that increasing supplies of "movable riches" were constantly being provided out of savings from previous incomes and profits. He believed that a greater amount of saving would lower the interest rate if the number of borrowers remained constant. Turgot also claimed that interest was the price of an advance of money. Although this last observation seemed obvious, it began a never ending series of speculations on the question of why interest was paid at all.

The more formal statement of the theories expounded by Hume and Turgot came from JEAN BAPTISTE SAY. His reduction of all prices to a matter of supply and demand was directly applied to interest. By dividing capital into disposable capital and production capital he made a notable advance in the understanding of interest. Only the former influenced interest rates, he claimed, for since the latter was already incorporated into enterprise there was no way in which it could affect the supply of disposable capital. Say also introduced the idea that not one but many factors may influence interest rates including risk and liquidity, *i.e.* the ease with which the loan can be converted into cash.

Another class of interest theories has been called the *indirect productivity* theories. The basis of these theories is the fact that the addition of capital enables a workman to produce in greater quantities. Therefore the one who supplies the capital is entitled to a share of the increase. Lauderdale was one of the first supporters of this theory. He believed in the independent productivity of capital. Although he did not distinguish between interest and profit, his argument showed that both would naturally come from the earnings of capital. VON THÜNEN in *Der Isolierte Staat* applied his theory of diminishing returns to the general productivity idea and proposed that the interest rate would be determined by the productivity of the marginal unit of capital, that is, by the unit whose cost just equaled the amount it could produce. Von Thünen went on to explain that the interest rate could not hope to be the total increase in production derived from the use of the capital, since competition tended to reduce the price of capital to the amounts paid by those who could profit by the capital least.

One of Ricardo's ideas on interest might possibly be classified here although it differs slightly in being simpler. He said that the interest on money is determined by the rate of profit which can be made by the employment of capital. Add the idea of diminishing returns, and the theory is not materially different from von Thünen's.

The Payment for Waiting: Time Preference—von Böhm-Bawerk

Developed at the same time as the productivity theory was another theory with which it was later linked to provide the most popular explanation of interest and interest rates. This was the *time-preference* theory, that is, the theory based on the contention that because present goods possess superior value over future goods a payment must be made for waiting. In his definition of capital as abstinence, Nassau Senior turned attention to the factor of waiting. In order to create capital it was necessary to abstain from present consumption. Abstinence was not pleasant, therefore payment was necessary in order to cause persons to endure the discomfort. No distinction was made among English economists between interest and profit, consequently it was assumed that waiting might be responsible for either one or the other or both. John Stuart Mill built upon the work of Nassau Senior and John Rae in elaboration of this point but he made no modifications of the general theory.

It was VON BÖHM-BAWERK who made the synthesis of the time-preference and the productivity theories of interest. After a laborious description and frequent criticisms of existing theories of capital and interest he proposed his own positive theory. He accepted the proposition that man generally prefers present to future values, although this might be greatly modified by the character of the individual and the security of the environment. He claimed, in addition, an economic as well as a psychological reason for present values being greater. Since the function of capital is to increase the productivity of labor, an article made today will have greater value than the same article in the future, as its cost of production is greater today. Because of these facts people were willing to pay extra for the use of goods in the present, rather than wait until the future, and those who abstained from the use of goods until the future felt the need for compensation. But added to these considerations was the diminishing productivity of capital. Consequently interest rates tended to be set at a point where the payment people were willing to make for present values against future values equaled the productivity of the last unit of capital added. This was not materially different from the von Thünen analysis except that the demand for capital was analyzed with regard to the time-preference theory. One might draw the valid conclusion that this was merely another manifestation of the process of synthesizing utility on the one hand with cost of production on the other, a relationship so frequently made in other theories.

Modifications of von Böhm-Bawerk, both in the sense of elaborations of and deductions from his theory, have appeared in vast quantity since his original work. General support for the theory came from such writers as the American economist Irving Fisher. Although using different approaches, even different language, the general idea of Fisher was similar to that of von Böhm-Bawerk. The interest rate was set when the marginal utility of the capital to the borrower, which consisted of both the psychological factor of time preference and the marginal productivity of the sum borrowed, was said to balance the lender's time preference and his estimate of the opportunity for investment. The general criticism leveled against this analysis was the inability to know what the psychological factors of borrowing and lending were and how they worked. Assumptions on the question could be made, but they provided a very artificial base on which to establish a theory. Furthermore, the assumption that time preference led one to prefer present to future values had so many obvious exceptions that it seemed unwise to believe that it applied generally or for the average man.

As opposed to the complicated analysis of von Böhm-Bawerk there was a tendency to return to simpler formulae for explaining interest and interest rates. ALFRED MARSHALL, although he made no systematic treatment of interest, made several miscellaneous observations on the subject which may be briefly summarized.

He believed that the interest rate was set by the supply of the money stock balanced against the demand for capital. In small localities the equilibrium would remain fairly constant because supplies of capital might be drawn from outside communities. In the case of larger areas, however, the demand for capital could not be met immediately because saving required time; hence, a rise in the interest rate would be inevitable until equilibrium was re-established by the withdrawal from the market of those persons to whom the marginal utility of the added capital would not warrant the payment of the added cost. He indicated an acceptance of the Say doctrine that previously invested capital did not affect the interest rate, since by no consideration could it enter the supply of money available for loans. From time to time he referred in a minor way to the time-preference idea which has led some authorities to link Marshall with von Böhm-Bawerk.

Now a note on the interest theory of John Maynard Keynes. He assumed, with some justice as far as our own society was concerned, that most people invest not because of the interest rate but because of the prospective yield or, in other words, the increase in value of the original investment. However, it was also true that a large number of persons would save even if there were no interest rate. Fundamentally the interest rates in vogue were a result of custom on the one hand and liquidity preference on the other. This line of reasoning dealt a mortal blow to classical theory, which was based, in the long run, upon supply and demand for capital.

Modern Protests Against Interest

These views have on the whole discussed interest as an economic fact of our present society and have sought to explain it in terms of economic processes. Another body of theory, harking back to the medieval period, attempted to deal with interest as an ethical problem. Using the statements of Smith and Ricardo —which give labor the entire credit for the creation of value—as a starting point, Socialist writers beginning with Sismondi claimed that interest was an unjust charge on the rightful earnings of labor. Sismondi believed that payment for capital was justified since capital was stored-up labor and consequently required remuneration. Whether the payment was equal to a replacement cost of the capital in terms of its labor cost of production, Sismondi did not say. This might easily be inferred. Marx and other Socialists contended that it was the stored-up labor in capital goods which was productive and consequently should be paid for only as its labor cost of production, not as capital or as waiting time. It was the superior bargaining position of the capitalist which allowed him to secure an interest that was fundamentally unjustified, and the institution of private property which gave him claim to it.

What Is Profit? The Classical Tradition

At many points the theory of interest coincided with the theory of profits. Indeed, some authors discussed them interchangeably, and others found that interest rates and profit rates were determined by the same factor—the earning power of capital. There are, however, a number of different theories as to the meaning, the origin, and the rate of profit. The early writers, prior to Adam Smith, made no clear distinction between interest and profit, although from the literature it is obvious that the businessmen of the time, conducting their affairs many times on borrowed capital, must of necessity have paid interest, and considered profit as the residue. The Physiocrats and Mercantilists failed generally to note any difference between interest and profit. Adam Smith tried to clarify the meaning of these terms. He pointed out that profits were not wages paid for any kind of supervisory labor, but were a distinct income derived solely from capital or stock, as he called it. He was careful to caution readers against an error quite common even today, namely, that of lumping both the earnings of capital and the wages of proprietorship as "profits," when a business enterprise was conducted by a person who furnished his own capital. This point was elaborated by J. B. Say, a close follower of Smith's theories. Although Say's terms *profits of industry* and *profits of capital* were in themselves somewhat confusing, he tried to separate the wages of the entrepreneur from his returns as an investor. *Profits of industry,* he said, included wages paid to common labor and to the supervisors and directors of the enterprise, whereas profits of capital included elements of interest and payment for risk. Say was extremely critical of the English language at this point, claiming that the absence of any word in English corresponding to the French "entrepreneur" was responsible for the failure to make the distinctions which he and Smith had pointed out. When the rate of profit in relation to the risk and the length of waiting time was low, capital would neglect such ventures in favor of more lucrative ones. This withdrawal would cause the competition to slacken (due to the lack of new ventures and the failure of old ones). A rise in profits would follow until risk and waiting were well enough rewarded to encourage the investment of new capital.

The classical tradition continued with the writings of Ricardo and Mill. Ricardo is never very clear on the meaning of profit. In some instances it was discussed as a residual amount after labor was paid. Since the subsistence theory of wages implied a stable amount for this factor, the increase or decrease in the total income would affect profits. In other discussions Ricardo stated the conviction that the return on capital was payment for past labor. It is always well to keep in mind that Ricardo speaks usually of long-term principles, under systems of perfect competition; although once in a while the peculiar movements of the present broke into the exposition. Certainly the reward of capital as payment for the labor necessary to produce it was a "natural" payment, as Ricardo saw it, modified at any given time by the short-term conditions of the market.

Both Mill and Ricardo were interested in the effect of population movements on profits. They both believed that the increase in population resulted in use of the less productive land; and capital, earnings, and, of course, profits would fall, tending to approach zero. Advances in civilization, however, of which inventions were an important part, would go a long way to preserving a substantial rate of profit.

In his discussion of the relation of profits to other forms of income, Mill incorporated into his own thought some of the ideas of J. B. Say. He advised that the returns on business enterprise should be broken down into the return on the use of capital, a payment for risk, and wages to the entrepreneur. Just which of these should constitute true profit, Mill did not say.

This discussion of the elements which constitute profit has continued on into the 20th century. Both Alfred Marshall and J. B. Clark proposed solutions to the difficulty. Marshall believed that profits were made up of the same divisions as described by Mill, but Marshall also added the idea of profits as combination earnings. This was an aspect of profit which appeared only as large scale industry began to take shape. Whereas, in earlier days the owner of a business enterprise invested his own capital, managed the business, and assumed the risk, in modern times each of these services could be and was frequently performed by a specialized group for a fee that was fixed in amount by market conditions. Profit, then, would be the result of the skill with which these factors were brought into combination in a particular branch of industry. This seemed to have certain advantages from a quantitative standpoint. If, as in large corporations, all the traditional elements of profit could be bought at a stipulated sum, even risk, the surplus over and above all costs could be nothing more than the earnings of an intangible aspect of the business enterprise best characterized as the skill in integrating the factors of production, at a certain time, for a certain purpose.

Not content with this explanation, Marshall and Clark

separately, proposed that profit be considered as the product of market disequilibrium. They assumed a hypothetical situation in which perfect competition and the free application of supply and demand brought all aspects of the economic process into balance. Under such a circumstance there would be no profit. Such a situation could never exist; however it was theoretically possible and interesting. Its failure to materialize was an indication of the operation of such unpredictable forces as unexpected shortages, losses, and demands. Marshall coined the term quasi-rent to cover the short-term earnings of the forces of production which arose because of the unbalance in the economic process. Although there is no reason why quasi-rent should not be substituted for the term profit to define such earnings, there does not seem to be any significant gain from so doing.

Contemporary economists have delved deeply into the elements of profit, hoping to grasp a factor which would seem to give a fairly adequate explanation of profit for the modern type of business enterprise. When, as in many industries, all of the constituents of profit, such as wages of an entrepreneur, return on invested capital, and payment for risk-bearing, are met in advance for a definite sum, the source of profit becomes an elusive and complicated factor indeed.

CHAPTER V

Foreign and Domestic Trade

MISSELDEN   MUN   PETTY   NORTH
QUESNAY   TURGOT   SMITH   SAY
RICARDO   MILL   MALTHUS
BASTIAT   VON THÜNEN   MÜLLER   LIST   RAE
HAMILTON   CAREY   PATTEN

*Is the policy of "sell more than you buy" as valid for nations
as for the individual businessman? Is money or useful goods
the better measure of an individual's wealth? Of a nation's
wealth? Will free trade or government protected business
produce the most profitable economic relations? Are there
stages in economic development when protection is more
advantageous than free trade? What are the modern
methods used by business to control the "market"?*

THE STORY OF THE TRANSITION from the self-sufficient manor of
the Middle Ages to the great systems of national economy of the
modern world is largely the story of the rebirth and maturing of
foreign and domestic trade. It is difficult, if not impossible, to
differentiate cause and effect in historical sequences. Was it the
Arab control of the Near East which caused the western voyages
of Columbus? Was it Watt's application of steam to hand tools
which set in motion the industrial revolution? One cannot give
an unqualified answer to questions such as these. Evidence is

ample, however, to show that behind the economic activity of the
latter days of the Middle Ages and the centuries which followed
lay the constantly expanding markets at home and abroad, spur-
ring on the increasing productivity of farm and factory. Without
a market for goods, few of the revolutionizing inventions of the
past centuries would have become so well known or so widely accepted. So it is first of all to trade that we must turn if we are to
understand the driving power and organizing genius which
guides and motivates our economy.

Trade in the Middle Ages

Trade, of course, never ceased even in the most static period of
the Middle Ages. Itinerant merchants plied their way from town
to town in spite of bands of outlaws, avaricious nobles, taxes, and
tolls. Goods from the East filtered through the Italian cities to
points in central and northern Europe. Soon merchants were buying articles made in one part of Europe to sell in another. The
knowledge that goods could be sold stimulated changes in
methods of production. Enterprising craftsmen became merchants. They secured raw materials and put them out to other
handicraftsmen who carried on small manufacturing in their
homes. For a time the merchant capitalist dominated the productive process. The expansion of markets called forth new forms
of manufacture; the power driven machine, the factory, wages.
The extensiveness of trade required money, banks, credit. And
so the economic system changed into modern industrial capitalism
at the heart of which lie trade and the market.

. The trade of the 15th, 16th, 17th centuries was carried on
mainly in the form of monopoly. The right to do business was a
privilege dispensed by the head of the state for a price. But perhaps more fundamental as a reason for the large scale of trading
organizations was the risk involved and the initial expense of
outfitting expeditions. Foreign trade especially was marked by the
monopolistic character of the participants. The MERCHANT AD-

VENTURERS, the MUSCOVY COMPANY, and the EAST INDIA COM-
PANY were synonyms for power and wealth. Their leaders were
merchants whose commercial and political influence put them
in the front rank of the nation's citizens.

Mercantilism

When Adam Smith was searching for a name to identify the
body of economic ideas generally accepted in the century or two
before he wrote, he called it Mercantilism, because of the emphasis placed upon trade. In earlier chapters we have already en-
countered the outstanding representatives of this general theory
of economic life: Mun, Petty, Child, Steuart, Montchretien, and
von Hornick.

Briefly stated the Mercantile doctrine identified wealth with
money. It therefore emphasized the necessity of a community so
conducting its affairs as to acquire an abundance of precious
metals. The surest method of doing this, especially for those
countries without mines, was to export the utmost quantity of
its own manufactures, and to import the absolute minimum from
other nations. The excess of exports over imports would be paid
for in gold and silver. A favorable balance of trade, that is, when
more coin is received than is paid out, was considered the only
satisfactory condition of commerce. The establishment and maintenance of such a favorable balance was not alone the responsibility of individual merchants; the government carried a
heavy obligation as well. It was agreed that by prohibitions
against foreign goods, subsidization of exports, restriction upon
the export of precious metals, and the creation of monopolies
among the trading companies, the government might assure the
nation of a steady influx of gold—as the means of making the
state strong and powerful.

While most economists of the period must be classed as Mercantilists, not all of them would subscribe to the above summary
of Mercantilist ideas. Many of them were too clear sighted to be

trapped by certain obvious errors in the Mercantilist line of reasoning. However, these men were in a sense merely expressing in terms of ideas what was the actual practice of the times. In spite of variations similar conditions gave birth to similar ideas. The growth of commerce and discoveries of the New World led to the rapid development of a common medium of exchange. Feudalism, with its barter and general self-sufficiency, gave way to an economy where buying and selling was important. The men of the time were impressed with the power of money. Money was always in demand. The more of it one had, the more goods he could control. Money would last. Tomorrow, or the next day, or years hence, money represented the power to acquire goods. The formation of great states, with powerful governments, great armies, luxurious courts, and hosts of officials, required the expenditure of vast sums of money. Dense populations and industry seemed better able to produce revenue-getting conditions than sparsely settled regions dependent upon agriculture. Hence industry and trade received the favors of government, while agriculture was left to seek its own survival. Colonies were sought as markets for goods, while severe laws restricted their economic freedom and made them dependent upon the grudging purchases of the mother country alone for commerce and trade. Duties on imports, barriers to the export of gold, and great trading monopolies were characteristic of every nation. These things were not theories; they were the most important facts of the times. The economists either summarized what was happening and found reasons to justify it, or they took issue with the turn of events and suggested alternatives. Such ideas compose the theory of Mercantilism. Whatever one may think of its practicability as an economic system, the theories of Mercantilism were truly representative of the times.

One of the early exponents of Mercantilism was EDWARD MISSELDEN, a merchant of the first part of the 17th century. His two pamphlets, *Free Trade, or The Means to Make Trade Flour-*

ish (1622) and *The Circle of Commerce* (1623) were written not as detached expositions of prevalent theory, but as tracts designed to secure favorable action on several proposals sponsored by the author. He wanted above all to curtail the activities of the East India Company, which he claimed was draining the country of its specie. Because the Company had a governmental concession to export large quantities of bullion on each voyage provided a similar amount was returned in six months, Misselden was led to believe that in being taken from the country economic depressions were the inevitable result.

In later years Misselden became a business associate of the East India Company and consequently discontinued his attacks upon that Company's privileges in his later work, *The Circle of Trade*. While recognizing the importance of rates of exchange as indices of the various market conditions for money, he did not believe that the balance of trade was dependent upon favorable exchange rates. He believed rather that one had first to determine whether a favorable or unfavorable balance existed between one nation and another. Once determined, it was the business of government to take proper measures to secure a favorable balance.

THOMAS MUN (1571–1641), perhaps the ablest exponent of Mercantilism, began his explanation of that doctrine while endeavoring to justify the practices of the East India Company, of which he was a director, against such attacks as those of Misselden. *A Discourse of Trade from England into the East Indies* (1621), Mun's first work, was not his best. It was a polemic against attacks on his Company, with an abundance of charges and counter charges and a minimum of considered thought. It was in his *England's Treasure by Forraign Trade, or The Balance of Our Forraign Trade Is the Rule of Our Treasure,* written about 1630 but published posthumously by his son in 1664, that Mun gave his most lucid explanation of the mercantile philosophy and presented a comprehensive plan to increase the wealth and treasure of England. The merchant, according to Mun, was a most important figure in the community since he was responsible for enriching the kingdom, for providing the king with revenue and maintaining his treasure. Although an academic education was not necessary for the merchant, he should be well versed in language and skilled in ship building and navigation. Mun accepted in principle the mercantile idea of a favorable balance of trade.

The ordinary means therefore to increase our wealth and treasure is by *Forraign Trade,* wherein we must observe this rule; to sell more to strangers yearly than wee consume of theirs in value . . . because that part of our stock which is not returned to us in wares must necessarily be brought home in treasure.

How clearly dependent the nation's welfare was upon foreign trade in Mun's opinion was indicated in the closing pages of his book.

So much Treasure only will be brought in or carried out of a commonwealth as the Forraign Trade doth over or under ballance in value. . . . Behold then the true form and worth of forraign Trade, which is the great Revenue of the King, The honor of the Kingdom, The noble profession of the merchant, The School of our Arts, The supply of our wants, The Employment of our poor, The Improvement of our Lands, The Nurcery of our Mariners, The walls of the Kingdoms, the means of our Treasure, The Sinnews of wars, The terror of our Enemies.

In addition to his elaborate praise of foreign trade, Mun made some practical suggestions as to how a favorable balance was to be maintained. The third chapter of *England's Treasure by Forraign Trade* was devoted to cataloguing the devices which might be used for this purpose. He advised England to cultivate waste lands, refrain from exclusive consumption of imported goods, set prices on exports as high as the traffic would bear, sell scarce necessities dear and plentiful goods cheap, ship only in English bottoms, be conserving in the domestic use of natural resources, compete with the Dutch in exploiting the fisheries off the English coasts, develop the carrying trade by creating facilities for storing and transshipment of goods, encourage the purchase of materials at their source of supply rather than through middle men, allow the export of money itself when used as stock, remove taxes on imports of raw materials used in manufacturing of later exports, and, finally, to make domestic goods serve the needs of the population. Such a program of industry and frugality seemed almost infallible as a guide to national wealth and power.

Thomas Mun was not uncritical of the system he so well described. For example, his proposal for the export of bullion was not readily accepted by his contemporaries. To them no bullion should leave the country save in payment of debts. Mun saw beyond the immediate present. He believed that the use of bullion to foster a carrying trade established by Englishmen abroad was a legitimate excuse for shipping gold out of the country, since a prosperous trade would in time return more bullion to the country than was taken out. The analogy Mun used to drive home his point has become famous: A farmer viewed only at seed time when he scatters his seed over the ground seems wasteful; but when his harvest is considered, the worth of his action becomes apparent. Thus Mun at this early date pleaded the cause of all foreign investors. The economic history of England amply proved his point.

On other aspects of mercantile theory and practices Mun was in advance of the men of his own time. He did not fall completely into the fallacy of thinking that wealth and money were identical. It was what money could buy that was important. Furthermore he denied the idea that in order to secure a favorable balance of trade it was essential for each merchant to have a favorable balance. The sum total of exports and imports for a given period was the important consideration. It was a hundred years or more before this last consideration led to a complete reappraisal of the idea of foreign trade.

There was great similarity between Mun's exposition of Mercantilism and that presented by Philipp von Hornick, an Austrian whose works appeared a half century later. His *Oesterreich Über Alles, Wann Es Nur Will* (Austria above all others, if it wants to be) was published in 1684. A greater interest in national self-sufficiency and power pervaded his work. The very emphasis upon the supremacy of Austria which appeared in the title gives a clue to the viewpoint expressed in the book.

There are of course a great many writers who in one way or another accepted the idea of a favorable balance of trade being essential to national strength. These men are frequently noted for the new lines of thought they opened up and have consequently been discussed in other chapters. Sir William Petty emphasized the monetary aspect of foreign trade; Sir Josiah Child, who venerated Dutch industry and Dutch moral character, saw economic success as dependent upon low interest rates; Sir James Steuart, whose excellent *Inquiry into the Principles of Political Economy,* had the misfortune of supporting a moderate mercantilism just nine years before *The Wealth of Nations* by Adam Smith appeared, nevertheless contributed greatly to latter theories of value and population.

Critics of Mercantilism

The mercantile system was the dominant form of economic thought in the 17th century, and it was clearly the pattern of the practical statesmanship of the times. Nevertheless, another system of thought hostile to Mercantilism was growing increasingly popular. While the origin of the new ideas was in England (for at least the first hints of the new doctrine appear in English literature) France was the first nation to adopt them as a natural philosophy and to give them practical expression.

Some writers in economic history look upon Petty, Locke, and

North as the authors who laid the foundations for the revolutionary doctrine of *freedom in trade*. Although PETTY is usually classified as a Mercantilist because of his general acceptance of the philosophy of Mercantilism, his greatest contribution was a destruction of the mercantile theory of money and prices. Hence his inclusion among the forerunners of free trade. He understood that a nation needed money, but he believed there could be too much or too little of it, thus affecting price levels. Although the idea of an automatic control of the quantity of money in a nation was not yet developed, Petty advocated the removal of all restrictions upon the export of money. His work in statistics on the commerce of Ireland showed that an abundance of exports under certain circumstances was actually harmful, and that other things than goods and money influenced a nation's economic position.

LOCKE's importance lay not in his economic ideas, but in the philosophical support he gave to the search for freedom generally. As a matter of fact, a survey of his purely economic writings might lead one to label him as a Mercantilist. He believed in the importance of a nation having a greater abundance of the precious metals than its neighbors, and maintained that in the absence of mines such abundance of gold and silver could be acquired only through conquest or commerce. But in his opposition to arbitrary authority and his explanation of the advantages of individual liberty he challenged the basic assumptions of Mercantilism.

For purely economic criticism of mercantilist ideas of trade no one in the 17th century surpassed the directness and forcefulness of the writings of SIR DUDLEY NORTH. In his *Discourse upon Trade,* published in 1691, he showed that wealth could exist independently of gold or silver. Agriculture and industry were the true sources of wealth. Money he conceded was one element of wealth, and it performed invaluable services in facilitating the exchange of goods. The quantity of money in a country might be in excess or less than the requirements of the nation's trade but this was something which would regulate itself without human interference. North's belief in the importance of domestic trade was extraordinary in a world so dominated by the concern over foreign trade, but it was quite logical considering the emphasis he placed upon domestic agriculture and industry. He condemned the practice of granting business privileges and concessions to one particular group of merchants, saying that every such exclusive privilege was to the public's disadvantage. North stands out as an independent thinker, as a herald of the new economic era that was ushered in nearly a century later by Adam Smith.

The names of Roger Coke, Nicholas Barbon, and Charles Davenant should be added to the list of critics of Mercantilism. Their work kept aflame the smoldering fires of discontent that were threatening to destroy the doctrine of foreign trade operated under government control for the sake of more metal. Coke pointed out the probable reaction of foreign nations to the tight-fisted money policy. He foresaw the diminution of England's foreign trade as rival countries refused to trade with a nation that would not reciprocate, just as he foresaw the stagnation of domestic industries when freed from competition. Babton showed how trade might increase rather than diminish if restrictions against imports were removed; and Davenant expressed the opinion that trade was self regulating and would prosper better if freed from control.

The reaction against Mercantilism was particularly strong in France where the evils of an exaggerated mercantilist policy had brought financial ruin to the country. The unrest among the people, oppressive taxes, and a depressed condition of agriculture led to violent protests against the financial administration of Jean Baptiste Colbert. Unwittingly Colbert became the chief exponent of Mercantilism in Europe to such an extent that the system became known on the continent as *Colbertism*. The extravagant demands of Louis XIV forced Colbert to find new and fruitful sources of revenue. He developed the pattern of Mercantilism in France not as a studied purpose but as the inevitable result of hundreds of independent moves to increase the revenues of the state.

Pierre Boisguillebert wrote voluminously in opposition to the mercantile school of thought. In his various works he insisted that national wealth did not consist in an abundance of precious metals, but in useful things. He protested against restrictions on both domestic and foreign commerce. Such artificial control of trade as occurred through government regulations was harmful, since there were natural laws of the economic order which could not be violated without undesirable consequences. To Boisguillebert the world was a unit. Economic prosperity could result only as commercial relations between all peoples were allowed to develop naturally. For France, he believed, the way to economic well-being lay along the road of a revived and prosperous agriculture.

The Physiocrats

Credit for the final destruction of mercantile principles both in theory and practice as far as France was concerned goes to those economists known popularly as the Physiocrats. To be sure, Montesquieu in the *Esprit des Lois* destroyed the philosophical basis of Mercantilism, much as Locke had done in England, by proclaiming the importance of natural law in social matters. However, his concern with economics was only incidental; and, as a matter of fact, he showed a general acceptance of certain mercantilist views. With the Physiocrats it was a different story. They broke completely with the past, and established a new order of economic life. QUESNAY and TURGOT were representative leaders of this school of thought. Their attitude toward trade was a direct outgrowth of their basic concept of a natural law which applied to all nature. The individual had a right to whatever natural enjoyments he could procure through his labor. The right to hold and transfer property was therefore undeniable. Once having granted these assumptions, it followed that competition should not be restricted by law, by the creation of monopolies, or by the granting of special privileges. On the other hand, Quesnay considered commerce as unproductive labor. The mere exchange of wealth, he claimed, was not the same as the production of wealth. The gain made by merchants was at the expense of the agriculturalists who alone were the producers of all value. He denied the value of a favorable balance of trade since its effect would be to raise prices; and the wealth of a state could not be judged by the quantity of money it possessed since money was sterile, having no value in itself except as it effected an exchange of commodities. To conduct commerce at the expense of another nation was impossible, since commerce can only take place as long as there exist reciprocal advantages. Nevertheless, the Physiocrat defense of free trade cannot be accepted as evidence of this high estimate of its worth. Just the opposite was the case. Foreign trade was a liability since the expenses of it were deducted from the real production of agriculture. Domestic trade at least kept all true values within the nation. Turgot modified some of the details of Quesnay's ideas but he changed no important feature. For example, in emphasizing the obligation of the state to prevent monopoly and special privilege to the extent of preserving natural liberty, he especially objected to extending the state's responsibility to the degree of a paternalistic care of the careless, lazy, or indifferent. Hence the free trade doctrine of the Physiocrats and their opposition to Mercantilism arose more from their philosophical world view than from any critical appraisal of the value of either in itself.

David Hume

The work of the philosophers during this period of transition to a new economic society was of incalculable value. They attacked existing ideas from an objective viewpoint, clarifying the economic issues and indicating the probable direction of future developments. No systematic analysis of economic life was attempted by them, this job they left for economists, who benefited, however, from their philosophic work. This in the main describes the relation which existed between David Hume and Adam Smith. HUME (1711–1776) was a learned man, able to write on many subjects with lively style and penetrating insight. He was never exhaustive about any of his interests, but his ability to survey critically and evaluate many aspects of human life in terms of history placed him in the front rank of the world's philosophers. His writings in economics consist of a few scattered essays. In the main these writings attacked the mercantilist ideas on the value of money and the importance of foreign trade. Hume denied that a nation's wealth was dependent upon the accumulation of bullion. In fact, he went so far as to state that regardless of the quantity of money, trade could be carried on effectively; for prices tended to adjust to the quantity of money in circulation. On the other hand, he contended, a nation's wealth consisted of its people and its industry; a nation would by natural forces and without effort get the money it required for its economic activity. One of his most amazing statements was to the effect that England's economic success depended upon the growing prosperity of countries in Europe, since only if they were prosperous could English merchants sell them goods. The basis for such a statement was Hume's idea of a territorial division of labor; consequently he condemned any artificial barriers to trade. Furthermore it was his belief that should foreign commerce cease, the stimulation which it had already produced in the desires and ambitions of men would find expression in the improvement of domestic commerce and industry to the greater benefit of the people.

A host of other writers might be mentioned as forerunners of the new era in commerce and trade. Exhaustive research has shown that all the elements of Adam Smith's doctrine of free trade were available before *The Wealth of Nations* was written, very often in obscure writings and in fragmentary form. For example, Paterson and Gervaise warrant mention as early free traders. Many minds helped to prepare the way for the new ideas and new methods that soon were to challenge men's thoughts.

Adam Smith

It is not Hume, North, Locke, the Physiocrats, nor any of the writers mentioned above, but Adam Smith who stands forth as the great critic of Mercantilism and the chief exponent of the doctrine of individual freedom in trade. It has often been said that there was more than coincidence in the fact that both the Declaration of Independence and *The Wealth of Nations* were given to the world in 1776. One was a declaration of political freedom, the other proclaimed industrial and commercial independence. Certainly strong ties bound the two together. Very little that Adam Smith said on the subject of trade was new, most of it had been said before; but the scope of Smith's work, the completeness of his analysis and the timeliness of its appearance all conspired to make *The Wealth of Nations* a landmark in economic thought.

The ideas expressed by ADAM SMITH on the subject of trade were rooted in his beliefs concerning the nature of man and society. Each man, he said, was more understanding than any other as to his own needs and desires. If each man were allowed to seek his own welfare, he would in the long run contribute most to the common good. Natural law, better than government restraint, would serve to prevent abuses of this freedom. It was self-interest, in the course of human history, which led to the subdivision of labor. The co-operation and exchange which naturally followed were responsible for the world's economic progress, and therein lay the road to future achievements.

It is obvious that Adam Smith favored free trade. Any restriction upon domestic or foreign commerce he believed unwise since it hampered the operation of natural law, and prevented the increase in benefits that further exchange would undoubtedly bring. A large part of *The Wealth of Nations* is devoted to an attack upon the principles of Mercantilism. That Smith's ideas of Mercantilism tended to exaggerate its evils is of small moment today. His work served to bring public confidence in the practices associated with mercantile policy to an end. He showed clearly how all forms of government interference whether the granting of monopolies, subsidizing exports, restricting imports, regulating wages, or the effort to acquire a stock of money hampered the natural growth of economic activity. It was, however, in his portrayal of the advantages of specialization by regions and nations that Smith secured his most general support. "It is the maxim of every prudent master of a family never to attempt to make at home what it will cost him more to make than to buy." Beginning with such reasoning, Smith showed how each nation would be far better off economically by concentrating on the thing it could do best, rather than following the Mercantilist doctrine of national self-sufficiency.

The new economic society which Smith proposed was to be regulated by competition. Economic privileges and monopolies were to be destroyed. Competition assured that each man and each nation would do the thing it was best fitted to do, and it assured each one the full reward of his services and the maximum contribution to the common good. One important function of government in relation to the business life of the community was to preserve competition.

Adam Smith's position on the question of government regulation was not absolute. He could be counted upon under most circumstances to defend free trade, but there were conditions which in his opinion required government action. For example, he did not believe that complete freedom in foreign trade could be achieved in England. He admitted that for political reasons the government might regulate trade. The Navigation Acts, requiring the use of English vessels to transport goods to and from England, Smith believed were necessary to safeguard the marine service as a matter of national defense. He was willing to compromise on the laws prohibiting the export of wool, accepting a tax instead of a full embargo. Although he disliked the use of counter restrictions in order to secure the reduction of barriers raised against English goods by foreign countries, he thought their use should be determined by the estimate of their success. Further departure from an absolute free trade position was apparent in Smith's suggestion that gradual steps should be used in restoring freedom to large industries heretofore maintained by government concessions, and that risky ventures from which the public would later benefit might be granted privileges of monopoly.

In spite of his defense of the *laissez faire* policy, Smith saw vast opportunities for a positive contribution by the government to its people. Necessary projects which were too large for private enterprise or for the voluntary efforts of a small section of the population should be undertaken by public authority. All institutions and works related to public defense, justice (especially the enforcement of contracts and the protection of property) were government business. He believed that education, licensing of professions and trades as a protection to the public, perhaps even the financial support of religious institutions, fell within the sphere of government action.

The effect of *The Wealth of Nations* on the thoughts and actions of the people was extraordinary. The ready acceptance of Smith's ideas seems to indicate that the people were waiting expectantly for his message even though the Napoleonic wars prevented direct application of these ideas to foreign trade for nearly forty years. As Eric Roll pointed out, Smith's analysis of trade gave businessmen a significant place in history, it justified their pursuit of profit, it gave them a social respectability as a class and identified them with great national destiny. In particular it voiced the ideas of many of them that opportunities for trade were practically unlimited, if legal restrictions and government privileges were removed. *The Wealth of Nations* simply removed obstructions and quickened a trend toward a new era in trade which was already well along but had thus far remained unobserved.

Later Exponents of the Free Trade Doctrine

The arguments for and against free trade following the death of Adam Smith were carried on by men whose names stand high in the ranks of great economists. J. B. Say in France was the first continental follower of Adam Smith to give widespread circulation to Smith's ideas. In addition to popularizing *The Wealth of Nations,* Say also made some clear observations of his own on the question of trade and the functions of markets. To him, as to Smith, money merely facilitated exchange of goods. It had no value in itself and it created none. Consequently, trade was really an exchange of goods for goods, and every supply of goods gave rise to a demand. Thus trade could be fostered if each nation would increase its own surpluses so that trade could take place. An over supply of goods generally he believed impossible, although scarcity and abundance might occur in particular commodities.

The protection of trade as a government policy died slowly in England, but many aspects of the theory of free trade were worked out in the controversies that accompanied every change in existing legislation. It was through Ricardo's participation in the protest against the Corn Laws that he clearly stated his position on free trade. Before Adam Smith a common principle of the anti-mercantilists was "that it pays to import commodities from abroad whenever they can be obtained in exchange for exports at a smaller real cost than their production at home would entail." This seems almost a truism. Obviously a nation is not going to engage in trade unless it seems less costly than to produce the commodities at home. Nevertheless, it is usually a different matter to convince a nation that this principle is worth following. Ricardo, in developing an idea which is known in economics as the *doctrine of comparative costs* was merely restating and amplifying a rule of trade developed much earlier. To make the idea clearer, Ricardo used an illustration which has continued in use ever since. In speaking of trade between England and Portugal he said that if Portugal could produce cloth with the labor of 90 men and wine with the labor of 80 men, and England could produce the same quantity of cloth with 100 men and the wine with 120, it would be advantageous for these nations to exchange English cloth for Portuguese wine. For by concentrating upon the thing each nation could do with the least effort each had a greater comparative advantage. Thus each nation had more wine and more cloth than it could have had by producing each commodity independently without the benefit of exchange. Ricardo used another illustration to drive home this same point:

Two men can both make shoes and hats, and one is superior to the other in both employments; but in making hats, he can only exceed his competitor by one-fifth or 20 percent—and in making shoes he can exceed him by one-third or 33 percent;—will it not be for the interest of both, that the superior man should employ himself exclusively in making shoes, and the inferior man in making hats?

It was Ricardo's contention that imports could be profitable to a nation even though that nation could produce the imported article at a lower cost. Consequently, it was not true, as some of the early economists had believed, that under free trade each commodity would be produced by that country which produced it at the lowest real cost. Ricardo had a great deal more to say on the subject of trade; but since his ideas were concerned with the money aspects of trade, they will be discussed in the following chapter.

Further elaboration of this method of calculating the advantages of foreign trade was made by JOHN STUART MILL. In his *Essays on Some Unsettled Questions of Political Economy,* he discussed the quantities of goods which would be exchanged under a system of free trade. He showed that prices of commodities in exchange would adjust themselves so that the quantities of each article imported would be just sufficient to pay for the article exported. He said that no nation would give more units of commodity A for commodity B than it could produce at a cost equal to that which it could produce B. Thus the law of comparative costs while indicating the advantage of exchange also indicated the limits beyond which exchange was unprofitable.

One of the most tantalizing problems connected with foreign trade was the degree of specialization that would bring the greatest economic advantage. Mill at first held that under free trade complete specialization would take place, but he later modified this idea to take account of the fact that although complete exchange might be advantageous the productive facilities of the producing countries might be such that one country would have to make up for a deficiency of supply by domestic production. Ricardo had made allowance for the fact that complete specialization might not be possible. He claimed that partial specialization might still be profitable. However, extensive discussions have taken place among economists on this point, many of them holding Ricardo in error.

Practical applications of the principles of free trade began to appear in England with the close of the Napoleonic wars. At the beginning of the Corn Law controversy, THOMAS MALTHUS made keen observations as to the effect of high duties upon imported corn. He said that the restriction upon imports caused a greater expense of raising corn in England due in a large part to the "necessity of yearly cultivating and improving more poor land to provide for the demands of an increasing population; which land must, of course, require more labor and dressing and expense of all kinds of cultivation." While this argument was used by agriculturalists to secure greater protection, the net effect was to open the minds of the people to the need for importing cheaper corn. Richard Cobden and John Bright, the recognized leaders of the so-called Manchester school of economic thought, several years later formed the Anti-Corn Law League to combat not only the Corn Laws but trade restrictions generally. Using Malthus arguments, they were able to show a greater advantage to England by allowing foreign corn to enter, which would lower living costs, eventually therefore lower costs of production through lower wages, and allow the concentration of land and men to industrial uses in which England had recognized superiority. The Corn Laws were repealed in 1846, the Navigation Acts were abolished a year later, and by 1860 protection was completely removed from English economic practice.

The English economists took the lead in the battle for free trade, but they received able support at times from Europe FRÉDÉRIC BASTIAT (1801–1850), a French politician who gave serious attention to economic matters, advocated the adoption of free trade as a government policy. His best known work on this subject was a satirical pamphlet purporting to be a petition of manufacturers of candles and wax lights—and all others in any way engaged in the production of lighting equipment—against the sun. Since the sun was the lighting industry's chief competitor flooding the market with light at cheap prices, the petitioners advised the passing of laws requiring the closing of all openings through which sunlight was accustomed to pass. Bastiat introduced a sly dig at the unreasonable animosity against England when he intimated that England had encouraged the sun to shine so brilliantly on France as contrasted with the circumspection the sun "displays toward that haughty island." The early writing of Bastiat indicated a thorough-going support of free trade and opposition to government intervention of any kind save in the interests of justice. His final work, *Harmonies Économiques* showed him to be less certain as to the degree of freedom from government control that was desirable.

JOHANN HEINRICH VON THÜNEN (1783–1850) is best known among economists for his method of analysis. His principal work, *Der Isolierte Staat,* was an attempt to set up an isolated community free from external contacts. In that rarefied situation, von Thünen proceeded to show how the important aspects of economic life operated. For his discussion of trade von Thünen divided his community into two parts, thus showing how exchange benefited both groups. Nevertheless, acquaintance with List's works gave him serious doubts about an absolute free trade position; he recognized, as Adam Smith did, and quoted Smith as an authority, that on occasion government regulation and protection was necessary. Von Thünen began a line of investigation which in modern times has had considerable bearing upon trade, both domestic and foreign. In his ideal community, which was primarily agricultural, he was able to reduce to mathematical precision the location of various crops and the type of agricultural techniques that would be used, depending upon size and distance from the market. This same principle applied to modern industry and transportation presents important aspects of the problem of locating industry in relation to the character of the market.

Although free trade ultimately became the keystone of classical economics, not all economists supported free trade. Indeed, outside of England, while strong groups of free traders were to be found, there were always those who criticized the *laissez faire* (or the government-let-alone) policy. This non-conformity was a product of different conditions in widely scattered parts of the world. Consequently there was little similarity either in the reasons for opposition or the alternative plans suggested for the control of trade.

Before going further in the discussion it may be well to point out that the opposite of free trade is protection which is usually achieved through the instrument of a tariff, or duty, on imports. Exports in the modern day have seldom been subject to duty; indeed, the American constitution forbids such imposts. Free traders as a rule do not object to a tariff as long as it is for revenue purposes only, that is, as long as it is low enough to allow for competition of foreign goods with domestic products. Protection means a tariff high enough to make the sale price of foreign goods prohibitive in the domestic market.

Opponents of Free Trade: The Nationalists

Among the first to oppose the economic ideas of Smith, as they related to trade, were the so-called nationalists. These were German economists in the main who believed that the individual's wealth was secondary to that of the state, and that the state should safeguard its own economic and political power by whatever means seemed expedient. The explanation for the rise of economic nationalism in the Germanic countries is not far to seek. First of all *The Wealth of Nations* grew out of English economic conditions and it was designed primarily for England. It naturally spoke of situations and propounded ideas which had little application to continental conditions. The reaction against Adam Smith in Germany especially should have been expected. Furthermore, the Central European nations were not so far advanced commercially and industrially as England. Germany was predominantly agricultural. An unfavorable geographic position had prevented the development of mercantile pursuits in Germany when the center of trade passed from the North Sea and Mediterranean to the Atlantic. The lack of political unity, and the accompanying petty jealousies of minor sovereigns hampered the growth of an extensive internal trade or common economic policy among the German states. Finally, a philosophical idealization of the all pervading influence of the state to which both Fichte and Hegel gave expression permeated German thought and allowed no development of individualism.

National Economy in Germany

ADAM MÜLLER (1779–1829), who is known in economic thought as a German Romanticist, was one of the first to oppose the individualistic, free trade doctrine of Adam Smith. He advocated the foundation of a national economic order. Home industry was to be protected, and wherever necessary, imports and exports were to be prohibited as a means of stimulating national feeling. Müller's conception of the state as something more than the individuals in it, with a power and spirit of its own, caused him to subordinate the individual to the larger entity. To him the individual pursuit of economic gain was a disrupting force in society; it was far better to return to the fixed and unchanging institutions of the Middle Ages. The state was responsible, he believed, for maintaining these venerable institutions and the individual property relationships which accompanied them. In spite of his opposition to many of Smith's basic teachings, Müller nevertheless regarded Smith as one of the greatest political economists of all times.

In the writings of FRIEDERICH LIST (1789–1846) the emphasis upon a distinctly national economy was given its strongest expression. The English title of List's most important work, *The National System of Political Economy* (1841), is clear evidence of the character of the author's thought. The original plan for this work called for three volumes. Only the first was finished and this dealt almost exclusively with the evolution of national economy and with trade. The economic development of a country passed through five stages, he said: a hunting and fishing stage; a pastoral stage—tending domestic herds; a settled agricultural stage; an agricultural and manufacturing stage; and finally a stage consisting of agriculture, manufacturing, and world trade. As nations pass through these various stages different measures are required for their development. List's criticism of Adam Smith was that Smith had written as though his principles were universally applicable, whereas they were only useful for England which had reached the last stage of economic development, or for some imaginary group of nations living in guaranteed peace and harmony. List, having lived in Germany, and then in America from 1820 to 1832, believed that these two nations were on the fourth stage, and therefore must of necessity follow a more controlled economic policy until such time as their manufacturing had reached a position to compete with those of any other country. In analyzing the economic activities of the world he came to two basic conclusions. The first was that the most desirable economic state of a nation could be achieved by arriving at a balance of its agricultural and manufacturing resources so that no interruption of exchange was possible. His second was that since some tropical nations have little adaptability to manufacturing but produce agricultural commodities which cannot be produced elsewhere, the manufacturing nations of the temperate zones therefore should bind these purely agricultural communities to themselves to the mutual benefit of both.

Following this line of reasoning then, it was desirable for a nation such as Germany or any nation which had the necessary requisites of a manufacturing nation, to adopt a policy of protection. Duties should be introduced gradually and reasonably, so as to achieve the maximum benefit. Agricultural products and raw materials should be exempt. After a reasonable number of years if an industry did not give evidence of being able to survive on a minimum of protection (List suggested twenty to thirty percent) it was evidence that the industry was not adapted to the country and all protection should be removed from it.

It is quite obvious that the ideas of List found fertile soil in Germany. The economic policy of the German nation has followed closely the general outline developed by him, and later economists and statesmen of that nation have constantly turned to him for the basic principles of a strong national economy.

Many practical developments and theoretical concepts of modern Germany are a testimony to his influence, for example, the system of national railways, the customs union or *Zollverein,* and the search for tropical areas to exploit. On the other hand, the criticisms levelled at List are more concerned with assumptions than with the practicability of his ideas. His absolute distinction between temperate and tropical nations is faulty; strong, manufacturing nations may also develop an extensive trade in raw materials, as for example the United States; and nations do not normally conform to the evolution by economic stages as List worked them out. However, if one may judge List's ideas as compared with those of Smith, he was at least as good an exponent of the economic tendencies of his own environment as Smith was of his.

About the same time as List there lived another economist who shared some of List's experiences and arrived at somewhat similar views. JOHN RAE (1796–1872) was born and educated in Scotland but he migrated and spent most of his life in Canada. Like List, he objected to Smith's emphasis upon individual freedom and individual wealth on the grounds that the national wealth and welfare were different from the sum total of individual wealth and welfare. Accordingly he believed that modified *laissez faire* was not a positive policy. Instead he advocated enlightened government control. He believed furthermore that legislatures had the ability and power to guide the economic activity of the country. To illustrate this, Rae used the analogy that a number of people passing between two points would in time wear a path. Would this path, he asked, being created without intention, be better than a path built under community direction? In matters of trade Rae was concerned with the most efficient method of establishing industries and the useful arts in a new country. He mentioned that these ends were better accomplished under the direction of the organized state, the public bearing the initial cost, than by private enterprise. To safeguard such efforts from foreign competition was also a legitimate use of government power.

John Stuart Mill's Compromise

Protectionism as a policy of international trade was not confined to the outspoken opponents of classical theory. Yet most of the other economists who supported protection against free trade tried to stay within the general bounds of classical tradition as outlined by Smith. John Stuart Mill, in spite of his adherence to classical economy, found certain instances where he believed protection was justified, when in a young nation new industries were being developed. Since the superiority of industries in older nations may merely be that of time, it is necessary to protect the new industry during the formative period when it is adapting itself to the new conditions and gaining strength to compete against the well established foreign firms. Mill warned his readers, however, that although a duty on imports was one way in which a nation could tax itself for the period of experimentation, it should not be conceived as a permanent subsidy to an industry unfitted by nature to its new location or extended beyond the time necessary for the industry to be fairly established. For the most part, however, Mill defended the doctrine of free trade against the arguments of the protectionists. He especially challenged the ideas of Henry Carey, who advocated a thorough-going nationalistic policy for America.

American Ideas on Protection

America seemed more fruitful soil for the growth of protectionism than England. From the earliest days of the United States there were sponsors for protectionist views. The burning resentment felt for the mercantilist policies adopted by England in the 17th and 18th centuries did not prevent several great Americans from supporting a paternalistic attitude of government toward industry. The economic ideas of ALEXANDER HAMILTON (1757–1804) were born out of his efforts to stabilize the financial structure of the new United States. Not that the ideas were original, for many of them had appeared centuries earlier in the writings of the English economists. Nevertheless, Hamilton wrote in the face of the growing popularity of the doctrine of free trade and the disappearance of protection as a national policy in England. As the first Secretary of the Treasury in the United States government, Hamilton was asked to assume the economic leadership of the new nation. He expected to exercise authority comparable to that of the English Chancellor of the Exchequer, but American political organization prevented the settling of such important powers outside the national legislature proper. In spite of this rebuff Hamilton continued to advocate programs of national policy in reports such as the one on manufacturers submitted to the House of Representatives in 1791. He was concerned over the fact that restrictions in foreign markets curtailed the demand for American goods, while at the same time, the American market was completely open. The need, as he saw it, was for a program that would insure more of the American market for American manufacturers. Moreover, Hamilton saw the possibility of developing new industries in America to the advantage of the people of the United States.

Hamilton was well acquainted with the arguments of Adam Smith in favor of agriculture and against protection, just as he knew the objections and distrust of his fellow citizens against any government participation in economic activity. Nevertheless, he fought for a protective tariff to retain the domestic market for those industries which were just getting started, and a government subsidy to start enterprises that seemed desirable. The use of the protective tariff and subsidy was not to be an indiscriminate matter, a careful analysis of the industries to be assisted was necessary to see first of all if American conditions would support the industry in question, and secondly if the demand for the article warranted the effort, and thirdly if the industry contributed to national defense. The general theory which Hamilton sponsored foreshadowed the later work of Friederich List. There was the nationalistic spirit, the same conviction that government should assist economic development, and the same idea that tariffs should be used only until an industry had had time to prove itself adaptable to the natural conditions of the country. Whether List became acquainted with Hamilton's papers while in America is difficult to say. It is not hard to believe, however, that an awareness to the same conditions gave rise to the same ideas.

HENRY C. CAREY (1793–1879) was one of the first of American economists to stand as an ardent advocate of protection. His success in managing a family publishing business enabled him to retire with a comfortable fortune at the age of thirty-five. From then on he devoted himself to writing on economic subjects. The most important work from his pen was *Principles of Social Science* (1857–1860) in which his system of social organization was outlined. It was in one of his earlier works *The Harmony of Interests, Agricultural, Manufacturing, and Commercial,* published in 1851, that he presented his views on industry and trade.

In general outline Carey's arguments were similar to those of Hamilton and List, but at various points he differed and took a more extreme position. Manufacturing was a socializing and a civilizing force, while agriculture—as List had said—held a population in ignorance and semi-barbarism. Furthermore, Carey believed that agriculture without a neighboring market could not survive, the cost of transporting produce to distant markets more than consuming the farmer's profit. But through protection the people of the nation would be knit closer together and the value of natural resources which America possessed would be retained by the people. A word of explanation will clarify these arguments. Protection would increase the diversification of occupations in America, bringing about cooperation and exchange among various elements of the population, and consequently the intellectual development of the nation as a whole. On the second point, Carey had a peculiar notion. Selling agricultural products and raw materials abroad took out of the earth its valuable qualities and left the people of America poorer. Produce sold within the nation was returned at least in part to the earth as fertilizers. It is difficult to follow this argument, for the sale of agricultural products would enable the people to import goods they considered more valuable than cereals or dairy products. If necessary, fertilizer could be artificially created or imported, as John Stuart Mill pointed out in his criticisms of Carey.

However, a later writer took pains to clarify this point. SIMON N. PATTEN (1852–1922), the well known economist at the University of Pennsylvania, followed Carey in the defense of protectionism. While economists in general throughout the United States were supporters of free trade in theory at least after the masterful arguments against protectionism made by William Graham Sumner, the nation in general supported protection; and political parties merely disputed with one another over a higher or lower rate of protection. Patten, on many things considered quite liberal, argued for the economically conservative policy of protection. This paradox is easily resolved. The so-called liberal strain in Patten consisted of his support of a policy of government intervention in the interest of labor, consumers, and of economic planning. This, of course, was not foreign to government protection of home industries, in fact, the success of the former might clearly depend upon the latter. For example Patten believed that economic prosperity depended upon building a market for goods in the immediate vicinity where they were produced. And he also believed, in the same vein as Carey, that free trade would lead to the exhaustion of American raw materials, since without the protection necessary to produce manufactured goods these would be the chief source of money income to the country. Exportation of natural resources would lead to exhaustion of soil and mineral wealth. The history of the American southern states where the tremendous export trade in cotton has led to most severe cases of soil exhaustion gives strong support to this idea. Finally, while subscribing to the "infant industry" argument as a bona fide reason for protection, he pointed out that a nation would always have "infant industries" as long as it continued a dynamic economic existence. There would always be efforts to start new manufacturers after their successful introduction in a foreign country. Thus protective tariff for that reason alone would be ever present.

Additional Arguments in the Free Trade vs. Protectionism Controversy

The question of free trade vs. protection has been a perennial one in American politics. The arguments for and against have become so commonplace that it is impossible to find the original authors of many of them. Some of the arguments are interesting in themselves even though originators remain in doubt. The modern defense of protection frequently begins with the Mercantilist idea that a nation must sell more than it buys in order to have a favorable balance of trade and an annual influx of gold. In spite of its age and its obvious fallacies this reasoning continues to be used. The most widely cited argument for protection is that cheap foreign products must be kept out of the country in order to maintain high wage scales and full employment. If foreign goods, made by working men who get half the wages of domestic workmen and who live on a much lower standard of living, were allowed to enter the country one of two things would happen: either the domestic workmen would have to accept lower wages so that the domestic product could compete with the foreign product, or the industry would shut down and the working men would be unemployed. Economists such as Ricardo and Malthus answered this argument long ago by showing that high wages and consequently high standards of living of wage-earners could be traced to superior skill, machinery, and capital, or advantages in the character and abundance of raw materials or both. Consequently, the question of protection has little bearing on wages. As to employment, Ricardo's analysis of the values of international trade showed that by free trade each nation would gain most by concentrating upon the production of those items in which it had an advantage and exchanging such items for other necessities. On the other hand, A. A. COURNOT (1801–1877) made it clear that the question of unemployment could not be dismissed unless both labor and capital could adapt themselves immediately to other pursuits, which in many instances would not be the case. Adam Smith, however, foresaw this type of difficulty and agreed that protection should be removed from any privileged industry by gradual stages so that severe dislocation might be avoided.

Both the infant industry argument and the transportation cost argument have been reviewed above. They are effectively used in popular discussions of the tariff question, but further exposition here is not necessary. There is one argument for protection for which there is no rebuttal except a change in outlook of the peoples of the world toward each other. It is simply this: that protection is necessary in order to assure the nation of a full supply of all necessary materials in time of war. List was a realist. He saw the virtues of free trade in a world in which order was guaranteed by a universal association or federation of all nations as a guarantee of perpetual peace. But he felt that as long as nations competed with a view to taking resort to war to settle disputes, tariff protection would be needed. This argument, of course, was not economic, it was political. Nevertheless, the economists, contrary to List, have frequently dealt with economic ideas as though the world were something different from what it is. This is not to say that List's view was correct, except in so far as he attempted to develop his ideas in close association with the real world around him.

Economic Nationalism

For more than a hundred years government intervention in matters of trade was confined to certain forms of protective tariff, mild subsidies for some industries, and occasionally an export bounty. These were very faltering introductions to the dynamic quality of economic nationalism which began with World War I and in no small measure was the cause of World War II. In the first place, the spirit of national supremacy which found its early expression in the work of the German philosophers spread across the world. It took hold of nations which felt themselves oppressed or cheated of a place of prominence, and it brought into positions of authority men who by domination organized these nations economically and politically for a vast effort to take by force the advantages which other nations held by rights gained long ago. Freedom of individual enterprise gave place to government regulated policies. Automatic processes were condemned as wasteful and inefficient. Regulation and planning were substituted. Dictation of imports and exports was merely one aspect of a dictator controlled economy, or autarchy. In the second place, these nations were dependent for their war effort upon raw materials which were owned and controlled by the nations upon which they expected to make war. During the period of preparation, while business was conducted as usual, the government regulated imports and exports so that vast stores of war materials could be accumulated. In the case of Germany, this meant extensive government subsidies for the export trade, so that merchants might continue to sell even below the prevailing price of foreign competitors, and thus acquire foreign exchange. Cost of production or the laws of supply and demand no longer entered the price fixing policies of the German merchants in their search for foreign markets. To fight this kind of competition rival nations were forced to resort to other means just as far removed from ordinary business practices. The conduct of international trade according to the previously held economic laws was no longer possible. National barter, in which for example so much machinery was exchanged for a certain quantity of oil, in many instances eliminated the necessity of money exchange altogether. Finally, both to increase national prestige and to assure the nation of dependent colonies to furnish raw materials and provide a market for manufactured goods, these nations began a war of territorial expansion. The theory, given wide publicity both in Germany and Japan, was that independent economic regions could be established with a great industrial nation at the head. Within each region would exist free trade and self-sufficiency. Since all regions would have at hand vast populations for markets, new materials, and industrial skills each would prosper, none would need feel inferior to the other. Opposition to the programs of these nations was instantaneous. Whatever might be the logic of their plans, their methods of unwarranted aggression, regimentation, oppression, and enslavement could bring nothing but war.

CHAPTER VI

Competition, Supply and Demand, Price

AQUINAS   MUN   PETTY   CANTILLON
STEUART   SMITH   SAY   LONGFIELD   RICARDO
SENIOR   MILL   SISMONDI
COURNOT   GOSSEN   JEVONS
WALRAS   MARSHALL   PARETO   VEBLEN

How are prices determined? Why will the same article cost more or less tomorrow than it did yesterday? Is the law of supply and demand really important in determining price? Is competition beneficial to the consumer? Does competition give the consumer better goods at lower cost than a government system of price fixing? What is utility? How does the utility of a good affect consumer choices? Why is it that perfect competition never exists in fact? What does the economist mean by imperfect or monopolistic competition?

Buying and selling has been one of the chief characteristics of economic activity for centuries. Although there has been much talk and some evidence of *barter* on an international scale, no one has had the temerity to suggest that our internal business should be conducted on a barter basis. Buying and selling are such com-

monplace activities for everyone that the many economic processes involved in the simple exchange of goods are ignored.
Suppose, for example, in the days before the war, a housewife
went to her groceryman on Saturday morning and after inquir-
ing the price of eggs, bought a dozen at forty-five cents, com-
menting that the price was a bit higher than the week before.
But why were eggs forty-five cents a dozen and not twenty-five
or eighty-five? Why were they higher this week than last? Who
or what sets the price of eggs anyway? Economists have devoted
no small amount of effort to find the answers to these questions.
Perhaps naturally enough the answers vary from age to age, indicating that there is no one eternal and universal way in which
prices are set. Prices perhaps are determined differently under
different economic conditions. Nevertheless there have been those
who sought to answer the questions of price determination by
presupposing an ideal situation in which economic forces worked
perfectly. With such an assumption it was comparatively easy to
work out a general formula that would explain prices. Others,
motivated by sentiments of justice or benevolence have been content to make assertions as to how prices should be determined.
In the historical development of the ideas of price, fanciful no-
tions as well as the more realistic ideas of the great economists
have a place.

In the days of THOMAS AQUINAS (1225?–1274) conceptions
of price could be summarized by the words: *just price*. Aquinas
lived in an age when small units of population were largely self-
sufficient. Exchange was little known and competition among
producers and sellers almost entirely absent. In the absence of a
market for goods there were no "economic" forces to determine
price. Therefore, the price of an article could logically be determined only by the amount of labor time which was required to
make it. This did not mean that every laborer's time was equal.
The social status of the laborer determined his standard of living, therefore a *just price* was one which enabled the maker of

the goods to maintain his accustomed standard. Economically speaking, the medieval period was comparatively unchanging, consequently such social facts as custom, status, and inheritance were of utmost importance.

Modifications of the *just price* formula, however, were being made continuously to allow for the practices of the market place. Risk was a consideration which permitted a merchant to add something to the *just price*. If a merchant bought when the market was plentiful and sold when goods were scarce some authorities believed a higher price was justified since the merchant had performed a useful service in holding the goods until they were badly needed. This, of course, was a remarkable change from the law of Charlemagne which held that no one should sell goods at higher than the legally fixed price either in time of abundance or time of scarcity.

The Views of the Scholastics

Whether as a result of the arguments of the scholastic philosophers, or due to the static nature of economic life generally, prices remained fixed until the close of the Middle Ages. Essential foods were sold at prices controlled by the public authority, especially in England. In England, too, the courts exercised some authority in setting wage scales for labor. Generally speaking, however, it was the guilds which determined prices and standards of quality for most commodities, in addition to prescribing conditions of work and regulating the supply of materials.

Regardless of the teachings of the ecclesiastics and the power of the guilds, the market had to be reckoned as a force controlling prices. Droughts, wars, and disease were natural factors which influenced both the supply and the demand for goods. The tendency for prices to rise or fall as a consequence of any of these could not be denied. For example, the Black Death, occurring about 1350, so decreased the working force that wages rose precipitously. Local magistrates were empowered to set wages and to enforce the terms of existing contracts. In spite of legal restrictions and the heavy penalties inflicted for violation, wages and the prices of commodities continued to rise. The information available on the general course of agricultural prices from the 13th to the 18th centuries indicates that prices were constantly fluctuating during these years. Devaluations in currency brought about by monarchs in their efforts to increase the state's revenue also affected the price level, causing prices to rise several hundred percent during the course of a few centuries.

The Mercantilists

The general trend not only in practice but in the theories of the economists was toward a price system determined by the forces of the market. This does not mean that controlled prices ceased to exist. The stabilizing effect of the guilds persisted. State-created monopolies controlled the amount and price of numerous products, and government regulation was still important. Nevertheless, those acquainted with such matters began to show a greater appreciation of the economic forces underlying price. JEAN BODIN in his *Réponse aux Paradoxes de Malestroit* (1569) gave a detailed explanation of price changes. The most important cause of the rise in prices, he said, was the increase in the amount of silver and gold in circulation, due to the expansion of trade and the influx of metal from America. Another important cause of rising prices was the control of products by monopolies. The emphasis upon export which caused scarcity at home, the extravagance of the nobility, and the debasement of the monetary unit, all played a part in the upward swing of prices. As a remedy for this condition, Bodin advocated free trade. Both the explanation and the remedy were far in advance of their time, for they were essentially the same points which Adam Smith discussed so effectively more than two hundred years later.

That Mercantilism underestimated the strength of economic

forces and relied almost entirely upon rigid control was nowhere
more apparent than in THOMAS MUN's suggestions concerning
a price policy. We might even say that Mun conceived of price
as an instrument of economic warfare. On goods of which England had a monopoly, he said, prices should be kept high, but
not so high as to be prohibitive. Goods which were highly competitive should be priced low so that England might continue to
hold a large share of the market. However, a policy designed
to drive competitors out of the market by extraordinarily low
prices only to be followed by excessively high prices was quite
unwise. He was aware, at least in domestic trade, that an increasing quantity of money raised prices. There is no clear indication
in his writings that Mun was aware of the close connection between money, supply of goods, prices, and the amount of trade.
But later economists of the classical school made much of this
relationship.

SIR WILLIAM PETTY introduced several ideas of price which
indicated the trends of thought in future years. He suggested first
of all that the price of a commodity would tend in the long run
to remain equal to the amount of silver that a man could mine
if he worked as long as it was necessary for another man to produce a unit of the commodity in question. This is how Petty himself explained it:

Let another man go travel into a country where is Silver, there Dig
it, Refine it, bring it to the same place where the other man planted
his Corn; Coyne it, etc. the same person, all the while of his working for Silver, gathering also food for his necessary livelihood, and
procuring for himself covering, etc. I say, the Silver of the one, must
be esteemed of equal value with the Corn of the other: the one being perhaps twenty Ounces and the other twenty Bushels. From
whence it follows that the price of a Bushel of this Corn to be an
Ounce of Silver.

Hence labor, in Petty's thinking, was the basis of value, or true
price. The political price, or worth in exchange, was dependent

upon a number of factors: excessive competition among those supplying goods to the market; an abundance of substitute commodities; custom; and the general relationship of supply to demand.

Locke and Hume increased the understanding of prices by making clear statements of the effect of the quantity of money on prices. This topic has already been discussed in an earlier chapter; it is sufficient to note that Hume believed that prices of commodities would always be influenced directly by the quantity of money available. Therefore, the actual money in circulation did not affect the exchange of goods. By using an imaginary situation Hume was able to show that with drastic reductions in the quantity of money to the extent of four-fifths of a nation's supply prices would immediately fail to accommodate the supply of goods to the supply of money. A reverse situation would produce just the opposite results, indicating that prices varied with the quantity of money to effect a stable basis of exchange. Hume was careful to point out that hoards of money and plate had no bearing on this process since it was only money in circulation which mattered.

Some references to the influence of both money and the law of supply and demand upon prices were also made by CANTILLON in his famous *Essai sur la Nature du Commerce en Général.* He said, by way of illustration:

Suppose the Butchers on one side and the Buyers on the other side. The price of Meat will be settled after some altercations, and a pound of Beef will be in value to a piece of silver pretty nearly as the whole Beef offered for sale in the Market is to all the silver brought there to buy Beef. This proportion is come at by bargaining. The Butcher keeps up his Price According to the number of Buyers he sees; the Buyers on their side, offer less according as they think the Butcher will have less sale; the price set by some is usually followed by others. Some are more clever in puffing up their wares, others in running them down. Though this method of fixing Market prices has no exact or geometrical foundation, since it often depends upon the eagerness or easy temperament of a few buyers or Sellers, it does not seem that it could be done in a more convenient way. It is clear that the quantity of Produce or of Merchandise offered for sale, in proportion to the demand or number of Buyers, is the basis on which is fixed or always supposed to be fixed the Market Prices.

Through the influence of price, he believed that supply and demand equalized themselves. Another of Cantillon's illustrations showed a farmer with a surplus of corn and not enough wool. Reversing the ratios next year the farmer found himself with too much wool and not enough corn. This alternation continued until the farmer found the correct proportion. The criterion of over-supply and under-supply is price, for the farmer with an over-supply finds his money income too small to pay his rent.

SIR JAMES STEUART was another who anticipated the work of Adam Smith by developing a theory of price based upon supply and demand. If supply and demand balance, the resulting price will be relatively fixed, he claimed. But the balance might be disturbed by any one of a number of factors. If an over-supply existed, seller's competition would reduce prices. If an under-supply appeared, buyer's competition would raise prices. Under ordinary circumstances Steuart believed the activity of merchants themselves would maintain a price equilibrium. Should any unusual change occur, however, he believed firmly that the Government should intervene.

The ideas of price held by the Physiocrats were not as clear as some of the writers we have discussed above. Their emphasis upon competition as the force which determined price was an obvious indication of their disapproval of fixed prices. They did have some idea of a natural price and a market price, but at no point did they give a very understandable explanation of how these prices were established.

Adam Smith and the Classical School

All of these men were laying foundations for the first major statement concerning price. The main points emphasized by Adam Smith differed but little from those of Cantillon; but it was in the greater detail, the completeness of analysis, and the abundance of interrelationship described, that Smith's work was outstanding. "The real price of everything, what everything really costs to the man who wants to acquire it, is the toil and trouble of acquiring it." Thus ADAM SMITH stated his theory of value. He continued to show that while the amount of labor necessary to produce them was the real value of all commodities, their value in exchange was seldom estimated by it, because of the difficulties of equating two different quantities of labor. Thus the process of exchange was carried on by the "higgling and bargaining of the market," in which money was the common unit of measurement.

In discussing the subject of price, Smith indicated that a number of factors influenced the formation of nominal or money price. The value of money itself fluctuated, since the amount of labor necessary to produce a given quantity of metal varied. This in turn depended upon the productivity of mines. To illustrate, Smith used the increased production of gold from the mines in America, showing how this additional supply of gold caused a tremendous increase in prices throughout Europe. Likewise debasement of currency caused an increase in prices, because values were normally equivalent to a quantity of gold, and if coins included less gold at one time than at another, they would purchase less goods, or in other words, cause an increase in price.

In continuing his discussion of price, Smith said, the true price of any commodity included the true price of all the factors making the commodity. "In the price of corn, for example, one part pays the rent of the landlord, another pays the wages or maintenance of labourers, and labouring cattle employed in producing it, and a third part pays the profit of the farmer." "When the price of any commodity is neither more nor less than what is sufficient to pay the rent of land, the wages of labour, and the profits of stock employed in raising, preparing, and bringing it to market, according to their natural rates, the commodity is then sold for what may be called its natural price. The commodity is then sold precisely for what it is worth, or for what it really costs the person who brings it to market . . ." However, "the actual price at which any commodity is commonly sold is called the market price. It may either be above, or below, or exactly the same with its natural price."

How then is the market price determined? Smith went on to explain. The market price is regulated by the quantity which is actually brought to the market and the demand of those who are willing to pay the whole of the natural price. Smith was careful to point out that the effectual demand is the important consideration and not the absolute demand. The former is the expressed desire for goods plus the ability and willingness to buy them, while the latter is the desire of all persons for an article whether they have the ability to buy or not.

When a quantity less than the effectual demand is brought to the market, rather than do without, some of the prospective buyers will offer to pay more than the natural price. Competition among buyers tends to increase the price. Where buyers of some wealth exist, a shortage results in exceedingly high prices if the acquisition of the commodity is of more or less importance to the prospective buyers. On the other hand, when the quantity of a good brought to the market exceeds the demand, it cannot all be sold to those who are willing to pay the natural price covering the true cost incurred in producing the good and bringing it to the market. "Some part must be sold to those who are willing to pay less, and the low price which they give for it must reduce the price of the whole." The degree to which the price sinks below the natural price is dependent upon the amount the excess supply increases the competition of the sellers. The perishable nature of the commodity will also affect the price since the sellers will be more anxious to get rid of perishable goods increasing competition among them.

It is to the interests of all that the supply and demand balance one another. The natural price is then paid covering all costs, all those exercising an effectual demand are satisfied, and there is no excess of supply to lower the market price. The natural price, therefore, is, as it were, the central price, to which the prices of all commodities are continually gravitating. Different accidents may sometimes keep them suspended a good deal above it, and sometimes force them down even somewhat below it. "But whatever may be the obstacles which hinder them from settling in this center of repose and continuance, they are constantly tending towards it."

Smith was quite well aware that sellers might seek to maintain a high price by artificial means. He knew that when a market price was established far above the natural price the producers tended to keep the matter a secret in order not to attract additional competitors. Processes which tend to cut costs, if retained secretly by a small group of producers, may keep prices from falling to the natural level. When the effectual demand exceeds the total productive capacity of the country, to use Smith's illustration, as in the case of some vineyards in France, the price may be sustained indefinitely above the natural price. Monopolies, too, exert the same influence as a trade secret or a commodity naturally limited. Monopoly prices differ from freely competitive or natural prices in that the former are "the highest which can be got" while the latter are "the lowest which can be taken." All kinds of monopolistic conditions prevent the free interplay of supply and demand, and may for years maintain a price more or less higher than the natural price. While prices might be kept above a normal level almost indefinitely, it would be impossible to keep prices below the natural price for more than a very short period, for those persons who suffered loss would reduce the amount of produce which they brought to the market, or withdraw from production altogether.

It is obvious that Smith's ideas on price assumed a freely competitive market as the ideal or natural market. As a consequence he was extremely critical of any monopolistic or regulatory force whether it came about as a result of the normal self-interest of men or the arbitrary extension of governmental power. However, he recognized the tendency for workingmen and employers to organize into combinations. Since their interests were by no means the same, Smith said, "The workmen desire to get as much, the masters to give as little, as possible." The tendency toward combination was less hampered among employers than among workingmen. The former were fewer in number and no acts of parliament forbade their organization as in the case of workingmen, and consequently they were always found in a sort of tacit agreement concerning wages and prices. Not only that, Smith also recognized that the employers were much more likely to call on the agencies of government for assistance in their competitive struggle with organized workingmen. This tendency of combination was noted in what has since become a classic quotation from Adam Smith. "People of the same trade seldom meet together," said he, "even for merriment and diversion, but the conversation ends in a conspiracy against the public, or in some contrivance to raise prices."

Not only the natural tendencies of individuals but custom itself acted to prevent freedom of competition and the unrestricted operation of the forces of the market. The law of primogeniture, Smith thought, had an adverse effect upon the economic conditions of the country. He compared the large increases in population in lands where inheritance of family holdings by the eldest was not a factor, as in North America, with the meager increases in Europe, indicating to his satisfaction the strongest argument against primogeniture (which gives the principal inheritance to the oldest son).

Of the general acceptance of the ideas of Adam Smith on the importance of freedom of business enterprise and the effectiveness of competition as a regulator of economic activity there can be little doubt. Smith's followers were innumerable during the next century. However, even those who openly claimed adherence to the classical ideas modified and pointed out inconsistencies in the generally accepted thought. J. B. SAY in France never tired of defending the importance of supply and demand in determining price. He was even less tolerant than Smith of government intervention and other obstruction to the free play of economic forces. Nevertheless, in his emphasis upon the importance of the utility of an object as a consideration in price determination he unquestionably turned the emphasis away from cost of production and supply in the direction of utility and demand. This general line of development was carried forward in England by writers such as MOUNTIFORT LONGFIELD, the first Professor of Political Economy at the University of Dublin. He accepted the idea that price was determined by supply and demand, but he followed up the general understanding of demand with the first generally accepted statement of the influence of marginal buyers on price. He pointed out that the intensity of a prospective buyer's demand was measured by the price he was willing to pay rather than do without the article. For example, he said, with each increase in price a certain number of the buyers will drop out rather than pay the additional sum. Thus the market price is measured by the least intense demand which results in a purchase. In later years this trend to emphasize the demand aspect of price attained great popularity, but in spite of these early hints as to the importance of demand, it was supply which received the predominant attention.

David Ricardo

Few men reflect the character of their times as clearly as did DAVID RICARDO. He lived in a period when free competition in economic matters was nearer perfection than it had been or would ever be again. Legislation restricting foreign trade which had been passed in the full glory of Mercantilism was unenforced. Only the first of the factory acts had been passed, and trade unions were still held illegal by the courts. The market was in reality almost free. It was Ricardo's method to examine carefully a concrete fact of his own times, and then with unusual intellectual daring to draw general conclusions from it. Ricardo contended however that these conclusions were not directed to temporary effects, but to the long run and fundamental factors, or as he preferred to call them, the natural factors controlling economic behavior. Consequently Ricardo's belief in the power of competition to regulate production and distribution is not merely an unquestioning acceptance of an assumption made by Adam Smith, it is the result of keen observation of the economic activity of his own times.

In the long run, Ricardo believed that the power of competition alone would determine prices, wages, profits, and rent. Further, under a system of free trade each country would devote its labor and capital to those pursuits which were most beneficial. Likewise the abolition of taxes on the transfer of land would tend to place land in the hands of those best able to use it.

Some authors contend that Ricardo accepted so fully his postulate of free competition as the basis of his analysis that he failed to concern himself with the economic problems which arose because of the absence of competition. He did note, however, the effects of government intervention, of wars, and of the immobility of capital and labor; but these obstructions he characterized as short-run effects, which delayed but did not prevent the operation of economic forces. Moreover, he advocated the direct interference of government in the regulation of money, drugs, physicians, and the issue of credit.

In addition to his assumption of free competition Ricardo emphasized the importance of exchange value in the organization of the economic system. Briefly stated, Ricardo believed that the exchange value of any commodity was determined by the quantity of the commodity which a given amount of labor could produce in a given time as related to the amount of another commodity produced by the same labor in the same time. This was different from Ricardo's concept of market price, which he believed was essentially the result of the operation of the laws of supply and demand. Throughout Ricardo's work is the same confusion between natural value and exchange value on the one hand and market price on the other. This fact is noticeable in his discussions of wages and rent. However, if one could assume— as Ricardo did—a freely competitive market, natural value, exchange value, and market price would tend to coincide.

Nassau Senior

NASSAU SENIOR was another who supported the classical ideas of competition, supply and demand, and price. But just as Say had unconsciously emphasized the demand-utility aspects of price, Senior emphasized the supply-cost of production side. Some authors have read this emphasis in Ricardo's writing, but Senior did not leave his principles to a confused interpretation. The limitation of supply, he said, was by far the most important consideration in the determination of price. Whereas Ricardo constantly referred to labor as the sole source of value, allowing little or nothing for the contribution of natural resources and capital, Senior rearranged these factors. He believed that supply was affected by the three elements of production, labor, abstinence (which is Senior's term for capital), and the forces of nature. The supply of any commodity was "limited by the difficulty of finding persons ready to submit to the labour and abstinence necessary" to its production. Hence the cost of production limited supply. When the supply of raw materials was accessible to all— that is, where free competition existed—prices would tend to equal the cost of production. Senior was aware that the forces of supply and demand could not cause an instantaneous adjustment of price; but gradually, barring some interference, the net effect of supply and demand would be to equalize price and cost of production.

A bit more realism entered the writings of Senior than that of his predecessors, for he acknowledged the presence of monopoly and attempted to show how it influenced price. The first class of monopolists, explained Senior, were those who had control of the use of some special facility in production but not of production itself. Hence, the producer in this case could expand but could not limit the supply. Nor could he set the price above the cost of production of his competitors who were producing without the use of the special facility which he possessed. The tendency of such a producer would be to set the prices below that of his com- petitors but above his own cost, and to expect thereby to increase his own sales. Except for the fact that exclusive rights to the new device might be guaranteed to the producer by patent, the condi- tions of free competition and the laws of supply and demand were not set aside in this instance. Indeed, the interests of the producer and of the consumer were identical.

Senior noted another type of monopoly. In this case although the monopolist was in complete control of supply, increase in supply was impossible. The lower limit of price would be set by the cost of production and while the monopolist might set his price at any point he desired, he had to recognize that the laws of supply and demand would ultimately determine the amount of sales and the market price. A third form of monopoly existed in which the monopolist had complete control of the supply and he had power to increase or decrease it at will. On the whole, in spite of the absence of an upper limit to the price the monopolist could charge, the tendency would be to increase production, and expand sales at a lower price.

Then a fourth and final situation appeared in which the monopolist while not the only producer had peculiar facilities for production which tended to disappear with increased production. Thus the producer, as long as he produced small quantities, could set his price just below that of his most efficient competitor; but if he expanded production, the peculiar circumstances which enabled him to produce a small quantity cheaply would not apply and his cost of production would mount. A piece of extremely fertile land, for example, would produce a certain quantity of grain with a minimum of labor and fertilizer, but productivity of the soil would decrease with each additional application of labor and fertilizer. Price under such circumstances, said Senior, would be set at the cost of that unit whose production was most expensive. The work of Senior, therefore, stands as a realistic application of the principles of Smith and Ricardo, especially the latter. The emphasis is upon supply and the factors which influence it. While demand is recognized as the counter force to supply, Senior makes no attempt to analyze it.

John Stuart Mill

Next in order in point of time as well as from the progressive development of ideas was JOHN STUART MILL. Mill recognized the idea of free competition for what it was worth; it was an abstract ideal accepted merely for use in logical analysis. Whereas Smith, Ricardo, and Senior had believed in free competition as a state which existed and asserted itself in the long run—even though various obstacles hindered the free play of economic forces—Mill understood that this process of reasoning did not fit actual conditions, and should not, therefore, be used as a guide to political or social behavior. Said he, "Assume competition to be their (economic affairs') exclusive regulator, and principles of broad generality and scientific precision may be laid down

. . . but it would be a great misconception of the actual course of human affairs to suppose that competition exercises in fact this unlimited sway." Mill conceded that competition was modified in matters of price by monopoly and custom, the latter being far more important than generally recognized. One of his more important contentions in connection with competition was that the laws governing production and exchange were in the nature of physical laws, while the conditions of distribution were man made. Therefore, free competition should be promoted in connection with production, while common sense and sound judgment should apply to the problems of distribution. There perhaps is no need for pointing out that such a rigid distinction between production and distribution is unfounded. There is such a clear dependency of one upon the other that any law which applies to one must of necessity influence the other.

In his discussion of the law of supply and demand Mill was able to show that previous interpretations concerning the operation of this law were incomplete. Generally speaking the law meant that supply and demand determined price; that is, an increase in supply caused the price to fall, an increase in demand caused it to rise. Mill said that while supply and demand controlled price, price also caused variations in supply and demand. Price was, for example, the guide to the producer. Falling prices warned him to turn his efforts in another direction. Rising prices indicated that supplies were insufficient and that greater profits could be gained by entering the field or by increasing output. Variations in price guided consumers' purchases, though not with the directness nor in the same degree that has been usually assumed. Consequently Mill attempted to restate the law of supply and demand to take account of this process of action and reaction. "The law is that the demand for a commodity varies as its value, and that the value adjusts itself so that the demand shall be equal to the supply." In Mill's exposition the law of supply and demand applied directly and completely only to objects absolutely limited in supply. For other objects whose quantity could be increased by the expenditure of labor and capital, the cost of production represented a natural value below which the market value would not fall. The force causing prices (market value) to fall to the cost of production but not below was competition; for if the market value was greater than the cost of production, producers would increase the supply so as to increase their profit and new producers would enter the field. Except for the restatement of some points, Mill does not add greatly to the general ideas of price expressed by Ricardo and Nassau Senior. His emphasis was upon supply and demand, as influenced by various factors of supply. Apparently Mill felt that demand was more or less fixed, for he devoted little or no time to an investigation of it.

Critics of Competition and the Laws of the Market: Sismondi

There were but few critics of the classical ideas of competition during the early decades of the 19th century. Most writers agreed that the economic system could regulate itself, at least within the borders of the nation if not in international trade. Yet there were some who at first subscribed to classical doctrine and later became severe critics of it. One of these was SISMONDI. Although a sincere admirer of Adam Smith, he was impressed by the poverty and the economic crises that accompanied the advance of industrialization. As a result Sismondi re-examined the assumptions which formed the foundation of classical doctrine, and for all of his admiration he eventually challenged the fundamental ideas of the master.

First of all, Sismondi was impressed by the immobility of labor and capital. It was all very well, said he, for the economist to claim that an oversupply of a product and a falling price would result in a decrease in supply until price was stabilized and supply and demand were equal. But looking at the human factor, the process was not so simple. The workingmen instead of giving up their jobs were likely to accept lower pay and work longer hours in order to hold on to their jobs. Competition became more bitter, wages were further reduced, and a lower standard of living became fixed. The owners reacted in much the same way, he continued. It is not easy to give up a business in which a major share of one's fortune has been invested, and to which years of effort have been given. Under certain circumstances the owner would not be able to withdraw his capital even if he could. Consequently, the owners of the business would continue to produce, cutting costs, piling up debts, finally abandoning their enterprises when ruin overtook them. This was the course of events as Sismondi saw them. He believed that equilibrium, that is a balance of supply and demand, was achieved in the long run but only at the cost of great suffering and hardship.

Sismondi was extremely fearful of an increased production that was not preceded by an increased demand. He could not accept the idea so generally held today that an increase in production might easily create its own market. Thus competition was only beneficial when it encouraged an increased production in response to an increased demand. If it encouraged production in advance of demand the result was distress and impoverishment for workers and manufacturers alike, for only by emphasizing cheapness could any manufacturer survive. But the pursuit of cheapness meant lowering of wages, lengthening hours of toil, and the employment of women and children. Sismondi asks, of what value are increased production and lowered price, if the net result is a poor and unhealthy class of workingmen?

It must be admitted that there was justice in much of Sismondi's criticism. As he said, his eye was not fixed either upon the long run effects or the mechanical perfection of competition and supply and demand as regulators of the market, it was fastened upon the obvious human consequences of the period of transition from a society based upon agriculture and commerce to one founded upon large scale industry. He was likewise concerned with what Sumner Slichter a few years ago called the human costs as related to the money costs of economic activity. Sismondi was not a Socialist, even though his writings frequently sound like the Socialist denunciation of capitalism. He justified the return to the land owner and the manufacturer, and his alternatives to modern capitalism have little in common with socialistic programs. At this point it is sufficient to note that he advocated the intervention of the state to safeguard human welfare. He suggested that the rapid increase in inventions be restrained and that competition in production should be controlled. Futher discussion of Sismondi's reforms will be reserved for a later chapter. Whereas Adam Smith had applied the doctrine of free competition to production and had judged it good because of the abundance of goods produced, Sismondi applied free competition to distribution and found its effect bad when judged from its human consequences.

The Socialists

Sismondi's criticism of competition and the reliance upon the law of supply and demand to determine price set the pattern for later socialistic writing on this subject. Briefly stated, the Socialists contend that when prices are set by the freely operating forces of the market, and when wages and employment are left to the competitive self-interest of employers, the result is exploitation and impoverishment of the wage-earning population. Marx goes even further; he adds that the disparity between what the employee receives for his work and the value he actually produces is confiscated by the employer. This process is the result of competition coupled with the institution of private property, and leads directly to recurring economic crises. This last paragraph has anticipated a discussion of business cycles which will be taken up in some detail in a later chapter, but it is well to point out at once the ultimate result of unregulated competition according to Socialist thought.

The line of classical thought on the subject in hand is broken frequently by sharp attacks, and by conflicting ideas developed by other schools of thought. The Socialist attack was one. There were others. List, as leader of the nationalist school, undermined the whole concept of free competition and dependence upon the law of supply and demand. Since industrial development was a source of national strength and enrichment, it could not be left to the free play of economic forces. The government, in the national interest, must regulate industry. While competitive enterprise might yield a greater abundance at present, the nation must bear the sacrifices necessary to increase the national productive capacity. There obviously is little room in List's economic system for free private enterprise, at least in the stage of economic development which he assumed applied to the Germany of his day.

Cournot

Another of the continental economists is credited with a criticism of the classical emphasis upon free competition which although milder in form has done much to shake the faith of modern economists in the ability of competition and the law of supply and demand to preserve equilibrium in the economic order. AUGUSTIN COURNOT (1801–1877) was a French economist who attempted to describe economic behavior in mathematical or quantitative terms. He is looked upon by many authorities as the herald of the mathematical school if not its actual founder. He questioned the ability of competition to guide the activity and set the goals of the economic system. Cournot very fairly asked what was the social good to which competition was leading? In Cournot's opinion neither the classical school nor any other group of thinkers knew what the social good really was. However, since the question of the final good could not be answered, Cournot did not believe that classical economists could assume that competition would inevitably produce this undefined good. He did not because of this view despair of all improvement. He believed changes for the better could be introduced in various parts of the economic structure one at a time and with care not to disturb other related parts of the system. To achieve such a purpose, state intervention would almost certainly be necessary.

Another of Cournot's important innovations in the analysis of economic activity was concentration upon exchange value or price as the truly significant aspect of economics. He disregarded the relation of utility to demand and emphasized only the visible aspects of supply. He did not say that utility had no bearing upon demand, but he assumed that investigation of it was impossible, and furthermore the important items to be considered were the concrete data of the market. Cournot accepted completely the operation of the law of supply and demand, but instead of starting his description with the assumption of a freely competitive market in which supply and demand operated freely, he recognized the imperfections of the market. Consequently, he first analyzed price when it was determined in a market controlled by one seller or monopoly; then in a market controlled by two sellers, or duopoly; and finally in a perfectly competitive market. It had been the contention of Smith, Ricardo, and Mill that the forces of supply and demand would in the long run produce equilibrium, when the forces themselves just balanced. In other words a price would be set at which the effective demand would be satisfied and the supply taken from the market. Cournot was able to show that when a manufacturer was able to expand his production and at the same time reduce his cost of production per unit, no stability was possible; for the producer was under compulsion to increase his output, lower his cost, and thus increase his profit. While not fully developed Cournot's ideas did much to turn the attention of the economists who followed him toward a more realistic analysis of the the processes of exchange.

The Marginal Utility School

Before completing the development of the thought of those economists who held with Cournot that a controlled market was more usual than a freely competitive market, we need to take note of another school of thought which influenced the consideration of question of competition, supply and demand, and price. For want of a better name this school is known as the *marginal utility* school. Briefly stated this school claims that utility is the fundamental characteristic of value, and as such its influence upon price and exchange is paramount. As we have noted in the chapter devoted to wealth and value, the credit for one of the first clear formulations of the conception of marginal utility goes to HERMANN HEINRICH GOSSEN (1810–1858). His work was ignored by later authors, a fact which distressed Gossen and caused him to withdraw his works from circulation. Gossen's basic conceptions were formulated in two laws. The first law stated: "The amount of one and the same enjoyment diminishes continuously as we proceed with that enjoyment without interruption, until satiety is reached." The second law stated: "In order to obtain the maximum sum of enjoyment, an individual who has a choice between a number of enjoyments, but insufficient time to procure all completely, is obliged—however much the absolute amount of individual enjoyments may differ—to procure all partially, even before he has completed the greatest of them. The relation between them must be such that at the moment when they are discontinued, the amounts of all enjoyments are equal." According to Gossen then, while it is impossible to satisfy all wants, the greatest satisfaction can be achieved by keeping the intensity of all wants at about the same level.

The development of the idea of utility was carried on by Jevons, Walras, and Menger. Our interest lies not so much in an exhaustive examination of their theories of utility as in discovering how they evaluated competition and the law of supply and demand as part of the economic process. The law of supply and demand is unquestioned in the writings of these economists. They assumed its validity and set themselves tasks first of expressing these forces of the market in quantitative terms and second of reducing demand to the psychological factors of which it was composed. Although JEVONS labored over the relation of price to subjective utility, and actually produced several important ideas, his statements remained cumbersome and vague. He is best known for his formulation of the law of indifference, which is, briefly, that where there are two or more identical articles on sale at the same time, it is a matter of indifference to the buyer which he chooses. Therefore there can be only one price at a given time for similar articles.

Menger, and Walras, on the other hand, began with Gossen's idea that the desire to maximize utility, or to increase the sum total of satisfaction, was the basis for exchange. The utility of every commodity to the purchaser sets the upper limit to the price he is willing to pay. Each prospective purchaser will put a quantitative measure upon the utility of the commodity to be purchased. This will express not only the desirability of the article itself alone, but its desirability in relation to a known number of other things which also have utility. MENGER proceeds to analyze price under different economic situations. In isolated exchange the price will be set somewhere between the buyer's and the seller's quantitative expression of the utility of the object. Price may be said to be indeterminate between these limits. In case of monopoly the seller will set the price at a point just above the price offered by that buyer who is necessary to clear the market, that is, the marginal buyer. However, the monopolist may choose to make individual bargains with each buyer.

WALRAS goes more deeply into the processes determining market price, although he uses the same concepts and much the same terminology as previous writers of the marginal utility school. To Walras, however, we owe the idea of scarcity as it applies to goods. It is the utility of a good accompanied by the fact of scarcity which gives an object value. Price, therefore, is the quantitative expression of utility and limited supply. When supply and demand are equal as a result of competition, the price will be what Walras termed the called price—that is, a price set by competitive bidding at an auction. Walras believed that equilibrium could be achieved, and he defended not only the freely competitive market but the doctrine of *laissez-faire*. The originality of this school lies only in the field of emphasis and the direction of its thinking. Whereas previous economists had been concerned with cost of production and supply, these men dealt with subjective utility and exchange in value. Thus there was common agreement among the members of this school on the importance of supply and demand and competition, but there was nevertheless a growing realization of the importance of external control of the market as found for example in monopoly. The special field of investigation that the utility school followed supplemented the work already done.

By 1890 all the essential fields of inquiry and criticism concerning the assumptions made by Smith and Ricardo as to competition and the law of supply and demand had been more or less catalogued. Some of them had been fully explored. There was first of all the socialist criticism that unbridled competition was detrimental, not beneficial. There was clear indication that some writers believed that a controlled market rather than a freely competitive market was typical, and that supply and demand never achieved or continued in equilibrium. Then there were some who said that cost of production and supply were the chief forces in determining price; while others took the opposite view, saying that utility and demand were most important.

The Neo-Classical School: Alfred Marshall

The materials for a restatement of the basic ideas in economics were present. They waited only for a mind with the breadth and skill to weave them into a comprehensive pattern. That man appeared in the figure of ALFRED MARSHALL (1842–1924). An English economist of the classical tradition, he brought together the best thought of his time into a description and explanation of economic processes which served as a model for economic thought in England for several decades. As of Ricardo, it can be said of Marshall: he was the most representative figure of the economic activity of his times. That many of his ideas have lost their popularity is testimony to the changed character of the times rather than to the shortcomings of Marshall's ideas. In most cases, even his severest critics found their inspiration in something Marshall said or hinted.

On the question of competition itself as a means of organizing the economic order, Marshall had some very definite opinions. He assumed that competition would produce those forms of business enterprise best adapted to their environment. This did not mean, however, that they were most beneficial to their environment. In fact Marshall said that he did not doubt that an economic order operated by virtuous men co-operating actively with one another would be superior to the best forms of competition. His question was, however, whether such a co-operative ideal could thrive in the present environment. Hence, we can assume that Marshall thought of a competitive economic order as a workable order under present circumstances but not necessarily the best order possible. Competition, in the sense that Marshall used the term, allowed for certain forms of co-operation among business men, and for some intervention on the part of government. As a matter of fact, he believed that enlightened government intervention might enlarge the scope of economic freedom. It is well to note, however, that free competition was not the perfect competition of the early economists, which assumed perfect knowledge of the market and perfect mobility of the factors of production. Free competition in Marshall's opinion required only the exercise of faculties possessed by the average well-informed man and a reasonable mobility of labor and capital considering the situation. Marshall was quite well aware of the forces tending to restrict the operation of economic forces. These were law, custom, trade union regulation, inertia, and sentimental attachments. Nevertheless competition and economic freedom were continuous and all-pervading.

In his discussion of the effects of competition upon the process of exchange, Marshall clearly deserted the idea of a perfectly competitive market. In the first place, he noted all kinds of different markets, each with its own peculiar characteristics. For example, at the two extremes there were world markets and isolated markets; and between, with innumerable valuations, lay the majority of markets with which business men normally must deal. Further, Marshall's idea of a normal market did not mean a freely competitive market, although one might assume that for illustrative purposes such was the case. But the ordinary market was subject to a variety of influences some of which were competitive and some were not.

The relation of competition to supply and demand, especially the former, was one of the chief points of Marshall's work. As we have noted before, the willingness of a producer to increase his supply depended upon the character of his costs of production, *i.e.* whether they were increasing, decreasing, or constant. Whereas the early economists assumed that all costs were constant, Marshall knew that costs varied greatly. The producer with increasing costs would expand his output only if an unusual demand so far outran the normal supply as to keep the price above the increased cost. The latter two cases, constant or decreasing cost, represented sources of instability since an increase in supply might prove quite profitable if some obstruction prevented the operation of freely competitive forces. But there were other modifications that required attention. One situation Marshall noted was the time required for a change in the market, especially as time affected the supply of goods. Marshall said, in speaking of exchange value: " . . . as a general rule, the shorter the period we are considering, the greater must be the share of our attention which is given to the influence of demand on value; and the longer the period, the more important will be the influence of the cost of production on value." Marshall knew that with the tremendous amounts of fixed capital tied up in business enterprises variations in supply to meet short run changes in market price or demand were unlikely. Business men frequently continued to operate at a loss rather than retire from business and lose the large original investment. Realizing the importance of long time trends, Marshall's price formula was expressed in terms of cost of production. He said that prices tended to be set at the cost of production of the most expensive unit necessary to meet the existing demand. That is if the most efficient producers could not supply the demand, less efficient producers would be encouraged to enter production, and the market price would be set at the cost of production of that one of the less efficient producers whose addition to the supply just met the demand.

When Marshall turned his attention to the effects of monopoly on the market, he made some rather striking comments. The rapid increase in capital and the intense drive toward greater specialization he knew constituted real threats to freedom of economic action. Yet he held that there was an element of monopoly in every competitive business, and that the power of monopolies was of "uncertain tenure; consequently every monopoly must give attention to the factors of present or latent competition if it intended to survive." In spite of the encroachment of monopolies and other forces seeking control of the markets, Marshall believed that such tendencies were counteracted by the development of new instruments of competition. Government intervention was one, greater consumer information was another, the increase of small investors a third, new emphasis upon trade morality, and a diminution of trade secrecy through newly developed avenues of publicity were others. Throughout, the net effect of Marshall's work is to emphasize the continuing power of competition as a regulator of economic activity. Consequently in spite of his emphasis upon the imperfect nature of competition, he remains in the classical tradition by accepting a freely competitive market as a starting point for his investigations and in his confidence that the power of competition would in the end establish equilibrium between the forces of production and consumption.

The Theory of Imperfect Competition

The importance which Marshall attributed to competition as a regulator of the market and a determinant of price was not shared by all of his followers. Marshall's influence over half a century cannot be denied, but in recent years new and challenging ideas have been presented. The recent trend in economic thought is unquestionably toward the analysis of exchange under conditions of monopoly and imperfect competition. It was not the challenge of greater minds, but the force of actual conditions which turned the attention of economists away from Marshall's ideas of a competitive market, toward the uncertainties of the controlled market. The selling of goods is such an integral part of large scale production that business cannot afford to trust the control of a freely competitive market. Consequently tremendous efforts have been made to devise methods of maximizing money value of sales and guaranteeing an adequate market. Devices such as class price, and the use of advertising to break down consumer indifference, as in trade names, are now commonplace. It is difficult to see how one could hold to a belief in a freely competitive market in the face of such developments. Titles such as E. Chamberlin's *The Theory of Monopolistic Competition,* and J. Robinson's *The Economics of Imperfect Competition,* are indicative of the recent trend. Briefly, the new line of investigation abandons the assumption of competition as a regulator of the market through the forces of supply and demand; instead it attempts to analyze the effective methods of control of the market now in practice, usually expressing the results of such control in quantitative terms. The emphasis placed upon mathematical formulae can be traced to the influence of Walras and the Italian economist PARETO (Walras' successor at the University of Lausanne) and to a revival of interest in the work of Cournot.

The goal of the newer school of economic thought is to establish a theory of price determination which will be applicable for both competitive and non-competitive markets. The initial formulations of the new doctrine were derived from an analysis of prices in monopoly markets, hence it was necessary only to expand the scope of the analysis so as to include a greater number of sellers while continuing to use exactly the same assumptions and methods. Authorities seem to agree on the practical success of the new departure and although little has been written concerning the theory of imperfect competition in recent years there is little doubt of its importance to economic thought.

Thorstein Veblen

The assumptions of free competition and the control of market forces emphasized by the classical economists came under attack from yet another source. THORSTEIN VEBLEN (1857–1929), father of institutional economics, believed that the fallacies of previous economists lay not in their logic but in their premises, for even the critics of classical economics accepted generally the basic assumptions of the school founded by Smith, Ricardo, and Mill. According to Veblen these basic assumptions were: first, that man inevitably sought pleasure and avoided pain; second, that each man through the pursuit of self interest (*i.e.* pecuniary gain, subject only to control by competition) contributed to the the well being of the community; and third, that because of self interest and competition, society inexorably ascended to greater heights of wealth and happiness. The facts of living, as found among primitive peoples and in historical civilizations, denied these assumptions, said Veblen. His principal works were devoted primarily to the accumulation of data to prove his contention. He believed that man is endowed with certain instinctive tendencies which condition his behavior, but that in every age the established customs and traditions of a society determine the specific direction such instinctive tendencies will take. In order to understand the economic activity in any age, therefore, one must study the interaction between man's instinctive tendencies and the institutional form in which they find expression. Since all economists up to the time of Veblen took human nature and social customs for granted and paid little attention to them, Veblen's method of analysis was a thoroughgoing innovation.

The most important of human instincts, in Veblen's treatment of the subject, is the *instinct of workmanship*. This innate force causes men to use care in the development of those material objects, especially tools, which enable men to exploit nature more completely and adapt it to their own needs. The institution of private property, however, which began in either fraud or force in the predatory stages of social evolution, subordinated the instinct of workmanship to the accumulation of property. With the outset of modern industrialism two new aspects of social organization became apparent. The first aspect called attention to a division of society into two classes: those who lived in ease and luxury off the accumulation of property and those who labored at routine tasks for a bare existence. The second aspect recognized the existence of envy and jealousy among members of society especially in matters of money and property. Veblen saw modern society as a seething mass of individuals, each one striving to outdo the individuals just above him in the accumulation and the display of wealth. It was to him a society organized on the principle of "keeping up with the Joneses." Veblen coined unique terms to designate this characteristic of contemporary life. *Pecuniary emulation* (imitation in the accumulation and use of money and property) and *invidious comparison* (the envious comparison of one man's social position with that of his neighbor) are becoming familiar words in economic literature.

Thus with Veblen as well as with later members of the institutional school of economic thought, competition was a prominent feature of economic behavior. It was competition for property, place, and power, however, and not merely competition in the buying and selling of goods. Competition as Veblen understood it has far more serious implications for society than the competition of the market place. To demonstrate his superiority over his competitors, the modern business man does not confine his efforts to producing better articles more efficiently to sell at cheaper price; indeed, the pursuit of wealth and power leads the entrepreneur to undermine the competitive conditions of the market by perfecting his control over all the factors of production and distribution. He strives to obtain a monopoly of raw materials; he seeks to restrict the use of the peculiar types of machinery necessary for production; he limits production in the interest of higher prices; he tries to make wage-earners dependent upon him alone for employment at wages he is willing to pay; he reaches out to control the wholesale and retail agencies responsible for the sale of his product; and through the use of trade marks, brand names, and advertising, he seeks to determine the choices of the consumer.

It is obvious that Veblen would seek some other explanation of price than the operation of supply and demand in a competitive market. When the rate of expansion of markets began to decline about the middle of the 19th century, price competition in the market declined with it. Competition and collusion were introduced as a means of insuring profits by restricting production. Whereas the classical economists believed competition to be the natural or normal state of the market from which monopolistic practices were but occasional and temporary deviations, Veblen held that free competition was impossible in an industrial society. Every successful business, he believed, was marked by monopolistic practices to some degree. Indeed, he held that the only source of profit in modern industry was the interference on the part of the business man with the natural efficiency of business enterprise, that is, a "conscientious withdrawal of efficiency" from economic activity. Thus the setting of prices, in Veblen's view, was not a matter of the free play of market forces, but the result of innumerable controls exercised over the factors of production and distribution.

Looking back over the development of economic ideas as they apply to competition, supply and demand, and price, one fact stands out clearly. The conceptions of the economists on these subjects reflect the times in which they lived. If for some reason the ideas expressed were in advance of their times, the author remained for years in obscurity, only to be brought forth and honored for his pioneer work. From Adam Smith to John Stuart Mill, English experience proclaimed the value of free competition. Writers in countries not so economically favored as England were critical of any policy which left the destiny of the business or the nation to non-human forces. When freedom of economic action finally produced an increasing number of monopolistic situations, the old doctrines were revived albeit somewhat slowly. In the present circumstances, where change and uncertainty are characteristic of economic life, the ideas of even the leading contemporary economists remain unsettled.

CHAPTER VII

Money, Credit, and Banking

ARISTOTLE   XENOPHON   AQUINAS
GRESHAM   BODIN   MUN   MISSELDEN
LAW   PETTY   VANDERLINT   CANTILLON
SMITH   MALTHUS   RICARDO   MILL
OWEN   PROUDHON   CASSEL   KEYNES

Why is money so important in modern society? Why have gold and silver been accepted as standard money? What gives paper money its value? Does it matter how much money there is in circulation? Is a nation more or less wealthy if it has a large quantity of money in circulation? Do banks create money? What is inflation? What determines the value of money? Would business be aided if the government changed the value of money to suit price levels? What is the effect of war upon the amount of money in circulation and its value?

THE TWENTIETH CENTURY is frequently referred to by economists as a period of *money economy*. The point they emphasize is that in order to get even the necessities of life, people must have money. In contrast to the self-sufficiency of the early agricultural communities, people today make directly or completely very few if any of the things they use. The adage that men must work for a living has changed. Men work for money to buy a living, and there is no other way in modern society to live and do the things which people want to do. It is not the intention of this chapter to discuss the merit of the emphasis upon money which is so common today, although modern literature is full of opinion upon that subject. Our interest lies in a statement and an explanation of what the great economists of history have thought about money in its relation to economic activity.

As Adam Smith pointed out so forcefully, although he was not the first to do so, money originated as the counterpart of specialization. When people ceased to make everything they needed, and began to emphasize the production of those articles in which they had special ability, exchange became an important aspect of economic life. As long as group A could exchange its grain for meat produced by group B in quantities satisfactory to both, ordinary *barter* was sufficient. When direct exchange was not possible the next best arrangement was for group A and group B to exchange this grain and meat with other groups for some one item that was generally desired by most people. Just suppose, for example, it were skins. Groups A and B then would hold the skins they got for their meat and grain until they could be exchanged for other commodities which they desired to use. In that way skins, while having some value in use themselves, actually would be in greater demand because they had become a medium of exchange, or money. This explains the origin and—as Othmar Spann suggests—perhaps the fundamental nature of money. Some objects are better adapted to this function than others. Perishable and extremely bulky commodities would not do. In the inevitable weeding out process objects such as shells, cattle, skins, tobacco, and beads proved serviceable as money. Due to their greater convenience modern society has grown accustomed to the use of precious metals and paper for money.

The Views of Early Religious Leaders and Philosophers About Money

A great deal of confusion has surrounded the discussion of money in all ages. For one thing philosophers and religious leaders frequently raised serious moral questions about money, and consequently anyone who showed more than a disdainful interest in it was thought to follow an unprincipled existence on a base level. For another, since money was such an important part of economic activity, economists and financiers often advocated unorthodox plans for the control of money which left existing theories in a state of collapse. Until these plans for monetary control were proved wrong or economic theory changed to agree with the schemes, an understanding of the role of money in economic life was impossible. It is no exaggeration to say that such confusion on the subject of money has been more or less usual throughout history. This chapter will describe the development of the theory of money, from the viewpoint of the great economists. Let us consider first, however, some of the religious and philosophic attitudes toward money.

The moral relationships associated with money have, naturally, been paramount in all religious teachings. The Mosaic code forbade the lending of money, or any other article, at interest. Exceptions to the law were made when the borrower was either poor or a foreigner. In the case of the Hebrews, however, all debts were supposed to be cancelled every seventh year. The idea of the seventh year was derived from the traditional story of Jehovah's fashioning the world, when for six days he labored, and then rested on the seventh. Obviously, when trade increased, this restriction was greatly modified through the wording of contracts or completely ignored by those to whom religious observances meant little. Along with the prohibitions against lending at interest, commerce and trade were never as highly regarded as agriculture. Throughout Hebrew literature the tiller of the soil and the herder of sheep were symbols of uprightness and stability. Wealth gained by trade was considered tainted and unstable; indeed, trade was usually left to foreigners.

These or similar teachings are found in the holy books of all faiths. Usually ascribed to a deity or an anonymous prophet, they sooner or later find their way into the writings of famous philosophers or ecclesiastics. The objections to commerce and trade expressed in the early religious documents were restated by Plato and then by Xenophon. Plato believed that certain occupations degraded the individuals who followed them. The manual skills and commerce and trade were so classified. Tradesmen were permitted in the city only as a necessary evil, and any citizen who degraded himself as a shopkeeper would be imprisoned. Such occupations were only for foreigners.

Xenophon also expressed the general distaste for commercial undertakings but elaborated in more detail his veneration of agriculture. No respectable citizen would engage in any other occupation than tilling the soil. So important did agriculture bulk in Xenophon's appraisal of economic life that he devoted the major part of his economic writings to it. In Xenophon's analysis of the function of silver as money, we have a preview of some of the less logical ideas which have from time to time marked the history of economic thought. Although the value of other commodities diminished as the supply increased, not so with silver. The more mines which were discovered and the more intensively they were worked, the greater the desire on the part of citizens to possess silver. He hinted that the use of silver as the means of hiring soldiers for war gave it an extraordinary value that increased quantity could not undermine. Hundreds of years later these very same ideas became the grounds for heated controversy.

Aristotle's conception of money has already been described above. When trade and commerce expanded, money became indispensable as a medium of exchange and a standard of value both for the present and future. However, it was wrong, Aristotle believed, to lend money at interest. Since money could not reproduce itself, the exacting of more than was given was unjust. Others of Aristotle's ideas on money were more modern. He realized first that money was a commodity. As such it was subject to the same fluctuations in value as all commodities, although it was his conviction that the value of money was more constant. He pointed out that money had no natural value but only value created by law. Money carried an inherent danger according to Aristotle, for its very possession led to speculation, by which he meant the practice of trade not for purposes of securing needed articles for use but for purposes of amassing an abundance of the precious metals for their own sake.

In Thomas Aquinas we can recognize the influence of the essential teachings both of early religion and the Greek philosophers. The admonition of the founder of the Christian religion to the effect that a love of money was the root of all evil very clearly restricted the thinking of Aquinas, as did the principles laid down by the Mosaic law. Money and trade were perhaps necessary, but they were both spiritually dangerous since they led to the search for wealth for its own sake. Following Aristotle, Aquinas believed that money was barren and could not reproduce itself; hence to require interest was taking from another what one had not earned. Allowance was made, however, for some compensation for loans in exceptional cases. Prices were the money expressions of fair value, or as Aquinas interpreted it, the value of a man's labor according to his station in life.

The Development of New Ideas About Money During the Later Middle Ages

What Aquinas had to say on economic matters was largely in the nature of ethical recommendation rather than a critical description of economic processes. The stability and self-sufficiency of the period of feudalism might have found the just price and non-interest bearing loans sufficiently practical to serve as working principles; but in the very century in which Aquinas lived, the Thirteenth, commerce and trade with their demands for money and credit were swinging into a rapid tempo. In spite of the toll houses, the laws against trade, the opposition of the church and the arbitrary restrictions of feudal lords, the small band of traders, many of them Jewish, which moved across Europe during the Middle Ages now swelled into a mighty throng of merchants. Strangely enough, conditions which at first retarded the flow of commerce were in the end responsible for many of the instruments of trade which are now held indispensable. The absence of an abundant supply of money led to the rapid growth of money-lending agencies, and according to tradition at least, the Christian prohibitions against lending at interest had the effect of giving to the Jews this whole economic function. Buying and selling between cities which lacked a common currency and adequate police to give the merchants protection led to the revival of the bill of exchange. Although its origin is unknown, the bill of exchange was used in the Italian commercial cities before the invading Arabs destroyed their sea-borne trade with the cities of the Eastern Mediterranean. Once brought back into use by the development of European trade, it has continued as an essential element of modern business. The operation of a bill of exchange is simple; it requires only that persons of wealth in different cities be known to each other and agree to act in trust and confidence with each other. Given these conditions, suppose a buyer of merchandise wishes to journey to a distant city to purchase goods. Since police protection is meagre, and restrictions against the exportation of money numerous, the merchant would rather not risk carrying a large sum of money on his person. He therefore goes to a resident of his city known to have acquaintances in the city to which he is going. Paying the necessary money, the traveller receives a letter authorizing the wealthy friend to give the traveller a similar sum when he calls for it. This essentially is the way a bill of exchange operates. Of course, the settlement between the two friends, or bankers, is an important matter, but it does not need to be described here. Suffice it to say that since the relationship between the bankers is reciprocal, many of their transactions over a period of time will cancel out, leaving only a small balance, if any, to be settled in cash.

Another of the practical developments of the later Middle Ages which gave rise to important new factors in economic life was the formation of the Hanseatic League. This was the name taken by a group of cities centering around the Baltic and North seas which bound themselves together for mutual aid in carrying on commerce and trade. The word *hanse* is a germanic term similar to the modern idea of corporation. The power of these cities was great. They cleared the sea of pirates, deposed monarchs who continued useless restrictions against trade, forced large areas into commercial bondage, and admitted powerful cities to the advantages of their association only on payment of heavy fees. The ships of the League were known in the Mediterranean as far east as Syria; warehouses and banks were established in London in the League's name; and branches grew up in the interior of Europe. Apparently only the lack of a strong central authority prevented this loose knit association of cities from a firm and well nigh perpetual monopoly of European commerce.

Out of the conflicts between the league and rising native merchants in England and Belgium came the important functions of commission merchants and politically controlled tariffs. The former was the answer to the demand by the League that European imports and exports be shipped through the League city of Bruges. To avoid this control, business was transacted by sample through men who lived in Bruges and acted as agents. They merely negotiated the sale of the goods; details of shipment and payment were later arranged between the parties concerned, the agent receiving a percentage of the sale price as his fee. Much as the League sought to prohibit and later control such practices, they found no effective way of doing so. The city of Cologne broke away from the League on this issue, and the number of commission agents rapidly increased and they have continued to play an important part in the commerce and trade of the present.

Tariffs, of course, had been known during the Middle Ages.

The toll charges of the feudal lords who controlled strategic places along the highways and waterways were levies designed to bring the lord a revenue. It was, however, only when Queen Elizabeth permitted the manipulation of custom house levies in order to combat the privileges enjoyed by a group of European merchants from the days of the Hanseatic League that the tariff became an instrument of commercial warfare. Briefly stated, certain German merchants were able to bring goods in to England duty free; they owned a section of the city of London which was reserved for their business enterprises; a special court handled controversies between English and League traders. To prevent this unfavorable state of affairs, trading companies of distinctly English origin were encouraged by the sovereign, and tariffs were shifted to put the goods of the League merchants at a disadvantage. Thus was born the practice of nationalizing trade.

One might add indefinitely to the list of new economic techniques which grew out of the activities of the Hanseatic League. Commercial insurance, for example, was certainly stimulated by this trade. In addition to the scores of companies operating in Bruges in the days of the League, one company confined its business entirely to the writing of insurance on sea borne cargoes.

Another aspect of the economic conditions of the centuries immediately following Aquinas needs to be discussed before any further development of the ideas of money can be attempted. The increase of commerce and its demand for money found the monetary situation in Europe chaotic. Kings, nobles, and cities issued coins differing in weight, stamp, and name. The lack of a common unit made the function of the money-changer important. Added to this, however, were two tendencies which caused increased difficulty. Since coin was so scarce, every independent state and barony established restrictions against the exportation of metal. Within the state the content of the monetary unit was frequently changed, either by the process of devaluation instigated by the rulers in their desire for more funds, or by citizens who habitually reduced the content of the coins which fell into their hands by scraping, cutting, or chipping.

Henry VIII of England, for example, was exceedingly hard pressed for money. On several occasions he lowered the gold content of the English monetary unit in order to increase his own revenues. Henry had also borrowed large sums of money abroad, principally from Dutch bankers. When he was on the point of repaying his indebtedness he found that English currency had lost much of its value in foreign exchange and only coins of poor value were circulating in England. Henry's financial advisor at the time was Sir Thomas Gresham, a member of the famous Mercers' company. In order to offset the disadvantage in English money, he required English merchants who sold English wool abroad to pay the King's debts with the money they received for their wool. The King reimbursed them in debased English coins when they arrived home. Experiences such as this made Gresham a staunch advocate of sound money, advising the restoration of the original gold content of English coins. He saw clearly that where two kinds of money were in circulation—one of full gold value and the other of only part of the stated gold value—that the people would hoard the good money and spend only the bad money. Although Sir Thomas Gresham did not originate this principle it became known as Gresham's law. It states briefly, that bad money will drive good money out of circulation and even out of the country.

Trade was well nigh impossible during this period. Although systematic economic thought was meagre then, many proposals were submitted to standardize the monetary unit and control its circulation. The question of money became serious when gold was discovered in America, for the enormous quantities which entered the European trade completely disrupted the existing standards of money and trade.

The Mercantilist Ideas About Money

The period of growing commercial activity, falling roughly between the Thirteenth and Sixteenth Centuries, was more a period of economic action than of economic thought. At least, it is difficult to find a figure whose ideas seem at all representative of the economic developments of that time. However, the influx of gold from America and the problems associated with it seemed to foster extensive efforts to understand and appraise the rapidly changing economic scene. The literature of the Fifteenth Century is filled with observations on the necessity of increasing exports in order to increase the stock of money within a nation. For those nations which lacked mines, a favorable balance of trade was thought to be the only means whereby coin might be secured. Those who accepted the fact of an important interrelation between wealth, an abundance of money, and foreign trade were the Mercantilists, whose theories of money and wealth were discussed in an earlier chapter. A few of the Mercantilists such as Mun, Davenant, Petty, and Steuart clearly distinguished between wealth and money, but by and large the mercantilist writers either considered the two identical or avoided a clear statement of their relationship. It seems fair to say, however, that the complete identification of money with wealth was an extreme position of mercantilist thought, exaggerated by critics of Mercantilism.

Although the assumption that wealth consisted in an abundance of money may now appear unreasonable, strong arguments were offered to support it. The financial stability of the state in those days depended largely upon a ready supply of precious metals. Since public borrowing was still undeveloped, and taxation was not as flexible as it is today, the security of a government was naturally assumed to lie in an accumulated reserve of coin and bullion. THOMAS MUN, in writing on this subject, admitted the necessity of such a reserve but urged the heads of state to restrict their accumulations annually to the excess of exports over imports, so that the people would have sufficient money for commercial transactions. Characteristically, however, Mun also advised that ships, stores of grain, war supplies, and loans to the people for use in production should be considered desirable employment for the state's reserve.

Not a little of the desirability of a store of money was directly traceable to the use of mercenaries in warfare. Even more than today money was considered the sinews of war. Only a ready supply of cash could provide armies, ships, and munitions. An empty state treasury was frank admission of military impotence.

There was some force in the argument, too, that more money in circulation brought higher prices, and stimulated trade. The beneficial influence of a large quantity of money on trade was quite widely accepted. Although none of the Mercantilists could explain clearly the relationship between the quantity of money in circulation and the price level, a few of them at least were aware that such a relationship existed and openly subscribed to an increase in the money supply in order to increase trade. The value of the circulation of money was usually derived from and frequently explained in terms of William Harvey's discovery of the circulation of the blood which had taken place in the early Seventeenth Century. JOHN LAW (1671–1729), perhaps better than any other, serves as the exponent of these ideas. He supported the belief that the wealth of the state depended upon a large supply of money, and that business activity was increased by the increased quantity and circulation of money. But the variation he offered to mercantilist theory was that the state, instead of depending upon a favorable balance of trade to maintain its supply of money, might keep the supply of bullion intact and issue paper money for domestic transactions. However, when Law gave practical expression to his theories by the creation in France of a bank which would issue paper money, he was instrumental in bringing on one of the greatest inflationary periods of modern times. Others beside Law supported increased circulation.

EDWARD MISSELDEN, an early Seventeenth Century English writer of note, was a staunch advocate of the idea that to increase money was to increase trade. Misselden's two works, the short titles of which are *Free Trade* and *The Circle of Commerce* were published during the severe depression in English industry during the years 1620–1624. He believed firmly that money was the "vital spirit of trade." His suggestion that the state should increase the money in circulation by depreciating the value of the coins is quite out of line with the sound money ideas of classical economics, but recent events give the plan a very modern cast. He saw no danger in the rising prices such tactics would bring on, indeed he felt that the stimulation of trade and the increase of money resulting therefrom would more than compensate for the high prices.

JACOB VANDERLINT believed that plenty of money made trade flourish since people were enabled to consume more goods. WILLIAM POTTER, a writer whose contribution to economic thought has been largely overlooked, said in his *Key to Wealth* that money had value only as it stimulated the production of more goods, since a nation's wealth consisted of all the goods it possessed. But he added that an increased quantity of money would result in greater sales and hence in greater trade. To make available a larger quantity of money he advocated the issuance of paper currency backed by land and other property. He argued convincingly that the only necessity for foreign trade was an artificial dependence upon gold and silver for money; therefore if some purely domestic standard of currency were established, concern over foreign trade and export restrictions upon gold could be abolished.

The issues aroused by the Mercantilists were numerous. Not a few of them continued in one form or another to engage the attention of eminent economists of later years even down to the present day. Such questions as a nation's supply of gold, the use of paper money, the relation of money to prices, and the extension and control of credit have not been solved to the satisfaction of all; and not a little of present day public policy emanates from the careless interpretation of these key points in economic thought.

The Origins of the Classical Ideas on Money: The Automatic Regulation of Foreign Trade

Although many of the Mercantilists themselves deviated at various points from the traditional pattern of mercantilist thought, none gave clearer indication of the changes in the fundamental ideas of money that were to come in later centuries than did SIR WILLIAM PETTY (1623–1687). He accepted most of the principles of Mercantilism but by his empirical methods and a liberal use of statistical data he was able to throw off the restrictions of mercantilist doctrine, and offer more advanced ideas. When most of his contemporaries were advocating stronger control of the exportation of money, he maintained that without governmental regulation a nation might achieve a sufficient quantity of money to meet its internal needs by lending excesses at interest and creating a bank to make up for deficiencies by means of credit. He also gave some intimation that the quantity of money in circulation affected prices. To be sure his discussion was concerned more with the fluctuation in the weight of standard coins as they affected prices, but his insight was in the direction of later advances.

It was DAVID HUME, however, who made the first comprehensive attack upon the idea that the measure of a nation's economic and political welfare was the size of its stock of precious metal. By these attacks he put an end to the hold of Mercantilism on English economic thought. In spite of the able writing of later economists, Hume's exposition of the fallacies of the bullionist position and his advocacy of automatic regulation of the flow of money is still outstanding for its clarity of reasoning and excellence of style. Good partial discussions of the self-regulation of trade and the flow of money are to be found in the writings of John Locke, Sir Dudley North, Isaac Gervaise, and Jacob Vanderlint, but it was Hume who, in his *Political Discourses,* assembled the several points of discussion and wove them into a masterful analysis of the total idea. The essence of Hume's discussion is that the monetary supply of a country is self-regulating and the best interests of the country will be served without government attempts to secure a favorable balance of trade or to prohibit the export of bullion. A decline in the quantity of money in England will cause a decline in the price of goods; thus foreign buyers will buy English goods and pay for them in money until the quantity of money in England is equal to that of other countries. If money should increase, prices will rise, foreign buyers will seek other markets, and imports will exceed exports until the level of money in the trading countries is once again equal. The flow of metal is also influenced by the rates of exchange between countries which act as forces similar to price levels operating to restore monetary equilibrium. Hume, it appears, believed in a direct and equal relationship between the quantity of money and the price level. The actual quantity of money, he said, made little difference since it was the quantity of money as related to the amount of goods available which determined the price. There was, of course, a temporary advantage to be gained from an increase in money. Since prices did not react immediately to increases in money, there was a brief period of adjustment when at the same prices the nation possessing more money could demand more goods.

This analysis by Hume was readily accepted by most of the economists who followed him. CANTILLON (a contemporary of Hume), whose works were not so long ago rediscovered, made a brilliant and detailed exposition of automatic adjustment of money in international trade in his *Essai sur la nature du commerce en général* (1755), but Hume's work is the better known. It has appeared strange to later scholars that Adam Smith made no reference to Hume in his work, although his statement of the self-regulating mechanism is similar to that of Hume, and it is known that the two men were well acquainted. In JOHN STUART MILL's discussion of this topic there is a general acceptance of the Hume point of view, but one important innovation was added. The increase of money in one country actually increased the demand of that country for its own and foreign goods. The effect of this was not only to increase the prices of domestic goods which turned away foreign traders, but it also started the flow of foreign goods into the country, thus sooner or later bringing about an equilibrium.

Little has been added to this theory of the flow of money and the balance of trade since first composed by Hume and clarified by such writers as Mill. Serious questions have been raised in modern time concerning its effectiveness. In practice, governments have manipulated their currencies and gold supply, hoping thereby to secure advantage for themselves; but as yet no new analysis of the process of international trade or international money supply has supplanted what for want of a better name is still called "classical" theory.

ADAM SMITH made no changes in the basic ideas of money that his predecessors had propounded. Explaining how the origin of money was due to the necessity of exchange arising from a sub-division of labor, he proceeded to show how the quantity of money in circulation was regulated. He conceived of money as both a medium of exchange and a measuring of value, but he denied that it had any value in itself other than that of facilitating exchange. Because of this factor, the greater economy in its use the better. To this end the use of paper money was eminently desirable, for this increased the quantity of coin which was available for purchases of instruments of production abroad without decreasing the supply for domestic use. Money was a commodity, Smith believed, and like any commodity the amount of it would be regulated by necessity. If a greater quantity was available than domestic trade required, the excess would be used for purchases abroad. In the case of paper money issued by banks an excess would be attended by a rise in prices, and foreign purchasing would result, requiring the exchange of bank notes for coin with which to make foreign payments. Thus Smith's real contribution to the theory of money seems to have been his emphasis upon the value of paper money as an aid to economic activity.

In a general way the monetary views of DAVID RICARDO follow closely the pattern of Adam Smith. In the movement of bullion and the effect of the quantity of money on prices in international trade he subscribed to the quantity theory and supported the self-regulating mechanism, adding the significant point that even before commodity prices the price of bills of exchange seemed to reverse the course of trade in the direction of equilibrium between nations. Ricardo's name became closely associated with the efforts to solve the monetary problems of his day, in fact he is looked upon as the best exponent of the bullionist position. Economic crises, the suspension of specie payments for two decades, and price inflation, all marked the span of Ricardo's life. They were so serious that the English government gave close attention to plans for combating them. In his pamphlet, *The High Price of Bullion,* Ricardo attempted to explain the monetary instability as an effect of poorly regulated paper currency. Although he believed as did Adam Smith that paper money should be substituted for coin wherever possible, he was convinced that in order to bring about economic stability the amount of paper currency should be reduced to conform to the quantity of specie on hand. On the other hand, he advocated as a long term policy the issuance of paper currency rather than specie to meet the demands of increased population and increased business activity, for which a reserve in gold would be kept at the bank. The banking legislation of Great Britain for the first half of the Nineteenth Century reflects the monetary theories of Ricardo, testifying not so much to his originality or the validity of his ideas as to the energy and clarity with which he presented them. There was one point concerning his theory of money that emphasized Ricardo's adherence to Adam Smith's ideas and the classical tradition. While the value of money was primarily determined by the supply and the demand for it as a medium of exchange, the cost of production of gold and silver also influenced the value of money just as the cost of production tended to influence the value of other commodities. Thus, the relative value of gold and any other commodity was the relation of their costs of production. It was at this point that Ricardo's ideas seem most confused. Nevertheless, classical economists of later years tended to follow the same line of reasoning without criticism.

The idea that the value of metal money was determined by its cost of production was taken up and elaborated by JOHN STUART MILL. He was concerned with showing that the value of money could be affected both by its quantity combined with rapidity of circulation, and by its cost of production. In the case of the former the effect was immediate; the effect of the latter would be felt only over long periods of time. Obviously, said Mill, the law of supply and demand operated more quickly upon money than on other commodities, but since the cost of production ultimately affected the supply of money, it must be considered as influencing value. The thoughts of Mill on this question can be applied only to metal money, but since he advocated the issuance of paper against adequate gold reserves, with the amount of paper money in circulation being controlled to vary as the amount of specie in the country varied, the principle still held. Hence, the value of currency, whether coin or paper, was still controlled in the long run by the cost of production of gold.

The Quantity Theory of Money

In discussing the automatic control of the flow of money and commerce over international boundaries and the relative merits of gold *vs.* paper currency, we have touched on other important aspects of money. No idea has been more important in economic thought than what the economist calls the *quantity theory* of money. In the brief summaries given above of the ideas of such men as Law, Petty, Vanderlint, and Hume, the question of the influence of the quantity of money in circulation upon the price level was constantly referred to. Vague and undeveloped as it was with those early writers, it became the subject of extensive inquiry in the centuries following.

One of the earliest writers to be concerned specifically with the function of money and its effect upon prices was JEAN BODIN (1530–1590). His explanation of the advance in prices during the Sixteenth Century, as found in his *Réponse aux Paradoxes de Malestroit* (1569) is far in advance of his time. He ascribes the current price changes to the abundance of gold and silver, scarcity caused by effort, and the debasement of currency. There is no doubt but that he had a fair understanding of the relation of the quantity and value of money to prices. He proceeds to cite historical facts to support his contentions. All in all, his analysis of French foreign trade during the period and the subsequent influx of gold is on a par with the thinking of a much later era.

To JOHN LOCKE, however, goes the credit for the first formulation of the quantity theory of money. He claimed that the value of any commodity, money included, was determined by the relation of the supply to the demand. As long as the quantity of money remained the same, he maintained, any alterations in price were due to changes in the supply and demand for commodities in terms of each other. If, however, the quantity of money was altered and the amount of trade remained the same, any change in price could be traced directly to the change in the quantity of money. Locke was aware also that in determining the quantity of money some consideration had to be shown for the speed of circulation, since a coin used several times would count for more than the same coin if used only once in the same period of time. The additions to the theory made by Cantillon, Vanderlint, and Hume were in the nature of refinements of detail. Cantillon showed that the increase in money due to the exploitation of mines first affected prices of goods used in the process of mining, and then it affected the prices of goods used by those whose incomes were increased as a direct result of the increased mining activity. A general rise in prices would follow sooner or later throughout the country, the net effect of which was the dislocation of domestic industry through a development of foreign buying.

The earliest statements of the quantity theory of money were all made when the chief circulating medium was coin. During the years which followed, first paper money, then bank credit were introduced, and they quickly pushed metal money into obscurity. Then paper money for a time was the chief medium of exchange for business transactions, but since the middle of the Nineteenth Century bank credit alone has kept pace with the rapid expansion of business enterprise. These innovations have made the quantity theory of money more difficult to observe in practice, but they have not changed the basic principle. Until the 1930–1940 decade, it was generally understood that a nation's currency would be backed by precious metals which would be used to settle balances in international trade. The dislocations of international economic life and the practices of most nations in controlling both credit and note issue with little regard to the quantity of precious metals on hand have made this commonly accepted rule inoperative, at least temporarily. However, in ordinary times, while the quantity theory did not assume that prices would bear a direct relation to the amount of gold or silver on hand, nevertheless—since the limits of note issue and credit were indirectly controlled by the quantity of metal a nation possessed—coin continued to hold an important place in the operation of the quantity theory. However, today in the determination of the quantity of money on hand at a given time, bank credit, note issue, and other forms of credit are far more important than metal.

The modern economists interested in this field have constantly sought to describe these newer and more complex aspects of the quantity theory of money in terms which could be understood and applied. The attempts at simplification by mathematical means are not new, however. Montesquieu used common numerical ratios in his description, and Sir John Lubbock produced a formula which could be applied to determine the price level. IRVING FISHER has been considered the best exponent of the quantity theory in modern times, and his equation is the present best known expression of the theory:

$$P = \frac{MV + M'V'}{T}$$

In the equation, P = the general price level, M = the quantity of metal money, V = the velocity of turnover of metal money, M' = the volume of bank deposits, V' = the velocity of turnover of these deposits, and T = the volume of trade, or number of transactions.

In simple language the formula means that the price level may be determined if the quantity of money in circulation—including both currency and bank credit—is multiplied by the number of times it changes hands, or turns over, in a given period, and then divided by the total number of business transactions which have taken place during the same period. The price level indicated will be in the nature of a number which—when compared to similar numbers applicable to different times—will show the exact amount of change in the price level.

The quantity theory of money has never been completely acceptable among economists generally. It was held first that the formula itself was meaningless, since each of the items in the formula was not an independent variable but was interdependent with each other item. Further, Othmar Spann claimed that the assumption that the doubling of the quantity of money equaled a doubling in the demand for all commodities was untrue since a doubling of the quantity of money had a very uneven result, affecting both production and the demand for money in very different ways under different circumstances.

The defenders of the quantity theory were hard pressed to explain the downward trend in prices during the last three decades of the Nineteenth Century and the upward swing of the first two of the Twentieth. They pointed out that such fluctuations were directly traceable to the decline in gold production during the first period and the discoveries of new mines at the beginning of the second period. Gustav Cassel, a contemporary writer of Swedish origin, has done much to explain the price changes of recent times in terms of the quantity theory. By his research he was able to show that an annual increase of 3 percent (allowing a small percentage for wastage) in the gold supply was sufficient to stabilize prices. Larger or smaller increases in gold he believed resulted in price fluctuation, and the changes in prices were in direct ratio to the variations of the additional gold supply from the norm.

J. H. Laughlin also took exception to the quantity theory. He ascribed the decline in prices of the 1865–1896 period to the tremendous increases in production of that time. The rise in prices in the decades following he claimed was due to the extension of credit based upon the increase in commodities which had already taken place. As business activity increased, the medium of exchange expanded with it. Hence, the quantity of money or means of exchange had no influence on prices. Obviously so complex a matter as the nature and behavior of money will not be represented by one theory alone. There are many different ways of thinking about money. Spann pointed out in his *The*

History of Economics that one group of economists claimed that the value of money as a medium of exchange lay essentially in its own commodity value. That is, money was readily acceptable by all people because it had a value in itself as a commodity. Thus, gold is acceptable because gold has value in use. The other group, he said, were those who considered the value of money to lie in the legal fact of its being designated as a medium of exchange by the state, or by mass agreement. As he described the groups, the former were the economists of the classical English tradition, while the latter included members from the German historical and the Austrian schools.

JOHN MAYNARD KEYNES has in recent years become known for his analysis of the place and importance of money in the operation of modern economic life. Both in his *A Treatise on Money* (1930) and his *The General Theory of Employment Interest and Money* (1936), he emphasized the fact that money had unique characteristics which set it apart from other commodities. While the volume of most commodities can be almost indefinitely increased by the application of labor and capital, that is not so with money. Money can be increased, but the amount of increase is a matter of arbitrary decision by government authority and is not self-regulated by production costs and selling price as are other commodities. Also, there is no substitute for money. When the exchange value of other commodities rises, substitute products usually are available; but not so with money. Further, money holds a liquidity preference higher than any other commodity. It is the one commodity for which there is always a market. And, finally, Keynes claimed that the importance of money lay in its being the link between present and future values. As a general statement of relationship, Keynes accepted Fisher's formula of the quantity theory of money, but he added so many possible variables—such as the demand for money, labor factors, and physical factors determining the rate of diminishing returns in production—that the simple formula for him had very little meaning and could only be used in relatively artificial situations where one of the variables arbitrarily was held constant. In the long run the effect of the changing quantity of money on prices has never been allowed to operate. The normal trend of prices and wage rates has been upward. If by chance a deficiency of the supply of money caused a decline in prices and wage-rates, the increasing burden of the debt structure which followed such changes was too painful to tolerate. Measures of debt relief and changes in the monetary unit were introduced by the state to curb the deflationary trend. Keynes' investigations into the role of money and its effect upon interest and employment resulted in a recommendation that has undermined the whole classical tradition. He suggested that depressions could be ended through a form of controlled inflation which would eliminate the necessity of raising wage rates, and would keep interest rates stabilized at a point high enough to insure continued investment.

Paper Money, Credit, and Banking

The great economic achievements of the Dutch in the Fifteenth and Sixteenth Centuries were a source of envy to many commercially minded Englishmen. Very humanly, their minds tried to ferret out some explanation of the prosperity of the Dutch, perhaps for the intellectual satisfaction they might get but more probably in the hope of achieving that high standard of living customary among the Dutch merchants. It is not strange that many of them located the source of the Dutch commercial success in the fact that a bank was operated successfully in Amsterdam, while none as yet had been started in England. Sir William Petty and Sir Dudley North, Seventeenth Century writers, both advocated the formation of a bank in England which might issue credit. It is clear that the ideas of these early writers were vague on what banks could and could not do. North's idea was that a bank should be created to lend money to the government; and as a matter of fact that was the chief reason for chartering the Bank of England. Banks served as repositories for coin which could be put out at interest, but the ideas of note issue and commercial credit were scarcely known, even on the continent, in the Seventeenth Century.

The banks at Amsterdam and at Hamburg were really not banks in the modern sense of the word. They were places where money could be exchanged into currency of recognized and standard value. Because of the variety of coins circulating in Europe at the time, and because the weight and fineness of the metal coins varied so much from that which was claimed by the state issuing them, some reliable method of testing and exchange was essential to the conduct of trade. The increasing amount of commerce passing through Amsterdam and Hamburg made these cities the natural places for the establishment of exchange banks. They weighed and assayed the coin which traders brought them; in exchange, they gave coins of certified weight and fineness or certificates of deposit. Banks of this type needed no capital of their own, since they exchanged value for value and were rewarded by the small charge they made for the service they rendered. English authorities of this period confused cause and effect. They felt that the bank was responsible for the growth in trade, and consequently they advocated the establishment of a bank in London. Strangely enough, in their appraisal of the bank of Amsterdam, the English merchants had their eye not so much on the principal function of the bank—which was the exchange of currency—but on a practice which was at first considered quite secondary. When the Amsterdam Exchange Bank was established in 1609, traders were allowed to deposit money in the bank to be withdrawn at any time by the depositor. The rules of the bank required that large payments of several hundred dollars or more be made by the transference of accounts from one firm to another within the bank. A small charge was made for the transference of accounts. Such transfers of accounts were later called "bank money." As one authority expressed it, the function of the bank was "the local manufacture of international coinage." According to the laws under which the bank operated, the bank was required to keep on hand one hundred percent of the coin deposited. Violations were frequent, however, in the later years of the bank's history. Loans were made to the Dutch East India Company and to the city of Amsterdam, and although these obligations were finally met the bank was forced to close in 1820 for failure to meet its obligations.

Banks created primarily for the purpose of accepting deposits and making loans were organized in the commercial city of Venice as early as the Fourteenth Century. These private banks were required by the laws of Venice to hold coin as security for their depositors. Public banks were established during the next two centuries to accept deposits from citizens, make loans—especially to the government—and to issue bank notes on government authority.

When the Bank of England was founded in 1694 it was designed to create a market for government loans. It accepted money from private citizens which it immediately loaned to the government. The time was one of financial instability. With new monarchs on the throne (William and Mary, 1688) and part of the population disgruntled at the change, it was not easy to secure money for public purposes. One is not surprised to note the close connection between the admiration that English commercial interests had for the Dutch, the enthroning of monarchs with considerable Dutch sympathy, and the establishment of the Bank of England by the descendants of James Houblon, a Flemish refugee who came to England to escape the persecutions of the Spanish Duke of Alva.

The Bank of England was the first bank in England to have government authorization, and it was the first of national importance; but private banking activity had been carried on for a century and more before by the goldsmiths of England and Scotland, some of whose names are still attached to private banks now operating. The goldsmith accepted money for deposit and paid interest at a stated percent. Their guarantees of security, easy withdrawal, and interest brought forth abundant money which heretofore had been hoarded or lent at interest on personal security. Members of the royal family, Cromwell, and other prominent persons were known to have had dealings with them principally as borrowers.

A further extension of the goldsmiths' banking activities came when the certificates of deposit were accepted in payment for financial obligations. These deposit receipts, at first merely the holder's evidence for his deposit and his right to withdraw the amount stated, soon began to circulate as currency. As long as the reputation of the bank and the depositor were good, people had no fear of accepting deposit slips instead of cash. This issue of certificates was followed by the issuance of notes, and then in 1781 by a book of checks. The right to issue notes was so much a part of private banking that legislation in the time of Queen Anne prohibiting this practice was believed to be an effective means of eliminating any but the smallest private banks.

The immediate effect of the organization of the Bank of England was the stabilization of public finance, but the long run effect was a serious inflation of currency and credit. Specie disappeared, the mint closed because no one brought bullion to be coined, and devaluation of the currency was advocated. JOHN LOCKE opposed devaluation, and in his essay, *Further Considerations Concerning Raising the Value of Money,* he argued for a sound money policy. He believed it unjust to deprive blameless men of one-fifth of their estates and income. Many men, he said, would be glad to give a much larger proportion of their estates if they were assured the nation would benefit; but to take from some men and give to others less deserving (the debtors) did not help the state at all. Furthermore, the function of government was to preserve contracts; how could the government require that some pay less than their contract and others receive less. Such a policy was no more just than requiring men to pay more than they had contracted to pay. Lastly, he believed, devaluation would undermine public confidence in the government and defraud not only the king but also the church, the universities, and the hospitals.

Locke's arguments were persuasive, especially to the class of landowners who continued to exercise control over the government. A period of deflation set in, but the hardship which the advocates of devaluation had foreseen never materialized. What might have happened eventually will never be known, for a wave of speculation founded upon colonial enterprises overtook both England and France and brought on a banking crisis in both countries in 1720.

The name of JOHN LAW (1671–1729) is closely identified with this period of speculation, inflation, and subsequent financial crisis especially in France. Law was the son of a banker, one of the goldsmiths who originated banking practices in Scotland; and by tradition and training he became an authority if not a genius in economic matters. His ideas were coldly received both in Scotland and England. Because of certain personal misfortunes of a social nature while living in London, he was exiled from England and forced to spend the rest of his life on the Continent. The financial difficulties of France following the extravagant reign of Louis XIV gave Law his opportunity, and in an amazingly short time he had established institutions to put his ideas into practice.

Law's principal work, *Money and Trade Considered, with a Proposal for Supplying the Nation with Money,* was written in 1705, as a plan to relieve Scotland of a severe financial panic following the failure of the Darien expedition. The plan was never seriously considered in Scotland, but it embodied the basic ideas which Law held on wealth, money, credit and banking, and to which he gave practical expression in France in 1716. Law denied the general contention of Mercantilism that money was wealth; he held that wealth in terms of goods did depend upon trade, and both employment and trade depended upon the quantity of money in circulation. Furthermore, he added, credit had all the beneficial effects of money. The quantity of specie need not be increased; but merely by the device of creating a bank, credit could be expanded. The bank which Law proposed was to issue notes backed by land. Credit expansion and note issue would be under rigid control, since the bank would be a state agency and the commission controlling it composed of government officials. The most daring part of the proposal was that foreign trade and public finance would be managed through one gigantic corporation, controlled by the state in the interests of the people, and carrying on business through the issue of an abundant supply of paper currency.

The story of Law's experiments in France reads like an economic fairy tale. During his exile he supported himself in luxury mainly through financial speculation and gambling. The chaotic financial situation in which Louis XIV left France on his death baffled the best financial experts of the time. A declaration of national bankruptcy was seriously considered. When an acquaintance of Law's, the Duke of Orleans, became Regent, Law was given an opportunity to submit a plan to stabilize the nation's finances. Opposed by the financial oligarchy in Paris, the plan was tentatively accepted by the Regent. The first step was the establishment of *La Banque Générale* under the immediate direction of Law. The capital of the bank consisted of shares of stock paid for in 4 installments, $\frac{1}{4}$ in cash and $\frac{3}{4}$ in the then nearly worthless paper notes of the French state. The privilege of note issue was granted to the new bank, the notes being redeemable in metal by weight on sight. Thus far the plan was a success. The fact that the bank was willing to accept the existing government notes raised the credit of the government; the bank's own notes became a most desirable medium of exchange since they had a fixed value in metal. The use of the notes for industrial transactions in the provinces, and the decree making the notes acceptable in payment of taxes created such a demand for the notes that new issues soon followed. It must be remembered that Law saw no difficulty in an unlimited issue of paper currency as long as there was a demand for it and as long as there was good security for it. An excess quantity of paper currency never worried him.

The success of the bank earned the immediate confidence of the Regent, consequently Law's request for permission to carry out the other parts of his program was met with approval. The Mississippi trading area was not prospering under the management of an incompetent speculator. Law took over the franchise and set up the *Compagnie de la Louisiane ou d'Occident* (Company of Louisiana or the West). Its capital was raised by the sale of shares payable part in cash and part in notes of indebtedness of the French state. The same confidence did not exist in the new company as had obtained for the bank. Consequently, the price of the shares fell below par. Law remedied this by agreeing as director of the bank, now an official state bank named *La Banque Royale,* to redeem the shares at par with notes guaranteed by the king. The favorable effect on the shares was immediate; their price rose on the exchange to above par. Law's next move was to unite the companies engaged in foreign trade into a single company, *La Compagnie des Indes* (The Company of the Indies), under his own direction. Without going into further detail, confidence in Law and the renewed vigor of business enterprise caused every new issue of shares to be grabbed up immediately at fantastic prices. To meet the demand for money caused by the accompanying price rise, the bank issued more paper currency. Finally, the more intelligent investors realized that the earnings of the companies were too meagre at this early date to pay a dividend commensurate with the price of the shares, and they began to sell. With the dictatorial power over French financial matters which he now held, Law introduced

measures to check the falling price of shares and the rising price
of metal and property. He declared a 40% dividend on the
shares, he forbade the use of diamonds and the manufacture of
gold and silver plate. A virtual embargo was placed upon coin.
But the shares still fell. Then Law made his most daring effort
to check the downward trend. He ordered the bank to buy and
sell the shares of the various trading companies at a fixed price,
payable in bank notes. The loss of confidence which at first only
affected the companies now extended to the bank and to the
paper currency. The latter soon became as worthless as the shares.
Law was driven from France and the bank notes were incorporated into the debt of France, the total of which was subsequently reduced by more than half. Much abuse has been heaped
on the head of Law for his mismanagement of French finances.
Mature judgment seems to indicate that while on the whole his
plan was admirable it was spoiled first by a fundamental misconception—that paper money could be issued in unlimited quantity—and, secondly, by a foolish gamble—ordering the bank to
buy the discredited shares at a fixed price. Except for the latter
action, the bank might have been saved and the credit structure
of France maintained. It is not an exaggeration to say that Law's
four years of experimentation with his "Mississippi Scheme"
stands as one of the most exciting periods in financial history.

While John Law was learning through bitter experience the
fallacies of some of his economic ideas, a similar course of events
was being pursued in England. In 1711 the South Sea Company
was incorporated. This was the first move in a scheme originated
supposedly by Daniel Defoe to reduce the government's debt
and stimulate foreign trade. The South Sea Company agreed to
pay the government several million pounds to be applied to the
national debt in return for a monopoly on trading rights in South
America and the Pacific Islands. The money paid to the government was to be raised by the sale of stock. In spite of trouble arising with Spain, the scheme was successful in its early stages and

a more ambitious plan was submitted to government officials. Under the new arrangement the South Sea Company would take over the entire national debt of over fifty-one million pounds on which it would receive 5% annually. It was the plan of the directors to contact the holders of government certificates of indebtedness and persuade them to exchange the government bonds for shares in the South Sea Company. Stimulated by the confidence of the French in the experiments of John Law, the shares of the company were not only readily accepted by the holders of government bonds, but their price on the exchange began to appreciate rapidly. Within six months the stock had risen from 128½ to 1000. Companies imitating the plan and organization of the South Sea Company began to appear, and speculation was wild. Then came word of the panic in France, and a similar loss of confidence began in England. The price of shares fell rapidly as insiders, sensing the situation, unloaded huge quantities of stock on the market. By December not only the South Sea Company stock but securities of sound companies such as the Bank of England and the East India Company went down rapidly, and Parliament was forced to take action. Investigation of the company showed both fraud and bribery and the leaders of the company were brought to trial and imprisoned. Those who had exchanged government obligations for the South Sea Company asked the government to guarantee them their original investment, but while not completely neglected they received only half of what was due them before the panic.

With these two major disasters in the background, it is no wonder that the more conservative economists were reluctant to give wholehearted approval to paper money and bank credit during the century which followed. This period was marked by bitter and continued controversies on the question of money and credit especially as they related to banking practices and government control.

In the midst of money and banking uncertainty, RICARDO endeavored to outline the function and methods of modern bank-ing, with the hope that a more general understanding of how and why banks operate would ease the mounting tension. In his *Proposals for an Economical and Secure Currency,* he described modern banking practices. He said the real advantage of banking to a community begins only when it employs the capital of others as well as its own. This additional money comes from deposits and the notes which it issues. Most of it is loaned to persons whose trustworthiness is assured, who intend to use the funds for business purposes, although a small part merely remains in the bank awaiting its depositor's decision to withdraw it. On the money loaned, the bank collects interest; some of the money deposited and some of the original capital may be invested in government bonds or other sound obligations which can be converted into cash on short notice. Another important function of the bank, said Ricardo, was the facility it offered in making payments be-tween merchants in near or distant towns, or foreign countries; checking accounts had not developed extensively at the time of Ricardo, but the use of the bank to make payments was wide-spread. Finally, banks could issue notes on the government bonds and specie which they held. The former not only furnished funds to the government but enabled banks to increase the paper money in circulation. The earnings of a bank arise through the interest it collects on loans to the government or individuals, the earnings from investments it makes, and the fees it collects for services. With these earnings the bank pays expenses, interest on deposits, and dividends to the holders of shares in the bank.

This outline taken from Ricardo is a fairly accurate description of conservative banking practices of his time. The simplicity of the description belies the problems and debatable issues in con-nection with it. As a matter of fact, at least two major issues stirred the financial world during Ricardo's lifetime. The first great controversy was between bullionist and anti-bullionist about which something has already been said in the discussion of Ricardo's ideas on money. The uncertain economic situation which could be traced to the almost continuous warfare during the Eighteenth and early Nineteenth Centuries upset the normal banking procedures. Specie payments were suspended in England; exchange rates were usually unfavorable; country banks failed; and the excessive government demands upon the Bank of England made uncertainty the keynote of the times. The chief point at issue throughout the period was the control of paper currency. Ricardo, Whatley, Malthus, and Thornton were the outstanding bullionists. They contended that the constant depreciation of currency was due to the over-issue of paper bank notes, and they advocated—in the report of the Bullion Committee which was largely the work of Ricardo—that a return should be made to specie payments, and that the difference in value between specie and bank note reflected the amount of over-issue of the notes. The anti-bullionists' position was presented in speeches and pamphlets by Nicholas Vansittart, Bosanquet, and Trotter. Their argument was that Bank of England statistics did not show that a greater note issue existed in periods when bullion was selling at a premium over paper money; and further, that in the years when large payments in specie were made by the Bank of England to foreign countries the premium of specie over paper was greater. Hence, the anti-bullionists refused to agree that depreciation in the value of paper money was due to over-issue. They believed that rather than set rigid limits to the amount of paper money a bank could issue by setting a fixed ratio to the amount of bullion on hand, the bank itself could control the issue simply by restricting issue when the interest rate began to fall. It is sufficient to note that the anti-bullionists' views were accepted until after the Napoleonic Wars, when specie payments were resumed. The immediate effect of the resumption was to set in motion a deflationary process which lowered prices and wages but continued fixed incomes and debts at previous levels. Objection to this economic condition was outspoken as it had been of the unstable inflationary period which preceded it.

Thus, the fires of controversy were kept burning. Did devaluation and the consequent inflation of currency stimulate business? Was the failure to honor the gold standard a breech of faith on the part of government? Could paper currencies be stable without being tied directly to the quantity of metal money on hand? These and other questions challenged the best minds of the times, and much of the best economic writing of the period is in the form of attempts to state an idea or a theory in language practical enough so that it might have a bearing upon the existing monetary difficulties. Further, refinement of the points at issue and sharper arguments were used as the currency controversies continued. The currency school advocated strict adherence to a metallic standard for paper money; the banking school believed that both paper money and credit could be regulated without government interference by the economic processes themselves. Nevertheless, government regulation became a fixture even though a specific metallic standard was a fiction rather than a reality.

The Views of the Historical School

An important deviation from the classical theory of money appeared among the writers of the historical school. Beginning with the work of Adam Müller and continuing down through the Nineteenth Century, German economists denied that the value of money was related to the use value of the metal of which it was made. They believed that the value of money was an act of the state. This theory was best explained in the writings of G. F. KNAPP (1842–1926) who became the outstanding exponent of "chartalism." Although in primitive societies money may have been an unconscious expedient to meet the need of exchange, in the highly organized modern community the government alone decrees what shall be the unit of currency and the value it carries. This dependence upon the state may have had a real bearing upon the currency manipulations in the Central European states in recent years. Certainly the recent departures of all modern states from the automatic monetary controls of classical economic theory in favor of managed currency gives a certain sense of reality to chartalist ideas.

Socialist Ideas of Money and Banking

While the classical economists were busy bickering over the relative virtues of metal money and specie and ways to control paper money and credit, ideas about money of an altogether different nature were being developed by other schools of economic thought. ROBERT OWEN in England, for example, was originating a socialist idea of money. His line of reasoning went something like this: The difficulties of modern economy could be traced to profit. Therefore it was necessary to abolish profit. Owen did not believe, as did his contemporaries, that through competition profit would gradually be eliminated anyway. Some active force must be found to destroy it. Now reasoning in another direction, he concluded that since profit was always expressed in terms of money, that is, the result of buying in the cheapest market and selling in the dearest, if metallic money could be eliminated so would profit. Therefore, he planned to substitute labor notes, expressive of hours of labor, for present money which had value in terms of gold and the amount of it in circulation. In practical terms, if a producer wished to dispose of an article, he received payment in labor notes according to the number of hours of labor spent in production. Ricardo had said that labor was the true source of value. Owen's plan was calculated to make the *labor theory* of value a reality by making the man-hours of labor the unit of currency rather than so many grains of gold.

Owen was not a person to remain content with the expostulation of a theory. He immediately established the National Equitable Labour Exchange in London to test his idea. Each member cooperating with the Exchange brought his produce to the Exchange and received labor notes in payment, according to the time spent in production. This member was then privileged to purchase any other produce on sale by giving the required number of labor notes in exchange. In this way, hours of labor were exchanged for hours of labor directly.

The Labour Exchange opened in 1832. Members numbered 840, and the initial success of the Exchange warranted the establishment of several branches. But difficulties were obvious. Members could not be trusted to state their hours of work correctly. When experts were employed to evaluate articles brought for sale, they did so by setting a money value and dividing it by a standard hourly wage. This, of course, was a complete reversal of Owen's intention. Furthermore, since the notes could be exchanged with non-members, neighboring merchants exchanged the notes for cash, then by buying the best articles at the exchange for the notes, they were able to realize a handsome profit by reselling in the regular commercial markets. In the face of such obstructions the Exchange soon found it impossible to continue operations.

Owen's failure with the Labour Exchange did not prevent later experiments intended to accomplish the same purpose. The Exchange Bank initiated by PROUDHON in 1849 was the next attempt to adapt socialistic theories to practical reform. His basic assumption was that interest was the cause of economic inequality and oppression. If one could make capital available to the wage earner at no cost, he would control the means of production and his produce, getting full value for the labor expended. To accomplish this purpose Proudhon advocated the establishment of an Exchange Bank which would issue paper money backed by the finished but unsold produce of those affiliated with the bank. Notes would be issued as a form of credit, and the notes would be acceptable as a medium of exchange among the members of the bank. Only a slight service charge would be made to cover actual operating expenses of the bank.

Since the notes in circulation would never exceed the demand for commercial credit, and would represent goods already produced, Proudhon could see no difficulty with his scheme. In two respects, however, Proudhon failed to see its consequences. First, the competition of the exchange bank notes with regular currency backed by gold would limit the circulation of the former and make the bank notes exchangeable with the regular currency, only at a heavy premium. Secondly, there would inevitably be a distinction between the members of the Exchange Bank who paid cash and those who demanded time, thus creating two different prices, since the use of discounting is merely a method of equating the same payments made now and in the future. In modified form, Proudhon's bank actually came into existence as the People's Bank. After three months of operation the bank closed its doors, due not only to the fallacies of its principles but to the fact that Proudhon himself was imprisoned for his literary attacks upon Louis Bonaparte. Although the practical experiment failed, Proudhon's basic ideas for an exchange bank have been incorporated into the modern cooperative and mutual credit societies.

The position of KARL MARX on the subject of money was confined mainly to two ideas. The first was the use of money as capital, and the second was the relationship of money to the operation of his labor theory of value and of surplus value. Marx did not go so far as to condemn money as the source of profit as Owen had done; but it is significant that the economy which Marx proposed made no place for the use of money. Goods were distributed according to need, not according to one's ability to pay. Since the state owned and operated all industries, there was no need for credit. In the early days of the U.S.S.R., LENIN attempted to operate the state according to the general outlines of the communist state. He soon found, however, that the absence of money was a severe handicap. Consequently, with the introduction of the *New Economic Policy,* money reappeared, and its use has increased rather than diminished in recent years.

Further attempts to do away with money have not been lacking. SOLVOY's scheme for a social accounting system was never put into practice. During the world depression of 1929–1939 many communities in America introduced a system of scrip payments to enable unemployed persons to work and secure wages without the use of money. An intensive system of social credit was planned for one of the provinces of Canada during the depression. These schemes generally, however, were in the nature of temporary adjustments to an emergency situation rather than plans for alteration of the basic money and credit structure of the nation.

CHAPTER VIII

Distribution of Wealth and Income

QUESNAY   SMITH   SAY   RICARDO
SISMONDI   MILL   RODBERTUS
OWEN   ROCHDALE PIONEERS   MARX
CAREY   BASTIAT   WIESER   THE WEBBS
MARSHALL   CLARK   HOBSON   VEBLEN   WARBASSE

Why do such extremes of wealth and poverty exist in modern society? What determines how much of the national income goes to the businessman, the landlord, and the workman? Are there productive and non-productive social classes? Whence do they derive their income? Is each person or each class in society rewarded according to the value of his productive effort in society? Is distribution of wealth the effect of man-made arrangements or of economic laws? Is unequal distribution of wealth wholly or partially responsible for depressions? In the long run is a disproportionate share of national income paid in rent as compared to the amount of wages, interest, and profit? How does Socialism attempt to provide a more equitable distribution of wealth? How exactly is the wealth of the United States and the national income distributed?

ONE OF THE MOST STRIKING ASPECTS of modern civilization is the inequality in the distribution of wealth. Granted that the difference between rich and poor is as old as the world, poverty has never been quite so apparent as it is today in the midst of such an abundance of material goods. Wealth and poverty are of course relative matters. No one would question the fact that the poorest classes of today have a greater variety of goods at hand than the most favored classes of the Middle Ages. But it is questionable whether there was as great a gap between rich and poor then as now exists. Both the rich and the poor today have greater possessions and a higher standard of living than the rich and poor of 1000 years ago, but the rate at which the rich increase their wealth is much greater than the rate at which the standard of living of the poor rises. It is these great disparities in economic position that are the source of unrest and discontent.

The conflict of the "haves" with the "have-nots" is an outgrowth of the envy and jealousy as well as the actual suffering which the great inequalities in wealth have fostered. In a day when political and religious inequalities have been brushed away it seems strange that inequalities in wealth should be more strongly emphasized. The problem of great wealth and great poverty is not merely the matter of the rich enjoying more leisure and more luxuries than the poor, though that might raise serious questions of ethics in the minds of some people, but also that wealth today is a source of power. Society is organized economically by those who possess wealth, our judgments are primarily money judgments, and success is evaluated in money terms. The pecuniary elements in modern society became the chief point of emphasis in THORSTEIN VEBLEN'S most stimulating analysis of contemporary civilization.

A great preponderance of individual incomes are small, derived principally from wages. This great number of small incomes really accounts for but a small proportion of the total income distributed. At the other extreme, a few persons have annual incomes running from several thousand to several million dollars and these incomes make up an extraordinarily large part of the total income. The larger incomes are almost entirely derived from the ownership of wealth.

Closely related to the inequalities in annual income are similar disparities in the distribution of wealth. In a capitalistic economy such as ours, this is natural. Except for those material goods used in consumption, wealth is expected to earn a return for its owner; hence those persons who possess wealth in large quantities receive large incomes, while those who own no wealth can receive an income only through the sale of their labor. The power of wealth to beget more wealth, however, is like the growing power of a snowball as it rolls down a winter hillside. Its increase seems to be inherent in its very nature.

Although a more complete résumé of distribution will be given later in the chapter, it might not be amiss to mention that in the United States in 1929, 40% of the families received an income of less than $1500. This was several hundred dollars below the income necessary for a decent living standard. As many as 65% had incomes of less than $2000. This latter group, the poorest two thirds of the population, owned but 15% of the total national wealth in 1929; while the very rich families, composing 2% of the population, owned 40% of the wealth. Such conditions could not for long escape the serious attention of economists. In America especially, much effort has been devoted to the search for principles underlying the facts of distribution.

Generally speaking, economists distinguish two types of distribution. First there is the distribution of income and wealth to individuals in the population, which has been discussed briefly above. This is known as *personal distribution*. The second type is the distribution which arises as a result of the remuneration paid to land, labor, and capital, for their services in production. The different types of income accordingly are: rent, wages, interest, and profit. This is *functional distribution*.

Early Views of the Distribution of Wealth

Attention to problems of distribution appears relatively late in the development of economic ideas. While ideas on production of wealth and the process of exchange find a place in the writings of early philosophers and ecclesiastics, distribution was not so honored. The relative simplicity of economic life and the social stratification which marked society in those days provide a reasonable explanation for the lack of importance attached to this phase of economics. One would not expect a society such as early Greece to be concerned with distribution, since the citizens of the Greek city states derived their livelihood from the ownership of farms tilled by slaves. Trade and manual labor were outside the sphere of respectability; hence the financial condition of those who followed such occupations was of little consequence. In the declining years of classical civilization—that is, from the Second to the Fifth centuries A.D., changes in the distribution of wealth caused serious upheavals in the economic and political life of Greece and Rome. The income from family lands proved no match for the greater affluence of merchants, traders, and financiers. The declining fortunes of the original ruling class forced the people of this class to loosen their hold upon social and political privileges, opening the way for the acquisition of power by financial oligarchies. The growing importance of money; the blurring of old traditional class lines; the crystallization of new social and economic classes; and the shifting of political authority from hereditary family groups to the *nouveau riche*—all these factors caused alarm among men of affairs as well as among the philosophers. Their reaction, however, was not an investigation of the economic principles of distribution. They attempted on the one hand to find some political means of adjusting the class differences and of maintaining some stability in a world which appeared to be crumbling at their feet; and on the other hand they sought for some principle of personal living that would give them security and satisfaction in spite of the disorganization around them. Hence, there is little in the ancient economic writings that has any bearing upon the economic aspects of distribution.

The Middle Ages

In the Middle Ages the self-sufficiency of the feudal estate and the rigidity of class lines in a sense made questions of distribution non-existent. When law and custom prescribe the amount of produce and service owed by one man to another according to his status; when the right of a man to receive these things depends ultimately upon military might; and when the supernatural and the hereafter so strongly influence the life of the people; there is obviously little room for the play of economic forces. One is not surprised then to find that men of the Middle Ages gave little thought to the problem of distribution. Where they thought about the matter at all it was to lay down rules of exchange that would preserve the traditional pattern of life and social relationship. In a sense, as we have noted before, the *just price* was merely a confirmation of the prevailing principle that in economic matters, as well as in all other phases of life, one treated a man according to his social status.

The expansion of trade had little effect upon the general understanding of distribution. Since the economic ideas of the time were fostered by the Mercantilists, interest was focused upon the money aspects of foreign trade. Production was subordinated to the demand of foreign buyers, and restricted by the production costs of foreign competitors. Distribution of the proceeds of commercial transactions was again a matter of politics, since privileges of foreign trade were granted by the sovereign to his favorites at the price of taxing their earnings to support his court. The powers of the state were enlisted to ensure a favorable balance of trade. This obviously was not an atmosphere which encouraged consideration of the problems of either personal or functional distribution. National distribution was all that mattered, and the prevailing ideas on this subject can be stated briefly: In the absence of mines to produce gold from natural sources, a nation could assure itself of political security and economic prosperity by the simple device of always selling more to other nations than it bought from them. In that way the stock of gold, the only source of economic and political strength, would be constantly increased.

The Physiocrats

Interest in the distribution of national income and wealth arose as a consequence of the reaction against Mercantilism. The Physiocrats, French economists and philosophers of the Eighteenth Century, were the first to protest against nationalistic commercial policies. They believed that a nation's wealth was derived from intensification of agriculture rather than from foreign trade. Since wealth had only one source, the Physiocrats felt it was important to show how this wealth was distributed throughout the population. For in their thinking, as Turgot said, the circulation of wealth was the "very life of the body politic." Modern critics are ready to admit that the investigation of the circulation of wealth was one of the great turning points in the development of economic ideas.

The investigation of the Physiocrats into the basic principles of distribution was elaborate and pretentious. The *Tableau Économique,* developed by FRANÇOIS QUESNAY (1694–1774), not only summarizes the ideas of distribution prevailing among the Physiocrats generally but it stands as the most significant single document in Physiocratic literature. In the *Tableau,* Quesnay described society as consisting of three classes: first, a productive class composed chiefly of agriculturists; second, a class of landowners and other persons who exercised power as a result of landownership and who were partly productive; and third, *la classe stérile* (the sterile class), consisting of merchants, manufacturers, and professional men who produced nothing, but drew the necessities of life from the productivity of the agriculturists. Nothing at all was said of wage-workers and laborers, although one author indicated that all such miscellaneous persons constituted a fourth class. The *Tableau* attempted to trace the circulation of a sum of money from the time of its investment in agricultural pursuits by the productive class until it returned to that class for further use in production. Quesnay estimated the return on the investment at one hundred percent. Now let the annual return equal the round figure of 100. It will be divided so that 40 is immediately used by the agriculturist to meet the expenses of next year's production, while 40 is paid to the proprietor and to the state in the form of taxes, and the final 20 going to the sterile class to pay for manufactured goods and services. The amount received by the landlord is the *produit net*. Now the landlord and the sovereign spend their income (40) as follows: half going to the agriculturists (20) and half to the merchants, manufacturers, and professional men (20). The sterile class must also spend their income (20 + 20). And since as a class they are unproductive, the total goes to buy raw materials and food stuffs directly from the agriculturist. Thus the total income received by others than the agriculturists soon gravitates back to the productive class and is used to increase real production from natural sources. Thus the process continued indefinitely to the advantage of all classes. The purpose of this analysis was not only to show exactly the source of income of each class, but also to state precisely how and why agriculture and mining were the only sources of real wealth. By concentrating its energies upon the improvement of agriculture and the extraction of minerals the nation would inevitably increase its wealth.

The important position accorded to the landlord and the failure to attribute any productive quality to the functions of the wage-earner and farm laborer indicate clearly that the Physiocrats believed firmly in private property in land. Indeed, the function of the landowner in preparing the land and in making it available for productive use was worthy of the highest honor, and, in the plan of distribution outlined by Quesnay, the landlord received abundant compensation though he actually lived in idleness. The claim which the landlords had to income was justified on the ground that if they had not cleared the land, prepared the soil by cutting trees, removing roots, and setting drains, and had not constructed buildings, the one source of wealth would never have been available for use. BAUDEAU, an exponent of Physiocratic doctrine, said, "A proprietor who keeps up the *avances foncières* (the capital equipment of a farm) without fail is performing the noblest service that anyone can perform on this earth."

In return for this income and honor, however, the proprietor was obliged to assume certain duties. He must of course keep the land up to its maximum efficiency by constantly improving its capital equipment. He was required to see that the *produit net* was adequately distributed and not appropriated for personal use. His leisure was to be spent in services for the general welfare. And, finally, landlords, generally, were forced to assume the entire burden of taxation for the upkeep of the state.

At best the Physiocratic scheme of distribution of wealth was a paternalistic ideal. Its manner of operation even from an academic viewpoint was unrealistic and confused. Fortunately it never actually faced the test of practice. TURGOT, during his brief term of office as minister of finance under the monarchy just prior to the French Revolution of 1789, was overwhelmed by the immediate problems which faced him; consequently experiments with Physiocratic doctrines were impossible. Yet however critical one may be of their practicability, the ideas propounded by Quesnay, Baudeau, Dupont, Turgot, and other Physiocrats were important, primarily because they directed the attention of later economists to the circulation of wealth as an important factor in economic activity.

Adam Smith and the Classical Economists

Authorities differ in their estimate of ADAM SMITH's treatment of the problem of distribution. It is quite apparent that Smith became conscious of distribution as an important phase of economics through his acquaintance with the Physiocrats. However, there is some reason to believe that Smith conceived of economics as concerned largely with production; distribution seems to be a hastily added appendage to his work. But it is true that the brief attention which he devoted to distribution set the pattern for later economists. Smith is concerned with distribution in the functional sense. Like the Physiocrats, he understood society as consisting of three economic groups, differentiated from each other by the source of their income: the landlords, the capitalists, and the laborers. These three groups deriving their income from rent, profit, and wages respectively, were not personalized in any sense. They were functional groups playing a necessary part in production. The return which each group received for its services was not a matter of equity or justice but of natural law. To be sure, some unfortunate situations occurred. Capitalists and landlords alike at times oppressed the wage-earner. But aside from minor variations the laws of the market place regulated the distribution of wealth and income.

How are the shares of the landlords, the capitalists, and the laborers determined? In each case it is the supply and demand for the various factors in production which set their price, and it is the contribution of each factor to the value of the article produced which determines the relative return obtained by land, labor, and capital. A greater supply of labor than is demanded, for example, lowers the price of labor and consequently reduces the income of labor. Such a situation was assumed to lead to a withdrawal of labor from the market until the price again rose to the natural or normal price existing when supply and demand were equal. Furthermore, if the article produced requires great labor but little or no capital, then the income derived by labor will be relatively large. Although it might be inferred from some passages in *The Wealth of Nations* that Adam Smith looked upon rent and profit as unjustifiable charges upon the value produced solely by labor, closer examination will show that he believed firmly that both land and capital were productive and hence entitled to a return commensurate with their relative contribution to the total value produced. In discussing rent, however, Smith seemed a bit confused as to its nature and source. Was rent an element which had to figure in the cost of production like wages, or was it a surplus which appeared on good land as the price of produce rose to higher levels? Smith never clarified this point. Later writers, notably Ricardo, finally worked out a detailed explanation.

J. B. SAY, the great French exponent of Adam Smith's ideas, improved Smith's doctrine of distribution. The principal change came in the concept of the *entrepreneur,* the person who brought together the necessary amount and type of land, labor, and capital to engage in production. Smith had assumed that the owner of capital and the organizer of a business enterprise were one and the same individual. Say understood that one individual might provide the capital as well as initiate the business activity, but he believed the process of distribution could be understood better by separating these two functions. Indeed, Say believed that it was only through the services of the entrepreneur that distribution took place at all. Land, labor, and capital might be readily available and the demand for goods might be great, but until the entrepreneur initiated an enterprise there was no demand for the factors of production or supply of goods. Thus the entrepreneur served as the intermediary through whom income was produced and distributed. It was in his opinion ultimately the productivity of each of the elements in production as regulated by the law of supply and demand which determined the return each unit of land, labor, and capital received. But it was the entrepreneur who in reality first estimated these factors and paid the sums necessary to bring these factors into productive relationship. Say was very emphatic upon the need of separating the return on capital from the earnings of the entrepreneur. His insistence on this point was largely responsible for the extensive use of the word entrepreneur in contemporary economic literature.

It was DAVID RICARDO who took the confused ideas of distribution propounded by his predecessors and worked them into a well rounded theory. He made the first real attempt to describe the process by which the various shares of income arise and how their quantity is determined. Although later writers have made it clear that Ricardo failed to clarify the problem of distribution, his ideas on that subject were accepted as authoritative for nearly a century. To Ricardo the problem of distribution was inseparable from the problem of value, for although in a letter to McCulloch in 1820 he denied that such dependence was necessary, his views constantly emphasized the close relationship of these two concepts.

First of all, Ricardo accepted the traditional division of income into rent, wages, and profit, corresponding to the three factors of production: land, labor, and capital. Thus no distinction was made between profit and interest. But that was secondary. The process of distribution, he believed, hinged upon the character of social development. As population increased, the increasing demand for food raised the price of food and brought into cultivation less fertile lands. Ricardo argued to show that in reality the rise in price of food was caused by the greater amount of labor necessary to produce food from the less fertile land. Be that as it may, each time additional land was brought under cultivation, rent—which is the differential between the costs of production on one piece of land as compared with the costs of production on the least fertile piece of land necessary to maintain an adequate supply—was increased. Thus rents continued to rise as civilization advanced.

Wages, on the other hand, were governed by the inflexible law of subsistence. Ricardo said, "The natural price of labor is the price which is necessary to enable the laborers, one with another, to subsist and to perpetuate their race, without either increase or diminution." The wages paid did not always correspond to the "natural price of labor." He maintained that when civilization is advancing, capital (including food, clothes, tools) increases and pushes upward the demand for labor. This is so because in such a state of civilization, the land under cultivation is the most fertile and consequently the productivity of labor is high, making the accumulation of capital more rapid than the growth of population. With the lapse of time this trend is reversed and population advances faster than the accumulation of capital because now the less fertile lands have to be used to supply the necessities of life. With less capital there follows naturally a decrease in the demand for labor, the surplus of which is ultimately absorbed in the greater application of labor required by less fertile lands. The net result is a decline in real wages. Subsistence represents the minimum point to which wages can fall. What subsistence is depends upon the habitual living standards developed by the community. So Ricardo arrived at the essentially pessimistic belief that as population increased more labor had to be applied to soil of decreasing fertility, which inevitably decreased wages. Where this vicious circle stopped or how it is stopped, Ricardo did not say. It is a safe guess that he shared Malthus' views that population would be curtailed to the limit of the food supply by the increasing severity of natural forces cutting down the population, for example: vice, wars, famine, and disease.

He went on to explain, however, that with rents taking an ever larger share of income, and wages commanding a relatively fixed minimum, profits alone must suffer the loss equivalent to the gain in rents. He put the case even more strongly. Profit is essentially what is left over after labor is paid for its work on land

which yields no rent. To illustrate, on a piece of marginal land—
that is, land which yields no rent at present prices—the sum
realized from the sale of produce is divided between wages and
profits. The share going to wages can never be lower than the
subsistence of the laborers; the amount going to capital must be
sufficient to encourage accumulation. It is necessary to point out
at this time that when the economist speaks of rent he usually
means economic rent. That is, the natural or theoretical return
which a piece of land should receive for its share in production.
If the selling price of produce just equals wages and interest,
there is no economic rent. Money rent, or the sum paid by a lease-
holder to a landlord, may be above or below the economic rent.
If above, money rent is paid by taking a share of the return rightfully belonging to labor or capital.

The net result of Ricardo's teaching was to emphasize the competitive nature of distribution; and this led logically to the idea
of the class struggle. Marx in later years saw the implication of
Ricardo's ideas, and built upon them his own system of the exploitive "squeeze" put upon labor by the landlord on the one hand
and by the capitalist on the other. In spite of his insistence that
distribution was the fundamental problem in political economy,
later authorities claim that Ricardo did not succeed in giving an
accurate description of how the relative proportions of income
were determined. Unwarranted assumptions and circular reasoning served in succeeding years to diminish the great respect with
which his work was at first received.

The basic assumption which preceded the ideas of the classical
economists examined thus far was that distribution was controlled
by natural forces which were interfered with by man to his own
undoing. Even the pessimistic trend described by Ricardo might
be made worse by attempts at human control. The more optimistic note struck by Smith assured all concerned that in spite
of the obvious inequalities in distribution the operation of self-
interest and natural law would result in greater abundance for

all. Ricardo was more pessimistic, but he agreed that in the long run land, labor, and capital received a return equivalent to their respective productivity. Hence, the mode of distribution was not only outside of human control but it also was essentially equitable.

The Socialists and Related Thinkers

J. C. L. Simonde de Sismondi (1773–1842) was one of the first to protest against the abstract and unreal thinking of the classical economists. Although he began his career as an ardent advocate of classical doctrines, he became keenly aware of the terrible human costs of industrialism and protested strongly against the complacent trust his contemporaries put in the operation of natural economic laws. Nowhere is this better portrayed than in Sismondi's explanation of the process of distribution.

Both in his travels and in his studies of history Sismondi saw repeated over and over again the same economic process. Everywhere, as a result of the competitive nature of economic activity, society was separating into antagonistic classes: those who owned land and capital and those who worked—the rich and the poor. The middle classes were gradually disappearing, leaving only the propertyless masses and the great capitalists. The gravitation of all property into the hands of a relatively few individuals materially affected the distribution of income. The wage-earner without property was utterly and completely dependent upon the sale of his labor for a livelihood. Since the numbers of workmen were far in excess of the demand for their services they were forced to accept the first wage offered them. It was Sismondi's contention that the independent artisan could estimate the need for his produce and his probable income and hence limit his expenses and his family accordingly. But under the existing system the workmen worked in a world controlled by others. Their incentive to foresight was lost. The size of families and the workmen's expenses fluctuated with the capitalist's demand for labor. Uncertainty, poverty, and misery became the inevitable lot of the working class. In spite of this, the capitalist and the landlord focused their attention on what Sismondi called the net product rather than the gross product. For example, while a plot of land might be fertile enough to produce abundantly, the financial interest of the landowner might be better served by limiting production, thus reducing not only the amount of produce available but also the opportunities for employment of workmen.

The actual process of distribution suggested by Sismondi began with the existence of an annual national revenue which consisted of rents and profits on the one hand and wages on the other. The claims of capital and land to a return were past claims based upon labor expended upon them in the year previous. The claim of labor to wages was a future claim, realized only as a result of opportunity for employment. Although these forms of income were in opposition to each other in the present, they were derived from the same source—labor. Sismondi believed that the revenues of one year were exchanged for the production of the next. In other words, the purchasing power of one year consisted of the wages, rents, interest, and profits paid in the previous year. When equilibrium was maintained, that is, when revenue and production exactly balanced, stability and prosperity were enjoyed by all. If, however, the owners of land and capital spend their income for consumption goods rather than for more capital; or if they consume too little so as to provide a disproportionately large amount for capital, the balance will be upset. If the amount of revenue allocated to the purchase of capital equipment could be increased slightly each year, the circular process of revenue, production, revenue, production could be raised to successively higher planes, increasing the standard of living year by year. However, one of Sismondi's emphases was that the failure of revenue to be distributed proportionately among rent, profits, and wages caused general overproduction of necessities for which there was inadequate income, while the unlimited desire for luxuries by the rich absorbed more and more of the consumers' power to purchase.

Thus according to Sismondi the real cause of the inequalities in distribution of income was first, the ownership of land and capital by a relatively few persons and the lack of any property at all by the working class, and second, the ruthlessness of economic competition under a regime of *laissez-faire*. To correct these ills, Sismondi advocated a vague and indecisive plan for the return of ownership to artisans and small capitalists with rejection of the doctrine of *laissez-faire* and a return to state paternalism. While these represented final goals, his intermediate objectives were the right of unions to organize, limitations on hours of labor and the work of women and children, and finally the "professional guarantee" which made the employer responsible for providing maintenance for the workman during illness, old age, and lock-out.

The importance of Sismondi's ideas in the history of economic thought lies first of all in the fact that he called people's attention to the human aspects of business activity, in a time when the classical economists were concerned only with economic matters and trusted implicitly in the natural benevolence of economic laws to safeguard the welfare of man. Of even greater significance was the influence which Sismondi's ideas exerted upon the important economic movements of the 19th century. Most of the latter can trace either their intellectual content or their inspiration back to the views expressed by this earliest critic of classical doctrine. Such development as the humanitarian reaction against the impersonal and coldly economic doctrines of Smith and Ricardo, the closer adherence to historical facts, the attack upon wealthy property owners for their complacency in the midst of human suffering and poverty, and the increasing demand for state intervention in economic matters were all foreshadowed by Sismondi. Very few of his contemporaries except the Socialists openly espoused his ideas, but as the years passed a much greater number came to acknowledge him as the source of their inspiration.

While the ideas of JOHN STUART MILL on distribution follow the general pattern of classical doctrine, he was influenced by the critical and humanitarian views of Sismondi and the Saint-Simonians. For example, he held to the classical doctrine that production was governed by economic laws which were in a real sense natural laws. With distribution he believed it was different. The factors governing that process were man-made and subject to human control. He said, "The laws and conditions of the production of wealth partake of the character of physical truths. There is nothing optional or arbitrary in them. . . . It is not so with the distribution of wealth. This is a matter of human institution solely. The things once there, mankind, individually or collectively, can do with them as they like." Mill stood between the full-grown power of classical dogma and the vigor and strength of newly born socialist thought. His writings show the preponderant character of the former, but the latter is responsible for a host of modifications which Mill felt it necessary to make in order to give his ideas a more humanitarian and social outlook.

The classical element in Mill's ideas of distribution represents a synthesis of ideas expounded by Ricardo and Nassau Senior. His division of income was traditional, consisting of rent, interest and profits, and wages. Rent he analyzed as the differential payment arising because of the higher costs of production on less fertile land. Mill was the first to use the term "unearned advantage" as a synonym for rent, meaning of course the same thing as the modern term "unearned increment." Assuming that an increase in rent and the value of land would arise from natural causes, he advocated a periodic revaluation of land leading to the levying of a tax which would absorb the increase. Profits and interest, however, which Mill treats together, are derived from three sources: abstinence, stored up labor, and the productivity of labor. Mill never really distinguished these three sources, his only clear contention being that profits depended on wages. When wages rose profits fell, and vice versa. Capital, Mill believed, consisted principally of advances to laborers, hence the productivity of labor would determine whether the surplus over and above the advances would be large or small. This return was presumably a payment for abstinence.

As to wages, Mill accepted with modifications the wages-fund theory. Wages he believed were determined by the amount of capital available out of which wages could be paid. In a sense the capital available was a demand for labor; the number of laborers available was the supply. Thus if the supply was large, wages declined; if the supply small, wages were high. The fund available for wages might of course increase from year to year, but in any given year the amount distributed as wages could not exceed the amount in the fund. Hence the way to raise wages was to limit the population. He said, "Only when in addition to just institutions, the increase in mankind shall be under deliberate guidance of judicious foresight, can the conquests made from the powers of nature . . . become the common property of the species."

The relative proportions of income which were distributed as rent, profits and interest, and wages, Mill believed, were affected by historical processes. The increases in population inevitably created a greater demand for living space and agricultural produce, hence rents tend to rise; but there was a corresponding tendency for the productivity of labor to increase, causing a fall in the price of manufactured goods which reduced profits to a minimum.

Mill was not merely an economist. He was also a philosopher and a student of politics. It is not strange, therefore, that he goes beyond the limits of economics to deal with the problem of distribution. As he saw it, the goal of mankind is to increase the sum total of human happiness. This could be done through the exercise of man's mental powers. "Poverty," he says, "like most social evils, exists because men follow their brute instincts, without due consideration. But society is possible precisely because man is not necessarily a brute." Since Mill had already indicated his belief that distribution was subject to man-made laws rather than natural laws he urged certain reforms in order to bring about more equitable distribution.

Each of the innovations advocated by Mill deserves attention. He encouraged both the co-operative movement and the reorganization of industry so as to include a plan of profit sharing. He suggested the repeal of laws against combinations, so that workmen would be free to join trade unions. That such a move on Mill's part seemed contradictory to his belief in the wages-fund theory has been denied. Rather than supporting a plan to raise wages, Mill was merely extending the principles of *laissez-faire* to workmen as they had been extended to employers. Trade unions he thought would die because of their failure to influence the wage rates. Whatever may be the truth of this argument, Mill clearly withdrew his support of the wages-fund theory when its fallacies were pointed out by Thornton and Longe. Mill advocated the use of preventive measures to check the growth of population in the interest of increasing the standard of living of the wage-earners. Complementary to these measures, however, should be set the education of the working class, which would result in a desire for higher standards of living to be achieved in part by family limitation. A land policy by the state was also suggested. In colonies and at home the government might strive to set up small independent landowners. Finally, positive legislation to protect the workingman from poverty and exploitation was not only necessary but quite within the function of government. Mill was not enthusiastic about minimum wage legislation, however, since he felt the security of such laws might result in irresponsibility toward the size and economic security of one's family. Inheritance taxes were an important item, since the perpetuation of inequalities in the distribution of wealth might thereby be checked. Mill, however, saw little chance for a solution to the problem of distribution aside from the radical change from a dynamic society to a static society. The possibility of such a development was fostered by Ricardo's theory of the diminution and final disappearance of profit as a natural consequence of economic development. Mill translated this idea into a belief in a completely stagnant economy. Much as he disliked the prospect of such a society he felt it necessary in order to eliminate the competitive struggle for wealth, which produced the inequalities and poverty characteristic of the population.

Amidst the firmament of economic thought John Stuart Mill stands like the Colossus of Rhodes straddling the sea, his one foot in the classical tradition of the past, his other in the social and moral idealism which marked the future of economic thought. The accumulated store of socialistic ideas which caused Mill to criticise and modify classical ideas at so many points completely captivated JOHANN KARL RODBERTUS (1805–1875), a wealthy German landowner. Rodbertus was elected to the Prussian national assembly after the revolution of 1848. Disagreement over attempts to discriminate among various classes of voters caused him to resign in protest and advocate non-participation in future elections. He was a nationalist, a monarchist, and a socialist at one and the same time. The all-prevailing will of the state seemed to him to be the most significant aspect of political organization. Consequently, although he agreed with the economic principles of Socialism he had no confidence in the socialists' political program. The rise of a strong socialistically minded German emperor seemed to him to be the ideal method of establishing a socialist state.

Rodbertus' economic ideas, expressed most completely in *Toward Knowledge of Our Economic Condition,* and *Letters,* can be traced largely to Adam Smith and Saint-Simon. This does not exclude, of course, a real measure of originality on the part of Rodbertus himself. From Smith was taken the concept of division

of labor, which as Rodbertus saw it was the most important socializing force in history. It brought the most divergent interests into
harmony and created larger and larger units of mankind into a
community of labor. A society which had been brought together
by specialization had three functions according to Rodbertus: 1)
the adjustment of production to need; 2) the maintenance of production at a point which would utilize all available resources; and
3) the equitable distribution of income among those who produce
it. It is the last function which is pertinent to our discussion, and
it is rather significant that Rodbertus should have singled out distribution of wealth and income as one of the three most important
social functions.

Rodbertus rebelled against the classical idea that these functions would be carried out automatically and in the best con-
ceivable fashion if men were free to pursue individually their own
economic interest. The kind of society men would have was the
result of their own decisions, he said; certainly it was illogical
to assume that the society which permitted its institutions to
grow haphazardly without plan or design would be better suited
to human needs than one which was consciously directed. The
goal of any system of distribution, said Rodbertus, was to assure
to everyone the product of his labor. In this he differed not at
all from the classical school. In the way this goal was to be
achieved he differed from them altogether.

Classical doctrine said that the process of exchange, controlled
as it was by the market forces of supply and demand, assured
to each factor in production the market value of its contribution
to production. Rodbertus maintained that while the theory was
excellent, it did not agree with the process of distribution in
practice. Since the value of all commodities was created solely
by labor, the charges levied upon the product by the landlord
and the capitalist were unjust. Raw materials and land were
the gifts of nature; intellectual effort was inexhaustible and required no expenditure of time; thus only manual labor which

required time and energy could be considered as productive. Like Adam Smith, whom he quoted, Rodbertus believed that labor was the only true source of economic goods. He never contended that labor was the only source of value, but he did believe that the ideal toward which the community should strive was an equality between the exchange value of an article and the amount of labor necessary to produce it. In the process existing at the time Rodbertus claimed that the owners of land and capital were able to control exchange so as to reap a benefit for themselves although they contributed nothing toward production. This control was made possible through socially supported rights of private property to exact payment when used in production. Hence society was really to blame for poor distribution, since as long as goods were produced and made available for use no thought was given to the justice of the rewards paid to such widely diverse elements as the continuous labor of the unskilled worker and the lazy indifference of the landlord and capitalist. The unearned return taken by the latter two, Rodbertus called rent.

Were this condition of maldistribution a temporary affair which would work itself out naturally as some of the classical economists claimed, Rodbertus would have been less concerned; but he believed the contrary. Wages were paid only in such quantity as to enable the workers to subsist and reproduce themselves. This, as Ricardo had pointed out, was the natural or normal price of labor to which all wages tended to gravitate. The amount of the product which went to labor remained constant, but the productivity of labor was always increasing; thus the share of labor was a constantly diminishing proportion of the whole product of labor. As a result it was perfectly true that the economic position of the worker became more degraded relative to that of other social classes.

The logical conclusion to Rodbertus' analysis was a program for the suppression of private property and unearned income. Instead of private ownership the state should own the land and capital, and labor should be rewarded according to its productivity. Labor time expended in production should be accepted as the real estimate of the exchange value of an article. The method by which this new program of distribution was to be accomplished, as Rodbertus suggests, was by the gradual establishment of state socialism which would compromise the issue to the extent of allowing private enterprise and private property to exist. Rodbertus was possessed by a sense of the inevitableness of history which would bring in the higher economic society based upon socialistic principles, and by a fear of the wild and uncontrolled action of the selfish masses in the face of the exceedingly complex problem of differentiating between the legitimate returns and rightful ownership resulting from labor and the exploitive charges made upon production by owners of land and capital used in production. The confidence which he expressed in the benevolence of the state was really an expression of the lack of confidence he felt in mass action. His immediate proposal for a period of transition was a plan similar to schemes of Owen and Proudhon. The state would supply to each employer a quantity of coupons equal to the labor value of the things produced and offered for sale. This process being followed in every enterprise, the employer and his employees together would be able to keep the equivalent of the article they produced. Periodic revision of the scale of payment would be made to take account of any increases in production or changes in proportion of the total product created by the workers as contrasted to the employer. This compromise between the forces of private property and those of labor was intended to be only temporary, and it could be accomplished only through the instrumentality of the state. Hence in the classification of economic doctrine, Rodbertus, frequently called the founder of scientific socialism, must be counted among the state socialists.

Emphasis upon the injustice of payments made to the owners of land and capital is characteristic of all socialistic writings. Only labor has a legitimate claim upon the final product. Saint-

Simon, Proudhon, Lassalle all follow much the same analysis. It was Proudhon who coined the famous phrase, "Property is theft." He considered labor alone as productive. Since land and capital were useless without labor, the demand by the owner of land or capital for payment was based on the false assumption that land and capital were productive in themselves. Hence any payment to landlord or capitalist was theft from the rightful earnings of labor. In the programs of reform or revolution submitted by these authors one would find a marked difference, but they explain their dissatisfaction with the existing order in much the same terms.

Although his ideas differ but little from those of other socialists, special mention must be made of KARL MARX (1818–1883). In terms of popularity, as well as in the profound effect upon socialist thinking of the 19th and 20th centuries, the doctrines of Marx stand supreme. It is doubtful whether any other non-religious works have been responsible for so much blind devotion, so much critical discussion, and so much emotional condemnation as the writings of Marx. Born of a moderately wealthy German Jewish family which followed the Protestant faith, he married into the lesser nobility. Educated to be a college professor, he forsook his career to become a leader of the revolutionary movement in Germany. He was forced on two occasions to flee the country because of his activities. Following his last departure he settled in London to devote the remaining years of his life (about thirty) to research and writing.

The initial chapter of Marx's great work *Capital* indicates his adherence to the classical tradition especially as it was presented by Ricardo. Indeed Marx, instead of disproving classical economic ideas, simply carried them to their logical conclusion. Annual income is divided into three classes—ground rent, profits, wages; these are the return on land, capital, and labor respectively. As a result of these three kinds of income there exist in society three primary social classes: the landlords, the capitalists, and the laboring class. What is the process of distribution of income to each of these classes, and what determines the share each shall receive? Marx said that there were really only two sources of income, namely, value and surplus value, both created by labor. Out of the former, labor was paid; out of the latter, rent and profits were paid. We have already noted that surplus value arose, according to Marx, because the capitalist paid only the wages of subsistence, while he was able to sell the product of labor in the market at a price determined by the laws of supply and demand. The difference was surplus value, claimed by the capitalist by his right to the product of labor as owner of the fixed capital such as machinery, and of variable capital out of which he paid wages. The capitalist's desire to augment surplus value was achieved in two ways: either through the exercise of superior bargaining power which enabled him to prolong the working day beyond the labor time necessary for the workman to produce the equivalent value of his subsistence, or by reducing the labor time necessary for the workman to produce his sustenance. The latter was accomplished through the increased use of machinery or the perfection of industrial organization.

In calculating cost of production the capitalist figured the payment of rent as a cost. This did not change the fact in Marx's mind that rent was an unearned charge upon the value produced by labor, as was profit. Essentially Marx followed the Ricardian explanation of rent with minor variations. Rent was for the most part a differential between the cost of production and the selling price of farm produce appearing on land which was more fertile than the average land under cultivation. He rejected the theory held by earlier economists that rent was interest on capital invested in the land. Instead he placed major emphasis upon the idea that rent was a monopoly price exacted by the private owner of the land because of the limited amount of land available for use. Under certain circumstances the landowner by his monopolistic power was able to extract from the capitalist the total amount of the surplus value as rent, leaving him only enough to pay other necessary costs of production.

Marx believed, as Rodbertus had suggested earlier, that this process in history resulted in the increasing poverty and misery of the wage-earner. Moreover the power of competition tended to reduce the number but to increase the power of capitalists and landowners, the losers dropping down into the laboring class. The remaining landowners and capitalists, having nearly identical interests, merged into a single capitalist class. Thus the process which Adam Smith believed would result in greater economic well-being for all men, Marx said would result in degradation of most men, the tremendous wealth and power of a few, and intense class conflict. It is important to note that as far as Marx was concerned the process was beyond human control. Legislation might slow the process and relieve the distress of increasing poverty, but the course of events was inherent within the process itself. The outgrowth of this economic process which took the value produced by labor and distributed it as rent and profits to the non-productive landlord and capitalist was a continuous class struggle. Whether Marx believed that the victory of the working class through revolution was inevitable is debatable. He most certainly believed that the class struggle was the basis motivating force in history. This is stated in the opening lines of the *Communist Manifesto,* "The history of all hitherto existing society is the history of class struggles." As a result of the class struggle the numerically important but impoverished working class, organized by the economic system itself, would eventually abolish private ownership of land and capital, the source of their impoverishment, and set up a socialistic community in which the means of production were owned by all the people.

Criticism of the Marxian ideas of distribution has come from within the circle of Marx's own followers as well as from his chief opponents. The surplus value source of profit has been discarded along with the labor theory of value. If land and capital are useless without labor, it is just as true that labor is useless without land and capital. The question is merely whether the present arrangement which makes it necessary to pay the owner of land and capital for the right to use these factors in production is socially efficient and just, or whether profit and rent when paid the owners who perform no essential social service represents what later authors have called unearned increment. The source of the criticism of Marxian ideas lies in the pattern of distribution in modern industrial society. The lot of the wage-earners has not steadily grown worse, as Marx said it would. Marx's followers have sought to interpret him to mean that in spite of an absolute rise in the standard of living of the working class the lot of the working man is relatively worse as compared to the rapid increases in wealth of the capitalist. Finally, the evolution of capitalism has not as yet caused the complete separation of society into capitalists and wage-earners by the annihilation of the middle class. The character of the middle class has changed. While Marx lived, the middle class was composed of the independent owners of small tracts of land and small business enterprises. This group is declining in importance both numerically and in the amount of business activity it carries on, but a new middle class has grown up consisting of highly skilled technicians, professional people, office personnel, and salesmen. More dependent upon the continued operation of capitalist business enterprise than their predecessors, the members of the new middle class—like the members of the old—act as a stabilizing force in society, resisting radical change but ultimately assenting to progressive changes in government and economics.

The Fabian Socialists

With the rejection of Marxian ideas of distribution, later Socialists have cast about for other economic explanation and justification for their social theories. Their principal ideas have been elaborations of the unearned character of rent. interest, and

profit. The Fabian socialists—consisting of such well-known per-
sonages in literature and economics as George Bernard Shaw,
Sidney and Beatrice Webb, and H. G. Wells—have proposed an
alternative explanation of distribution. They contend that wealth
is social. Modern industry makes it impossible to distinguish the
contribution of each individual or each factor in production to
the final product. Hence any attempt to distribute wealth and
income according to the labor expended is likewise impossible.
The only alternative is to declare wealth the property of all.

The Fabian explanation of distribution hinges on the idea of
rent as a differential payment made for the productivity of good
land over bad. If the same amount of labor were applied and
rewarded exactly the same, the greater production of one piece
of land over another would not be the result of labor or of ownership but of the nature of land itself; yet by the fact of private
ownership this surplus accrues to the owner. This same process,
however, applies to all kinds of capital—machinery, building
sites, soils, and forms of skill. Labor which works with the least
productive tools produces barely enough to pay its wages, while
those working with superior tools provide a surplus which is taken
by the owner of the tools. Even ability is rewarded as a differential rent. Marginal knowledge and skill produce only subsistence,
while superior talents produce a surplus which is claimed by the
owner of the superior talents. In their pamphlet entitled *English
Progress Toward Democracy* the Fabian Society states its position
on distribution: "The individuals or classes who possess social
power have at all times, consciously or unconsciously, made use
of that power in such a way as to leave to the great majority of
their fellows practically nothing beyond the means of subsistence
according to the current local standard. The additional product,
determined by the relative differences in productive efficiency
of the different sites, soils, capitals, and forms of skill above the
margin of cultivation, has gone to those exercising control over
these valuable but scarce productive factors. This struggle to

secure the surplus or 'economic rent' is the key to the confused history of European progress, and an underlying unconscious motive of all revolutions."

The Fabian program for more equitable distribution, unlike the Marxist doctrine, does not require that the economic surpluses be returned to the wage-earner. It does call for the confiscation of these surpluses for society as a whole. Thus everyone will become a wage-earner, receiving the means of subsistence as wages in return for labor. The standard of living of all will rise, however, as a consequence of equitable distribution of additional goods and services by the state. Revolutionary measures are quite unnecessary, for natural evolutionary processes will bring about the decline of the capitalist and landowner. The growing intervention of the state is the means by which the change will be brought about. Already, say the Fabians, profit and rent are drastically reduced through taxation; the use to which property may be put is restricted by legislation; the state has developed industrial enterprise which it owns and operates for the public service; and relationship of employer and employee are closely supervised by the state. "On every side the individual capitalist is being registered, inspected, controlled, and eventually superseded by the community."

Robert Owen and the Co-operative Movement

We must examine one other unorthodox explanation of distribution before returning to the main stream of classical economic thought. Those who advocate co-operative democracy as the most desirable program of social reform are seldom very specific in their description of the operation of the existing economic system. Vague generalizations and implications provide the principal sources for a review of their ideas. ROBERT OWEN (1771–1858) believed that the existence of profit was an unjust addition to the cost of goods. The just price of an article was its cost of production, consequently the process of exchange which allowed producers to charge more than the cost of production, and to lay claim to the excess because of their ownership of property, created a system which was not only unjust but unworkable. He pointed out that the wages paid represented the income with which the articles produced had to be purchased. If the price was increased above the cost of production to allow for profit an economic crisis would ensue when laborers could no longer buy back the articles they produced. Thus the combination of private property, profit, and rent made for an inequitable system of distribution. Owen disagreed with the other authorities of his time that this seeming injustice would disappear if competition were free and perfect. A different system of exchange was necessary in order to assure to the worker his right to consume what he produced. To achieve this end it was necessary to eliminate profit and suppress the desire to buy cheaply and sell dearly.

Owen's ideas of co-operative association and his plans for co-operative communities sprang naturally from his ideas concerning economic processes. Since money was the instrument which made profit possible, Owen advocated the replacement of money by labor notes as a first step in the elimination of profit altogether. He gave practical expression to his ideas in the organization of the National Equitable Labour Exchange. In this plan those producing articles for exchange would be given labor notes equivalent to the labor time expended in production. The price of the article in exchange would be an equivalent number of labor notes. Thus through a co-operative association articles would be exchanged for their labor equivalents and profit would be eliminated. The history of the Exchange has already been described above. It is sufficient to note that like other of Owen's experiments it failed in short order. Nevertheless the idea of a co-operative association continued to live; and, embodied in the Consumers' Co-operative Movement, it continues to challenge the basic principles of modern economy.

In 1844, in the village of Rochdale in Lancashire, England, the poverty and insecurity among a group of textile workers caused the formation of a co-operative society as a means of improving their lot. A previous co-operative venture had already failed in Rochdale, but the new society was organized on different principles. The missionary zeal accompanying the co-operative idea is attested by the fact that a follower of Robert Owen, a man named Holyoake, was the guiding light in the second Rochdale enterprise. The success of this second co-operative was so notable that the principles upon which it was founded have been adopted as the basis of consumers' co-operatives everywhere.

The Rochdale Society of Equitable Pioneers, for such the new society was named, began as a small retail store. Its original capital of £28 was secured through small subscriptions from those planning to participate in the store's activities. The intention of the founders of the store was to provide goods of high quality at the lowest possible price, by eliminating profit. Ultimately they planned to establish a self-supporting community. Although the latter aim has never been achieved, the value of the co-operative store has been clearly demonstrated by the rapid spread and continued existence of consumers' co-operatives in England, on the Continent, and in America. The success of the Rochdale Equitable Pioneers as compared to previous societies has been attributed to the new principles which they followed. Briefly stated, these were: capital investment would receive a return of no more than 5%; prices at the store would be the prevailing prices in the area; the surplus over and above the amount necessary to pay interest on capital would be returned to those who purchased at the store in proportion to their purchases; membership would be open to all who would pay a small entrance fee (1 shilling or 25 cents) and agree to purchase a £1 share ($5), which could be paid out of purchase savings. Control of the society was democratic, each shareholder being entitled to one vote regardless of the number of shares he possessed. Although the co-operative movement has grown tremendously since these early beginnings, little change has taken place in co-operative principles. A minor variation has occurred with the development of producers' co-operatives. Emphasis in these ventures is upon the rights of employees. Consumers' co-operatives have also allowed employees to participate in the earnings of the co-operative. In the last half century the kind and type of co-operative society has increased notably. Housing, credit, shipping, restaurants, clothing, books, are now produced and distributed through various types of co-operative enterprises. Failures have been frequent. In general the causes of failures could be traced to inexperienced management and the power of malicious competitive practices of private enterprises which sought to destroy the co-operative.

The ultimate goals of the co-operative movement are far-reaching. JAMES WARBASSE, the outstanding advocate of co-operation in America, says: "A co-operative society is a voluntary association in which the people organize democratically to supply their needs through mutual action, and in which the motive of production and distribution is service, not profit. In the Co-operative Movement the ultimate tendency is toward the creation of a social structure capable of supplanting both profit-making industry and the compulsory political state." These goals were implicit in the first articles written by the Rochdale Equitable Pioneers setting forth their aims. They were to start a store, build houses, commence manufacturing giving employment to those without work, purchase farms, establish a hotel ("for the promotion of sobriety"), "and as soon as practicable the Society shall proceed to arrange the powers of production, distribution, education, and government; or, in other words, to establish a self-supporting home-colony of united interests, or to assist other Societies in establishing such Colonies."

The Optimists: Carey and Bastiat

In spite of these conflicting and critical ideas offered by advocates of socialism and co-operation, classical ideas of distribution continued to be generally accepted by the majority of economists. Following the work of John Stuart Mill who accepted the basic formulas of Smith and Ricardo while compromising at various points with Socialism, there appeared further elaborations and modifications of classical ideas. Bastiat and Carey, respectively French and American economists of the middle 19th century, gave an optimistic turn to the analysis of distribution made by earlier economists. The similarity of the ideas of these authors was the cause of much comment; indeed, Carey insisted that Bastiat had plagiarized his work. There is little need, therefore, to differentiate between their ideas. In the opinion of these authors annual income is divided into three portions: rent, interest and profit, and wages, corresponding to the three factors in production: land, capital, and labor. Whereas Ricardo had stated that as population increased less fertile lands were brought under cultivation, and rent (the differential payment received by the good land) increased accordingly, the Optimists (especially Carey) held that the less fertile lands were the first to be cultivated and more fertile lands, which usually required clearing and draining, came into production later. While the total rent might increase, rent tended to decrease in proportion to wages, because as richer land came into cultivation labor's productivity increased and the price of farm produce would tend to fall.

Very much the same view was taken of capital. Indeed, Carey claimed that no distinction existed between land and capital. Thus as capital accumulated, the interest rate (and rate of profit) fell; so that while the total amount paid as a return on capital increased, the rate of return decreased and the proportion of total income taken by capital got smaller in relation to wages. Interests of owners of capital and workers were therefore not antagonistic; in fact the evolution of economic society would ultimately bring about equality between labor and the capitalist since the wages earned would in time equal the amount received by the owner of capital. Proof of these ideas was offered in the form of tables and historical summaries. For the most part, however, the tables were merely hypothetical situations reduced to quantitative terms, and the historical data was sketchy and obviously selective. For example, in spite of Bastiat's contention that the interest rate tended to fall, during the 19th century it appeared to rise and profits to increase proportionately much faster than wages.

The Austrian School

The attempt to explain distribution in terms of the utility of the three factors in production (land, labor, and capital) was pursued most ardently by the members of the Austrian school of economic thought. The names of Menger, von Wieser, and von Böhm-Bawerk are associated with the most elaborate development of the explanation of economic processes in terms of utility, that is, the want-satisfying power of economic goods. The process of distribution is based upon the power of each factor in production to impute value to the final product. It is the value contributed by the last unit added (marginal unit) which determines the return of all the units used. Thus the difference in the return obtained by labor in a productive process as compared to the return of capital and land is judged by a comparison of the value contributed to the final product by the last or marginal unit of labor as compared to the last or marginal units of land and capital. This is essentially VON WIESER's explanation. VON BÖHM-BAWERK confused the issue terribly by ignoring the idea of a factor of production imputing value to an article, and emphasizing the reverse and unreal process of the value of the final product as judged by its utility, back-tracking to the factors of production. How this could be done was never clarified. Von Wieser seems to be on fairly firm ground when he says that payment is determined by the value produced by the marginal unit of land, labor, and capital.

The Views of Alfred Marshall

The idea of marginal production as applied to distribution was worked out more intelligently and more concretely by ALFRED MARSHALL. In the final section of his *Principles of Economics,* which is entitled "The Distribution of the National Income," Marshall devotes a great deal of time and attention to clarifying the baffling problem of how income is distributed. One is forced to note at the outset Marshall's warning that the explanation of economic processes is by no means simple. First of all there appears an annual dividend which consists of the material and immaterial goods produced in a given year. This "National Dividend" is divided up into wages, the interest on capital, the rent of land, and profits on organizing ability. The problem of distribution is essentially one of describing the forces which determine the relative quantity of income received by each of the factors responsible for producing it. In such fashion does Marshall state the problem. His answers are not so easy to grasp. In simplest language Marshall's explanation is this: The price of any commodity is determined by the operation of supply and demand. In the case of the factors in production, the *demand* is determined by the entrepreneurs' estimate of the value of the land, labor, and capital, in production. The *supply* is determined by the costs (sometimes discussed as subjective costs, sometimes as real costs) of producing land, labor, capital. Land, of course being irreplaceable, has only a money cost figured in much the same fashion as Ricardo's differential payment for more productive land; labor's cost is essentially the cost of maintaining a family at a customary standard of living; capital's cost is the cost of abstaining from consumption, or the estimate of the superiority of present value over future value.

In determining the actual return which each factor is to re-

ceive, Marshall makes use of the concept of marginal productivity. Land, labor, and capital receive a return equivalent to
the productivity of the last unit of the factor used, as judged
in relation to its supply. Marshall then analyzes the way returns
on land, labor, and capital are determined under different economic conditions. In each case the analysis rests upon the general
idea that the return of each of the factors of production depends
upon the price it can command. This price in turn is fixed by all
the factors affecting demand on one side, that is, the marginal
value to the entrepreneur; and all the factors affecting supply
on the other. If a homely illustration may be permitted, the price
paid for any of the factors in production (and hence its share
of income) is like a large rubber ball held in the air by an indefinite number of streams of water playing upon it from every
angle. Roughly speaking these streams appear to line themselves
off into two groups (corresponding to supply and demand), each
group exerting a counteracting pressure to the other in order to
hold the ball in suspended equilibrium. Marshall's explanation
of distribution is still generally accepted among economists primarily for its realistic and penetrating examination of all the
separate factors representing distribution rather than for the
clarity of the theory itself.

Ideas similar to those of Marshall were being expressed in
America at about the same time by JOHN BATES CLARK (1847–
1938). He is the chief exponent of neo-classical economics in
America, and according to eminent authorities ranks among the
best five or six Anglo-Saxon economists of all times. A Professor
of Economics at Columbia University, his reputation rests principally on his *Distribution of Wealth*, published in 1899. Briefly
stated, he believed that functional distribution—that is, distribution of shares of income to the factors of production—was in
proportion to the marginal productivity of each of the shares.
Thus labor would receive what labor had created, capital would
receive what capital had created, and so on. To demonstrate his

idea Clark assumed the existence of a static society in which the amounts of capital and labor were fixed and considered as a fund, that is, a fund of social capital and social labor. To the entrepreneur who organized production by assembling land, labor, and capital the value of each of these factors would be equivalent to the value of the last unit of each of these he engaged to produce. In order to make this situation clear Clark assumed that the entrepreneur would hire units of land, labor, and capital until it was a matter of complete indifference in production whether additional units were hired or not. Clark engaged in a bit of circular reasoning here when he said the entrepreneur would continue to engage additional units of production until the value contributed by the last unit hired equalled the expense incurred for that unit. Such a statement apparently means that the return for each of the factors of production is already determined by forces other than the productivity of the factor. This confusing thought is overcome by the Ricardian explanation that the "long-run" and not the short-run process must be considered. In the light of Clark's direct statement on the subject, marginal productivity is the key factor. The idea is better stated by saying that the wages of labor or the interest on capital is equivalent to the loss in production when the last man hired is again withdrawn from service.

By the law of diminishing returns this unit does not and cannot produce as much as the next above it. Whether it is profitable to keep the marginal unit working or not is determined by the price at which the final product is sold in relation to the value of the marginal unit in production. There are innumerable assumptions made by Clark in order to set forth the above explanation. He assumes, for example, that all units of labor are completely interchangeable, that capital is entirely fluid and can be adjusted to any number of workmen, that no distinction exists between the rent on land and the interest on capital. In addition to criticism leveled at the abstract nature of Clark's explanation of dis-

tribution, Clark himself has been criticised for seeking two
mutually exclusive things: the unchanging natural laws which
govern distribution, and a method of eliminating the injustice
existing in present distribution. It has been asked why, if natural
laws govern distribution, should one seek a more ethical plan of
distribution? Like all classical economists Clark believed in the
existence of the natural laws and in the essential justice of their
control; the injustice arises not from the laws but from the obstructions which stand in the way of their full operation.

In recent years there has been in evidence a growing tendency
to scrap the marginal productivity concept of distribution in
favor of a more realistic and simpler *bargaining* theory. Maximum returns in this explanation would be determined by the
profitability of any factor of production to a business enterprise;
the minimum would be set by the peculiar circumstances underlying the supply of land, labor, and capital, and the alternative
uses or opportunities in which these factors might engage. The
work of Alfred Marshall is not discredited. His analysis of the
factors affecting the supply and the demand of the various factors in production is extremely pertinent, as the work of JOHN A.
HOBSON (1858–1940) very well illustrates. Hobson, writing a
few years later than Marshall, built upon Marshall's work. He
was essentially a social reformer, but he realized the necessity of
bringing economic theory more into harmony with the economic
development of the times. Hobson conceived of distribution in
the classical sense, as a payment to the factors in production.
Over and above the money payments necessary to bring these
factors into production there were surpluses. Some surpluses were
productive, that is, needed for growth; some were wholly unproductive and came about as a result of scarcity, as for example
rent on land beyond the sum necessary to improve it, or interest
beyond the rate necessary to increase the supply of capital for
natural growth. These unproductive surpluses, Hobson believed,
should be used as the most available source of state revenue. Two

additional ideas on distribution constitute Hobson's special contribution to this subject. In the first place, instead of just a general return paid to each of the factors in production, Hobson introduces three levels of return. These are: returns necessary to maintenance, necessary to growth, and surplus unnecessary to social production. These levels apply to rent (return on land), wages (return on labor), interest (return on capital), and profit (return on enterprise and organization). In the second place, it is the surpluses which cause so much dissatisfaction in society. If there were just sufficient to provide each factor of production with a return necessary for natural growth, no injustice would result, but in an expanding industrial economy surpluses are produced, and they are grasped by the elements in the strongest bargaining position.

Hobson's ideas have been stimulating to progressive economists but few of them have been persuaded to accept his explanation because of his interest in social reform, and because of his tendency to be careless of factual details.

The average citizen finds little satisfaction in the economics of distribution, for even the best of the ideas are weighed down by assumptions and abstract reasoning which eliminate all sense of reality. In conclusion, therefore, it might not be amiss to present additional information on the actual wealth and income distribution as it applies to the United States today. A study of the functional division of national income made recently by reliable authorities indicated that the proportion of the income which is received by labor (wages and salaries) has been increasing while the proportion received by property (profit, interest, and rent) has been decreasing. In 1900 labor received 53% of the national income, while property received 47%. In 1939, labor received 68% and property only 32%. The trends have been constant, each year noting an increase for labor and a decrease for property. However, by dividing the total income of labor into its component parts of wages and salaries, one notes that wages have accounted for about 40% of the total income, while more than 20% has been devoted to salaries. One further fact is worth noting. During the last 40 years the number of wage-earners and salaried workers has been growing steadily, while the number of those deriving their income from the earnings of property has steadily decreased proportionately. For example, according to Professor W. I. King the number of wage-earners and salaried workers increased from 24,410,000 in 1909, to 35,572,000 in 1927. In the same period, however, the number of independent business men declined from 9,845,000 to 9,801,000. Income from independent business enterprises has declined sharply while interest and dividend payments of corporations has been increasing.

The continued existence of rich and poor even in a nation as economically favored as the United States is clear evidence of the persistence of the problem of personal distribution. Indeed, some writers contend that the extreme inequality of wealth and income which marks American society is its most significant characteristic. A number of recent studies of personal income distribution in the United States all testify to the tremendous differences separating poverty and wealth. The richest 2% of the American population owns 40% of the total national wealth, while the poorest 65% owns but 16% of the wealth. A study made by the Brookings Institution in 1929 showed that over eleven million families, accounting for more than 40% of the population, received annual incomes of less than $1500 a year, a sum which at best would provide bare subsistence; while 160,000 families, composing 0.6% of the population, had incomes of over $25,000 per year. A more recent study made of consumer incomes throughout the United States in 1935–36 by the National Resources Committee, revealed more striking inequalities in distribution of income. Families and individuals with incomes of less than $1000 represented about 47% of the population, yet they received only 18% of the total national income. Put in a different way the 1% of the families and individuals with the highest incomes received almost as large a share of the national income (14% of the income) as the 40% of families and individuals at the lower end of the scale. About half of the families in the United States received less than $1160 a year.

A great deal of the disparity in income distribution can be attributed to the disproportion in the ownership of wealth. Federal income tax figures indicate that those with incomes of from $1000 to $2000 received approximately 82% of their income from labor and 18% from property. Those with incomes of over $500,000 obtained more than 95% of their income from property. By means of inheritance these extremes of wealth and poverty are perpetuated.

The Standard of Living

Granted that great differences exist in the distribution of wealth and income, what do these differences mean when translated into the life of the people? One of the first obvious effects is that differences in income make possible different planes or standards of living. Some confusion exists as to the exact definition of these terms. The standard of living at one time meant actual living conditions. Later *standard* more frequently meant the ideal or desirable condition of life that people wanted. Recently, economists have been using *plane of living* to designate actual conditions, while standard of living has been reserved for the theoretical or ideal life which should be obtained by certain groups of individuals.

In 1935–36, at prices which prevailed for that year, it was estimated that, for a family of four, $1000 per year would be needed for bare subsistence, and $1500 per year for a standard of health and decency. The National Resources Committee survey revealed that 41.8% of all American families received less than the minimum of subsistence, while 64.8% received less than enough to provide for health and decency. These percentages, of course, include families on relief. Subtracting the 10% of all

American families which were on relief in 1935, the proportion of the American population living below reasonable standards is considerable. Even in more prosperous times, 1929 for example, 20% of the population had incomes of less than $1000, while 40% had incomes of less than $1500. Adjustments upward in the money equivalents of the subsistence and the health and decency standard would put more families below the minimum standards.

The economic consequences of the inequalities in wealth and income are extremely important. Many of these are connected with the business cycle and will be discussed in the following chapter. However, in the early part of the 18th century the close connection between income and economic progress was discussed by Bernard Mandeville in a poem called *The Fable of the Bees*. He pointed out that while saving and being frugal were calculated to increase the estate of the family, such was not the case with the nation, since a balance of spending and saving needed to be maintained if stagnation was to be avoided. MALTHUS in 1821 was even more explicit. He said, "We see in almost every part of the world vast powers of production which are not put into action, and I explain this phenomenon by saying that, from the want of proper distribution of the actual produce, adequate motives are not furnished to continued production." The wide variations in income he thought led to the over-saving of some and the under-consumption of others, but this was bad for a country since it impaired the usual motives of production.

Adam Smith and his followers reasoned from the analogy that what was good for a family must be good for the nation, as expressed by Smith when he said, "What is prudence in the conduct of the private family can scarce be folly in that of a great kingdom." They believed that economy and frugality throughout the nation were desirable. It is clear, however, that if everyone saves and consumes at a minimum, the incentive to increase production disappears. JOHN MAYNARD KEYNES in recent years has done much to clarify the relationship between income, consumption, saving and investment opportunities. He points out that as income increases there arises an increasing gap between income and consumption which remains as savings. With the rise in incomes the amount of saving increases, or, as he puts it, "the propensity to consume" decreases. Under such circumstances the lack of consumption decreases the need for new instruments of production. Consequently investment opportunities decline as savings increase.

In addition to its effects upon economic processes directly, the unequal distribution of wealth and income has serious implications for the social structure as a whole. The vast differences in wealth and income have divided society into competitive economic classes. Although the activities and interests of people in America have not been regimented by their membership in one economic class or another, there is no doubt of the tendency for persons deriving their income from a similar source to unite for economic and political action. Their main purpose, of course, is to increase their share of the national income.

VEBLEN viewed society as a pyramided structure of people on various economic levels; each level aping the mode of life of the group just above, and all of them imitating directly or at second hand the characteristics of the leisure class at the top. Since the basis of distinction between the economic levels was pecuniary, that is, expressed in money terms, and since the distinction of the leisure class was its ability to engage in wasteful and conspicuous consumption without work, the tremendous stress placed upon income in society was inevitable. The ruthless competition for an increasing share of the world's goods was the dynamic force of modern civilization. Where a society so motivated would end, Veblen did not say. Indeed, one might justly conclude that Veblen saw the evolution of human institutions as utterly painless. Karl Marx, on the other hand, as we have already noted, contended that the economic struggle of class against class was the chief character-

istic of history, and that history could only be understood in terms
of the class struggle. Contrary to Veblen, however, Marx believed
that a pattern of evolution was inherent in the class struggle. In
every stage of civilization the struggle resulted in a new synthesis
of the elements of society in a more productive economic order.
The transition from capitalism to communism was the expression
of the class struggle, because under communism economic inequalities would be dissolved. From each according to his ability
to each according to his needs has been the economic ideal of the
communist state. This aim stands in striking contrast to the most
widely accepted statement of present distribution, that each factor
and each person tends to receive in the long run the equivalent
of what he has produced. There is no valid evidence to prove that
this theory of distribution works out in practice; in fact, the very
reverse is often the case.

CHAPTER IX

Business Cycles

HALES   MISSELDEN   LAW   SAY
MALTHUS   SISMONDI   OWEN
RODBERTUS   MARX   HOBSON   HAWTREY
VON HAYEK   WICKSELL   CASSEL   CLARK
CARVER   PIGOU   MITCHELL   JEVONS
MOORE   FISHER   KEYNES

What are business cycles? Are depressions caused by events outside the economic order, or by the nature of economic life itself? What is the government's responsibility in preventing depressions? Are depressions inevitable or can they be prevented? Have pump priming, public works, and social insurance brought about recovery or merely relieved the suffering of the depression? Do wars cause depressions?

THE REGULARITY with which depression has followed prosperity—bad times followed good times—has led economists to think of fluctuations in business in terms of *cycles*. Furthermore, the recurrence of these fluctuations has made many writers think of them as inherent characteristics of our present economic order. The pattern of events which marks the course of the business cycle is now so well known that it can be described with precision. Although names may differ, economists seem to agree that the business cycle passes through certain well-defined phases.

253

Professor WESLEY C. MITCHELL, whose work on business cycles is the best known and the most substantial of all the modern works in this field, identifies four phases: prosperity, recession, depression, and revival. Additional phases have been added. Certainly as information on business cycles becomes more extensive refinements will become desirable. As matters stand, however, the four phases seem to be sufficient. The words crisis, panic, and boom which have been so frequently associated with business cycles are reserved to indicate degrees of recession and revival.

Now what are the peculiar characteristics of business enterprise in each of these phases? It makes little difference at what point in the cycle we begin, the fluctuations constitute an endless chain of events; but the sequence is perhaps clearer if we start with revival. During the phase of revival, production increases. Unemployment begins to diminish as new jobs are opened. Prices start to rise and profits enter the range of possibility. New opportunities for investment appear. Stocks are traded at higher prices, and fewer bond issues are defaulted. Commercial bank loans increase. The prosperity phase is merely an extension of revival. Prices continue to rise. Consumers' demand reaches the heavy industries. Unemployment is reduced to a minimum. Security prices continue to increase, encouraging speculation. The demand for bank credit rises to a point where interest rates also rise. Profits are high and wages increase, but signs are already apparent of a slowing down in the movement of goods; inventories appear complete and opportunities for new investment seem fewer. Recession sets in as rising costs of production cannot be met by any further increases in the demand for goods. Inventories are so complete that wholesalers resort to a lower price policy in order to move their supplies. New building ceases. It becomes more difficult for debtors to meet their obligations. Speculators and investors in the security markets strive to sell, causing rapid decline in the prices of stocks. Banks recall their loans, and their reserves mount steadily. Unemployment begins to appear. Depression is the bottom point of the downward turn of business activity. It may affect only banks and commercial enterprises, or it may shake the economic world completely and bring business activity to a standstill. The marks of this phase are rapidly falling prices in consumers' commodities, goods moving slowly, stock market collapse, an increase in bankruptcies, some bank failures, and almost a complete absence of operation in heavy industry and in the building trades. Unemployment figures mount. Bank loans and new investment opportunities are negligible. However, economies in methods of production are introduced, a new product or two comes into large-scale production, stocks begin to move at the low prices, interest rates are set at a low figure, and bank credit is made easier. These characteristics indicate that the road is being cleared for an acceleration in business activity.

Business cycles as we have described them have been known for the past century and a half. Before that, the facts are not clear enough to speak with any certainty. But beginning with the earliest reliable information we can trace the cycles in business activity with a fair degree of assurance. A chart produced by Leonard P. Ayers of the Cleveland Trust Company presents graphically the rhythmic rise and fall of business activity since 1790. The chart indicates 23 major depressions, the one occurring during the 1930s being by far the worst. The significant facts indicated by the chart are the almost complete absence of what one would term normal years, and the almost equal division between depression years and prosperity years. The close association of war periods first with prosperity and then with depression is clearly demonstrated by the chart. Prosperous periods are associated, aside from the early days of war, with the opening of new industrial opportunities such as maritime commerce, land and railroads, corporate enterprise, and gold mining.

The Mercantilists' Knowledge of Cycles

Events of such major importance as prosperity and depression, booms and panics, could not fail to receive the attention of economists. While much of the search for causes of business cycles and the efforts to analyze and describe their various characteristics must be credited to modern economists, there is evidence of concern about the subject among earlier writers. It was in reality a depressed state of commerce and trade which was responsible for calling forth much of the early literature devoted to economic thought. JOHN HALES' *A Discourse of the Common Weal of This Realm of England,* was written during the unsettled conditions accompanying the enclosure movement of the 16th century. Turning of peasants from the land resulted in widespread poverty and the rise of food prices in England. Journeymen demanded higher wages to meet higher prices; masters could not afford to support apprentices; laborers could not find employment. Hales pictured the conditions during the depressed state. Houses, streets, highways, and bridges were left without repair; prices rose but markets decreased, for no one had money with which to buy. Charities were not maintained, and the universities were empty of young men. The cause of such conditions appeared to be twofold. First the enclosures reduced production of foodstuffs, raised the price of remaining food, and threw large numbers of persons out of employment. Secondly, debasement of English currency caused the prices of foreign goods to rise. As a remedy for depressed conditions Hales offered a mercantilist policy: Manufacture necessities at home, buy abroad as little as possible, and sell more than you buy. In addition he condemned debasement, advocating a return to a currency of established weight.

A contemporary of Hales, EDWARD MISSELDEN (1608–1654) also offered explanations of trade depressions. He lived in a period when the efforts of strongly organized wool merchants succeeded in enlisting the power of the king in order to break the hold of a rival group of traders called the Merchant Adventurers. The latter group had developed strong trade relations with Dutch merchants to whom they sold undyed and undressed cloth. The Dutch traders completed the processing and sold the cloth to northern European cities. The new rival company attempted to dress and dye cloth in England and sell directly to Europe. This move brought on a trade war with the Dutch in which English merchants not only failed in the new effort but lost the original Dutch market as well. This brought on a depression throughout England. Since Edward Misselden was caught in the ensuing battle, his analysis of the causes of depressed economic conditions bears reviewing. He noted four basic causes of the downward swing of the trade cycle: too large an importation of luxuries from abroad, the export of gold (especially as it applied to the policies of the East India Company), too much competition among English merchants, and the failure of the government to inspect carefully the quality of exports. In the remedies which he offered in his essay *Free Trade, or the Means to Make Trade Flourish,* Misselden proposed strict mercantilist principles. He suggested a means of preventing the exportation of English coins, while by a process of over-valuation foreign coins would be attracted to England. The coin export privileges enjoyed by the East India Company, he felt, should be curtailed. The low value of English money as compared to foreign money should be remedied by agreements with foreign nations concerning the stabilization of currencies. Some of the shallowness of Misselden's thinking on these subjects is apparent when he reversed many of his former ideas after becoming a member of the East India Company.

Daniel Defoe in *A Plan of the English Commerce* was able to analyze the phases of the business cycle in very modern terms, indicating clearly the frenzied activity of the merchant proprietors when excess demand skyrocketed prices, and the poverty and distress which accompanied business collapse. He ascribed the causes of booms and depressions to "Accidents in Trade" which first cause an unforeseen demand. Merchant proprietors, careless of the future, expand their production, hiring new workers, setting up more looms, increasing wages. Instead of confining his production to the orders in hand, he produces to excess, and when the "Accident in Trade" is over, the proprietor finds the market glutted with his goods. The distress of declining business falls hardest upon the new workmen who have been called from the farm to operate the spinners and looms, who, after a short period of work, are dismissed and find it impossible to return to their original employment.

The most dramatic of all the early trade cycles occurred in England and France in 1720, in connection with the Mississippi Scheme of John Law in France and the South Sea Bubble in England, both of which we have already discussed. Since both of these events were closely related to the use of paper money, discussion of trade cycles, or crises, was largely confined to debate upon the value of paper currency. These ideas have been reviewed in the chapter on money and banking. There is no need to do more than mention that, beginning with the first Mercantilists, economists have been interested in explaining the relationship of money to prices and to fluctuations in trade. Edward Misselden advocated increasing the supply of money, and overvaluing foreign currencies as a means of encouraging the revival of trade. Thomas Mun, on the other hand, said that increasing the quantity of money would raise prices and reduce trade, especially with foreign countries. William Potter wrote in the 17th century that prosperous trade resulted from an increased quantity of money and greater rapidity of its circulation. The line of authors who have advised increasing the amount of money in order to promote prosperity is long. It includes the familiar names of John Law, Jacob Vanderlint, Sir Josiah Child, and David Hume. It must be admitted, however, that these authors were not concerned with the business cycle except in a vague and secondary manner. Indeed, it may be questioned whether the idea of an actual cycle was ever a clear picture in their minds. Their chief concern lay in the use of money as a stimulant to trade, not in the variations in the quantity of money as an explanation of why business cycles exist.

Say's Theory of Markets

It was the economic upheavals following the Napoleonic Wars which excited the interest of economists in business cycles. One must remember that economists of the 18th century had few intellectual tools with which to analyze the processes of business. Only after the Physiocrats and Adam Smith had systematized economic ideas were those interested in economic problems able to go beyond the superficial descriptions that marked the earlier authors. JEAN BAPTISTE SAY was the first of the professional economists to treat business cycles systematically. In most things he was merely a popularizer of the idea of Adam Smith. His interest in the recurring booms and crises which marked economic activity is his only original work. However, his contribution is mostly negative, for he adopts the familiar ostrich method of hiding his head in classical theory and maintaining that crises do not exist because in theory they could not exist. To prove that this was so he developed his idea of markets. Since goods were exchanged for goods, all goods produced represented a demand for other goods, therefore increased production merely increased demand and over-production generally could not exist. He admitted that there might be a greater supply of one commodity than another, but—since goods were exchanged for goods—there never could be general over-production. In order to be free from the inconvenience of an over-supply of some goods in relation to others it was merely necessary to free the market from unnecessary restrictions in exchange.

Over-production and Under-consumption

Modern economists have pointed out that the real thinking upon the topic of business cycles was done originally by the non-professional or the unorthodox economists. It is true that Say's work was an attempt to refute the charges made against current practices by Malthus and Sismondi. The classical economists of the 19th century investigated chiefly the phases of economics which hold in the long run or apply to the normal or natural state. The "rhythmic rise and fall of business activity" received little attention. The search for additional explanation of the business cycle leads away from classical economic theory and into the domain of its critics. ROBERT MALTHUS, whose niche among the world's great thinkers is due to his ideas on population, was also a truly great economist. Malthus was the first to admit that crises might arise from conditions inherent in the capitalistic system. His ideas on the causes of crisis can be stated briefly. Production he believed depended upon the continuation of effective demand. This effective demand was one which established a price high enough to allow a producer to pay all expenses of production and still provide a profit. But he pointed out that the value of products was always more than the sum paid for the labor necessary to produce them. Hence the body of laborers themselves could never represent a demand big enough to enable the producer to obtain a profit. The additional demand for goods must of necessity come from another source. The capitalists themselves could not be depended upon to provide the necessary demand since they were more interested in saving than in spending. Consequently, the demand must come from what Malthus called *unproductive consumption*. As unproductive consumers Malthus enumerated landlords, menial servants, statesmen, soldiers, judges, lawyers, physicians, and clergymen. If, however, the rate of capital accumulation in a very progressive country was rapid, and if the non-productive classes were encouraged to save rather than consume, effective demand would fall and industry would come to a standstill.

Malthus was the forerunner of many who believed that crises and depressions were the result of under-consumption. In the light of later economic thought, Malthus might at first glance be classed among the revolutionary economists. He was no doubt one of the first to note the inconsistencies and contradictions in capitalism, but he noted its flaws with regret, for the ability of capitalism to produce was fully known to him. The salvation of capitalism as Malthus saw it was the encouragement of unproductive consumption. Whether his support of such a program was merely the detached and objective suggestion of a scientist who saw no other alternative, or whether his close connection with the unproductive classes led him to the sentimental support of their interests one will never know. By his own act, however, he identified himself with the forces of reaction rather than with the liberal and progressive groups that gave dynamic leadership to economic thought for the century to come.

The implications of Malthus' exposition were taken up and elaborated by a highly competent continental writer, J. C. L. Simonde de Sismondi.

The ideas of SISMONDI on business cycles illustrate how a slight change in perspective can identify a man of thought with the future rather than with the past. Sismondi, whom we have referred to several times before, was an Italian Swiss who began as a close follower of Adam Smith's economic ideas. These ideas he reviewed for European readers in his first work entitled *De la Richesse commerciale*. Following the publication of the work, Sismondi spent several years in historical research dealing especially with medieval Italian cities. After nearly 15 years of separation from active work on economic subjects he was asked to write an article on political economy for the *Edinburgh Encyclopaedia*. The period intervening between his first work on economics and the encyclopedia article had been one of great economic changes. The Napoleonic Wars had resulted in several crises. When Sismondi began to write his article he found that the generally accepted principles about which he had planned to write no longer stood the test of reality. In rearranging his ideas to fit conditions as they existed, he found that he had actually arrived at conclusions which diverged from the accepted thought. These ideas he set down in his *Nouveaux Principes d'Économie politique* published in 1819.

Sismondi's new ideas of political economy arose from his efforts to explain why it was that in a nation where relatively complete freedom of economic enterprise existed there continued to exist individuals who did not have enough money to buy what they needed to consume. In brief the explanation of crises was over-production and under-consumption. The analysis which Sismondi made of this situation involved four distinct conditions. In the first place knowledge of the market is imperfect. The nature of the market is really an unknown quantity to the producer. He has no exact information as to the taste, purchasing power, and quantities demanded. He depends upon price in relation to cost of production to dictate whether he should produce more or less. A high price in relation to production costs encourages greater production because of the desire to increase profits. But one producer has no means of knowing how much other entrepreneurs are increasing production. Consequently, over-production of certain commodities is always in evidence.

Sismondi suggests in the second place as a contributing factor the unequal distribution of income. While wage-earners' incomes are constantly depressed to the level of subsistence the surplus purchasing power gravitates into the hands of the wealthy. The reason for this maldistribution is that the ownership of private property includes the power to demand a part of the value produced by labor; and the severe competition among workmen for jobs results in subsistence wages. The wealthy, having sufficient income for necessities, can use their surplus only for luxuries, but for psychological reasons foreign luxuries are more attractive than those produced at home. Thus domestic production is forced to find foreign markets. This is difficult. New luxury industries are slow in starting because of foreign competition, hence workmen are dismissed, surplus stocks accumulate, and a crisis results.

Thirdly, since the purchasing power available to purchase consumer's goods is equal to last year's income, any increase in production will result in a surplus of commodities. This is true because the income of last year is less than the value of the goods produced in the present year. Hence increases in machinery are frequently responsible for gluts upon the market.

Finally, production under a capitalist economy is determined by the amount of capital available for investment rather than consumers' needs. In a prosperous period the accumulation of surplus funds in the hands of the wealthy is frequently turned to the production of goods for which there is no existing market. The result is the building up of inventories which ultimately cause a curtailment of production, unemployment, and crisis.

Sismondi described clearly weaknesses of the economic system which classical economists were likely to overlook. He failed, however, to give an explanation for these weaknesses which could find a place in the system of economic ideas prevalent at the time. His unorthodox conclusions and explanations formed an important point of departure for later socialist thought, and the realism of his observations had an important bearing upon the thinking of later classical economists even though they rejected his ideas. No one can take from him the honor, however, of being the first to present a systematic treatment of business cycles.

The interest which Sismondi exhibited in business cycles did not end with their description. His humanitarian principles led naturally to proposals which would eliminate the evils of business crisis and poverty. He suggested state intervention to regulate production and restrict the use of inventions in the interest of a more stable economy in which production and purchasing power would be kept approximately equal. Since inequalities in income were due principally to the separation of the wage-earners from property, Sismondi suggested a restoration of paternalism in industry and the return of the independent artisan. Until such a reunion of the worker and property could be achieved Sismondi believed that poverty and human suffering should be modified by laws permitting workers to organize, protecting women and children in industry, limiting hours, and guaranteeing workers against the hazards of unemployment, illness, and old age.

About the same time ROBERT OWEN in England was writing on the trade cycle, expressing ideas similar to those of Sismondi. Like Sismondi, his interest in business cycles was aroused by the depressions following the Napoleonic Wars. In his *Report to the Committee of the Association for the Relief of the Manufacturing Poor,* published in 1817, he stated that the introduction of machinery caused production to exceed the revenues of the world available to purchase these productions. He was quick to see that while some persons became wealthy as a result of machine production, wealth was so poorly distributed that the increases in production could not find a market. "The markets of the world are created solely by the remuneration allowed for the industry of the working classes, and those markets are more or less extended and profitable in proportion as these classes are well or ill remunerated for their labor," he maintained. "But," he continued, "the existing arrangements of society will not permit the laborer to be remunerated for his industry, and in consequence all markets fail." (*Report to the County of Lanark,* p. 252–253).

The effort to describe and explain economic crisis was ignored by the classical economists, but Rodbertus, a German economist of the middle 19th century, elaborated and clarified the ideas of the trade cycle advanced by Sismondi and Owen. Many of RODBERTUS' ideas were French in origin; and although research into the background of his work does not show an acquaintance with Sismondi, one must assume, because of the similarity in many of their thoughts, that Rodbertus had some knowledge of Sismondi's work. Rodbertus' explanation of crisis begins with his conception of distribution. Although in theory land, labor, and capital receive a return corresponding to their respective services as estimated by the market, actually capitalists and landlords are able to manipulate exchange so as to take from labor part of its legitimate share. Moreover, the present economic system recognizes the right of owners to a share of income although they have contributed nothing toward production. The loss of income by the wage-earners to landlords and capitalists is a permanent factor in the economic system and the loss increases rather than decreases as time goes on, ultimately returning to labor only enough income to provide subsistence. In spite of the declining income of the workers, capitalists continue to expand production to meet the total demand represented by the income distributed. But since much of the income goes to those who either save or spend only for luxuries over-production follows sooner or later. During a period of depression the surpluses are disposed of and equilibrium between supply and demand is established.

Like Sismondi, Rodbertus felt an obligation not only to describe the business cycle and identify its causes, but also to suggest remedies. As one might imagine from his theories of distribution, he proposed that means of production should be owned socially. Unearned income should be eliminated. Income should be distributed in proportion to the labor of each. These objectives were to be achieved gradually by the establishment of a socialistic state under a benevolent monarchy.

In his explanation of the evolution of capitalism into socialism KARL MARX ascribed a major role to economic crises. He was one of the first authorities to point out the fact that crises recurred periodically in capitalistic society, and perhaps without adequate proof he contended that crises were becoming more severe. *Das Kapital,* Marx's chief work—which explains in terms of economic processes his conception of the inevitable transition from capitalism to socialism—devotes several hundred pages to economic crises.

The Marxian analysis begins with the assumption made by classical economists that the normal state of the market is a state of equilibrium in which the supply of goods just equals the consumer demand for them. Anything which disrupts either supply or demand, therefore, disturbs the equilibrium of the market. In a crisis, immense quantities of unsold articles accumulate, while thousands of people go without basic necessities. An economic crisis, which is essentially a disturbance in equilibrium where supply outruns the demand for commodities in general, is peculiar to capitalistic economy. It could not exist in a society where each man produced for his own needs. When division of labor and specialization are introduced, the balance between supply and demand becomes delicate and a rupture of the equilibrium is possible. However, in the Middle Ages when each community was self-sufficient and the market for goods steady and well defined, no crises occurred save those which could be traced to external causes. Under capitalism crises are the result of the nature of capitalism itself.

What then are the significant aspects of capitalism which cause crises? According to Marx there are two. First, production ceases to be governed by the needs of the consumer; it is now controlled by the needs of production. Because of the interdependence of specialized labor in a factory, an employer sees to it that his entire labor force is utilized, but this may result in a productive capacity above the market needs. Nevertheless because of the interdependence of all workers and the necessity of maintaining the maximum efficiency, no workmen can be discharged. Instead the producer endeavors to create a market for his surplus. Although originally designed to satisfy more fully consumers' needs, size and the intricate nature of production now determine how much will be produced. Thus over-production is not only possible, it is usually present, for adaptation to the size of consumer demand is well-nigh impossible.

In addition to the impossibility of balancing production and consumption in such a complex system, because production now determines its own ends, the inequalities of income distribution add to the difficulties of maintaining equilibrium. Since the employer is able to exact surplus value from his workmen in the form of extra production which he places on the market for sale, it is obvious that the wage-earners alone cannot buy back the commodities they produced. The capitalist, instead of spending the surplus money which he receives on added consumption of the product, uses some of it upon luxury commodities and uses most of it to purchase additional machinery (constant capital) which enables him to produce more goods and to exact a still greater amount of surplus value. And since, regardless of the laborer's power of production, he is paid only a subsistence wage, a market surplus appears which cannot be sold at a profit or even at cost. The paradox of idle manpower and idle capital is the great paradox of capitalist crisis, and it is only by resolving the paradox that crisis turns to economic revival. This is accomplished by two movements. The first is the elimination of the surplus capital. Some of it disappears through business failures and the physical destruction of plant and equipment; the rest disappears through shrinkage in value. The second is the reduction of wages to a point where it is again profitable to produce. The number of the unemployed competing for jobs sooner or later reduces wages to the required level.

The inevitable consequences of this process are crises of increasing severity. On the one hand unemployment increases, and the wage-earners, growing in number, are impoverished. On the other hand, the mounting surpluses of unsold goods lead to bankruptcy of the smaller business; large corporations increase in size; ownership becomes merely a claim on surplus value without direct control or responsibility; and concentration of power in the hands of a few owners finally results. It is at this point that the wage-earners become conscious of the inability of capitalism, in spite of its huge accumulation of the means of production, to provide and distribute the needed commodities, and the transition from capitalism takes place.

The explanations of crises given by Malthus, Sismondi, Rodbertus, and Marx laid the general pattern of all under-consumption explanations. Until the latter part of the 19th century these were the only systematic treatments of the subject. Since then theories of the business cycle have come from the pens of economists in ever-increasing numbers. To discuss these ideas in chronological sequence would be confusing. A more intelligible method is to group the various ideas according to their principal emphasis. Such a process sorts out the theories into groups which stress the following factors as causes of business cycles: underconsumption, money and banking operations, over-investment, psychological and emotional factors, the weather.

JOHN A. HOBSON was one of the first of the modern authors to champion the idea of under-consumption. He believed that in modern society the incomes of the wealthy rise more rapidly than their expenditures, which leads naturally to greater saving. When invested in productive enterprise this new saving increases the supply of goods, and it also increases the incomes of the investors. Ultimately markets become glutted with goods that cannot be sold at a profit, because too much of the potential purchasing power has been saved. The upswing comes when prices fall sufficiently to clear the market of goods. Saving and spending once again balance, and profitable investment slowly returns. But soon the process begins again, resulting in a new crisis. The immediate cause of the crisis is over-saving; fundamentally it is caused by the great disparities of income between rich and poor which make saving automatic for the wealthy.

Present-day Socialists and many others subscribe to the foregoing explanation, giving more or less attention to the processes underlying the unequal distribution of wealth. In recent years it has been called variously by such names as over-saving and— more popularly—lack of purchasing power. Although this idea has been the intellectual justification for much of the "New Deal," orthodox economists have been slow to accept it. One of them has said: this idea "can be dismissed off-hand as wholly unfounded." To the general public the purchasing power or under-consumption explanation of crises seems to make the most sense.

There are several other interpretations of under-consumption as a cause of business cycles. Under-consumption may mean that purchasing power is lost. With the disappearance of money from the economic system the value of money rises. This deflationary process causes a fall in the price level and sets in motion the recession phase of the business cycle.

Under-consumption may also mean over-saving. This is the most generally accepted meaning of the term and is implicit in all the previous descriptions, especially in the ideas of Hobson. The essence of the argument is that savings lead to a decrease in demand for consumers' goods and an increase in production. The natural result is a fall in prices and a decline in business activity.

Not all authorities believe that under-consumption is a cause of depressions. Criticisms, however, are usually due in part to adherence to another explanation of the business cycle. While the over-saving idea does not seem to accord with the facts of investment, these alternative views of under-consumption which are worth consideration are claims that prosperity turns to recession when the full power of production made possible by the increased saving in the early part of the revival is finally brought into operation. Thus not over-saving or under-consumption but an over-supply of consumers' goods causes the recession. Another explanation claims that wages fail to rise swiftly enough during the boom period, causing excessive profits. A dangerous credit inflation follows which ultimately collapses when wages finally reach their normal relation to profits, and raise costs of production.

Too Much Money and Too Little Money

One of the most prevalent and widely discussed explanations of business cycles involves the flow of money and credit. One of the outstanding exponents of this general idea is Professor IRVING FISHER, but this school of thought includes many well-known economists. Moreover, its effect upon the monetary policies of both England and America during the depression of the 1930s has been profound. It is Fisher's belief that depressions are caused by fluctuating price levels. Since production in modern society is constantly increasing, if the volume of money remains fixed prices will fall and a crisis will ensue. One must bear in mind that money as here discussed means not only cash but credit as well, and the rapidity with which money and credit circulate must also be considered. In the midst of the recent depression Professor Fisher advocated an increase in the volume of money in circulation in order to re-establish 1926 price levels. This practical suggestion was indeed followed by the Democratic government then in office.

Contrary to the theory of Professor Fisher, who contends that too little money is the real cause of depressions, Professor ALVIN H. HANSEN of Minnesota believes that too much money is responsible. He describes the situation this way: Purchasing power consists of the cash in circulation and the volume of bank credit available. Restrictions placed upon the extension of credit prevent its unlimited expansion but credit varies greatly. If in a period of rising prices banks extend credit, they increase the purchasing power without increasing the amount of goods available. This process accelerates the rise in prices, and the purchasing power of consumers generally is actually reduced since bank credit is usually issued to entrepreneurs to facilitate business transactions. The rising price levels encourage new production in the anticipation of profit; this is but a transitory period, since the inability of banks to extend more credit and the recall of bank loans reduces purchasing power and turns the price level downward. As a consequence business activity is reduced to a minimum. The downward movement comes to a close when the accumulation of bank reserves leads to a lowering of discount rates to a point where use of credit is profitable. Exchange and new issues of securities are again in evidence, credit is extended, and the upswing of the cycle is on.

In England the monetary explanation of business cycles has been sponsored by R. H. HAWTREY (1879–   ) of the British Treasury. His understanding of the causes of the fluctuations in business has been colored by the ideas of Fisher and Hansen. On the one hand he believes that the rise and fall in business activity is due to variations in consumer's expenditure out of income. Changes in consumer's outlay, however, are due principally to the quantity of money. If the quantity of money is diminished, demand slackens and the goods produced move slowly, resulting in heavy supplies, curtailed production, unemployment, and decreasing wages. If the reverse be true, and the supply of money increases, demand increases, prices rise, stocks are depleted, production, wages, and prices increase. So far this statement is in accord with the general quantity theory of money. Hawtrey's peculiar contribution lies in his emphasis upon bank credit as the motivating power behind changes in the quantity of money. In precipitating such changes it is the discount rate which he feels exerts the greatest influence. A reduction in the discount rate causes merchants to borrow in order to increase their stocks. They give larger orders to producers. Increased production means larger incomes and consequently increased demand for goods generally, and depletion of stocks. The cumulative expansion of productive activity is pushed forward by a continuous increase in credit. Rising prices and the velocity of circulation add to the upward pressure upon business activity.

When credit can no longer be extended, the turning point in the cycle has been reached and the downswing is set in motion. The end of credit expansion is controlled largely by law, that is, by the acceptance of some standard of currency such as gold, and an established reserve ratio of cash to credit. The marks of the downward motion are those noted previously, namely the specific difference given to the importance of credit contraction in bringing about lower prices, smaller orders, higher inventories, and lower production. Implicit throughout Hawtrey's discussion is the fact that both the upswing and the downswing are cumulative; that is, each part of the cycle influences and builds upon itself. Therefore once set in motion the various phases of the cycle generate their own power of movement.

Over-investment

The next explanation to be examined is known as the over-investment theory. The essence of this theory is that industries producing machinery and other equipment (producers' or capital goods industries) expand faster than consumers' goods industries. The former are not as sensitive as the latter and react more strongly to fluctuations. That is, an increase in demand for capital goods reflecting an increase in demand for consumers' goods sets in motion a production process that is not closely adjusted to demand and may easily over-supply the market. Since many economists hold this theory, in general, it is natural that great variations should exist in the way they work out details. GOTTFRIED VON HABERLER, in his extensive treatment of the theories of business cycles entitled *Prosperity and Depression,* classifies the explanations of this type into three groups: Over-investment which appears as a result of monetary and credit changes; over-investment which arises from non-monetary influences such as inventions, discoveries, and the opening of new markets; and over-investment which is caused by changes in the demand for consumers' goods—which reacts more slowly but more violently upon capital goods industries. We shall review the general explanation and each of these modifications briefly. Since all three represent the particular viewpoints of several noted economists we can do no more than mention their names in connection with the discussion.

The monetary explanation of over-investment differs only slightly from the monetary theory of business cycles itself as discussed above. In fact this doctrine differs from that of R. G. Hawtrey primarily in the question of emphasis. The representatives of this body of ideas include FREDERICK A. VON HAYEK, formerly of Vienna, now of the University of London, LUDWIG VON MISES (1881–   ) the Austrian economist, and KNUT WICKSELL (1851–1926), the Swedish economist, all of them outstanding in the contemporary period. As in Hawtrey's explanation, the interest rate is here believed to be the key to credit expansion and contraction, which in turn controls prices and the demand for goods. When low interest rates set in motion the sequence of events leading to greater demand and still higher prices, the tendency is for investments in capital equipment to increase, since by the use of machinery expenses are reduced and profit is made larger. The increasing emphasis upon the building of capital goods reduces the consumers' goods available and naturally increases their price. But by the introduction of machinery, production is made more roundabout and less flexible. Consequently when banks can no longer advance more credit to meet the rising costs of consumers' goods the interest rate rises. The result is a complete stoppage in the production of new capital equipment, for the high margin of profit necessary to encourage production of capital equipment is no longer present. Frequently it is impossible for manufacturers to maintain the long and expensive mass production methods that capital equipment makes inevitable. Booms slow down and ultimately turn into recessions. Haberler in describing this process uses the Russian 5 Year Plan as an illustration. When the first 5 Year Plan was introduced it called for unprecedented building of capital equipment. Consumers' goods were produced at a minimum. If the strain of low consumption had been too great for the Russians, the government might have been forced to abandon its capital equipment program and resort to the quickest and most direct method of meeting consumers' needs. The cause of the crises, without the use of money, would have been the neglect of consumers' goods for producers' goods. The depression would have been increased in severity because of waste in the abandonment of the capital goods program. If the condition in Russia had existed in a free exchange economy, the net effect would have been to raise the prices of consumers' goods to extremely high levels. Profits from the production of consumers' goods would have been high and the surplus would have been used to finance the production of more capital equipment. But interest rates would rise and the amount of credit would be curtailed by the simple fact that saving does not keep pace with investment. The hardship of higher interest rates hits the capital goods industries first, for although consumer demand is brisk it does not bear directly upon the heavier industries. If credit could be expanded indefinitely, new borrowing could always keep pace with the demands of industry brought on by higher prices. But since credit does have limited expansion, when it is curtailed and eventually contracted, the high price structure which it supported inevitably collapses.

The difference between the monetary and non-monetary overinvestment theories of the business cycle lies mainly in the fact that money and credit are paramount in the former and merely passive agents in the latter. Professor GUSTAV CASSEL, the great Swedish economist, is an advocate of the latter explanation of the business cycle, although his explanation of the depression of the 1930 period emphasized the monetary causes. In the early period of the upswing the increase in production is caused by or encouraged by an increase in saving which goes to increase capital equipment. But near the end of the boom, wages tend to rise, reducing the amount of ready capital which can be used to purchase equipment. By this time, however, the huge productive mechanism necessary to turn out such equipment, made possible by investments and credit advanced in the early period of the upswing, is just hitting its full stride. Thus the demand for capital goods, that is equipment, falls, while the production of such equipment rises. It is this shift in the flow of money, from saving to payment of wages, which eventually brings about the crisis and the subsequent depression. The real cause of the depression is an over-estimate of the supply of ready capital, or the amount of savings available to purchase the capital equipment produced.

Now the revival begins not as a result of the more rapid movement of consumers' goods, as so many economists contend, but because of increased investment. The principal stimulus to investment is the decrease in production costs such as wages, price of raw materials, lowering of interest rates. Professor Cassel looks upon the fall of the rate of interest as the most powerful influence. Other authorities following this general analysis consider the appearance of new inventions, the opening up of new territories, and the introduction of new business techniques as necessary to encourage new investment.

A further modification of the over-investment theory is that changes in consumers' demand are the real cause of over-investment. One is seldom successful in pigeonholing the ideas of different men on a given subject. To say that J. M. CLARK of Columbia University, THOMAS N. CARVER of Harvard, and A. C. PIGOU of Cambridge have done much to formulate this explanation of the business cycle would be open to fault. However, they seem to emphasize what has been called the acceleration principle, which implies that the effect of variation in consumers' demand for finished goods increases as it moves backward to the heavier industries which produce unfinished, durable goods. In other words, minor variations in consumers' demand for finished goods may produce violent fluctuations in the demand for capital goods and equipment used in their production. This happens because a small acceleration in demand, if it is to be met, requires an increase in equipment which is expensive and long-lived. Haberler in analyzing this proposition shows by hypothetical cases that a 10% increase in demand may lead to a 100% increase in the production of durable equipment. As John M. Clark points out, this condition stimulates the business cycle when the new productive equipment is fed by an expansion of credit. From this point on the description of the business cycle follows the pattern described by those adhering to a monetary explanation of the cycle. Credit advanced for new capital equipment feeds consumer demand which continues to expand. The principle of acceleration causes a new demand for capital equipment. But the necessity of restricting credit and the rising interest rate, or the failure of investment, sooner or later react upon both consumer demand and production of capital equipment. Then the principle of acceleration acts in reverse. The decline in consumer demand causes a complete and immediate cessation of production in the capital equipment industries. Since the payments of these industries for raw material and labor contributed largely to consumer demand, their closing further reduces consumer demand. The depression is then inevitable.

Too Much Debt

The idea of over-investment may be viewed in reverse as over-indebtedness. Professor IRVING FISHER of Yale University has taken this view of the business cycle. Actually there is no real distinction between over-investment and over-indebtedness. Professor Fisher's viewpoint has been helpful, however, because undoubtedly debts do intensify the fluctuation. Investments in capital equipment in the boom period are made with borrowed money. If business becomes unprofitable the debt structure remains but earnings are not sufficient to support it. Consequently the downward trend is encouraged. As prices fall the burden of debt becomes heavier; but to meet debts business men continue to sell, thus depressing prices further. No industry has illustrated this condition half so well as agriculture. During World War I when the prices of farm produce reached fabulous heights, farmers mortgaged farms to secure new lands for cultivation. With the collapse of foreign markets following the war, farm prices dropped, but the farmers still had to meet debts contracted when wheat was selling at $2.20 per bushel. At $.50 or $.75 per bushel they had to sell two or three times as much wheat to meet their debts. This of course further depressed the price of grain. The depression in agriculture was much deeper and longer lasting than it was in other industries.

Another explanation of the business cycle has been suggested by Professor W. C. MITCHELL, Professor of Economics at the University of California and Director of Research in the National Bureau of Economic Research. Encouraged by the decline in costs which accompanies the depression, business men are stimulated to produce. This brings on the period of revival. The tendency to increase production, however, will eventually bring about increased costs. Business men produce beyond the efficient capacity of their present equipment; less efficient plants are brought into production. The increase in demand for labor brings in the less efficient members of the labor force. In spite of this decline in efficiency, wages, rent, interest, and prices of raw materials all increase, many of them at a faster rate than the prices of finished goods. When, therefore, the inevitable point is reached where the margin of profit is insufficient to warrant continued production and the credit structure will not support higher prices, the downswing sets in.

Climatic Changes and Business Cycles

Finally, two non-economic theories of the business cycle have at times secured popular support. The first of these claims that business cycles are induced by changes in climatic conditions, sun spots for example playing the role of the villain. The other maintains that depressions are caused by states of mind—optimistic and pessimistic mental states—which determine the course of business activity.

WILLIAM STANLEY JEVONS (1835–1882), one of the great English economists of the last century, is responsible for the first statement introducing the importance of climate. In two works, *The Periodicity of Commercial Crises and Its Physical Explanation* (1878), and *Commercial Crises and Sun-Spots* (1879), he suggested that business cycles were caused by solar cycles. He investigated the history of trade fluctuations and the appearance of sun spots in England from 1721 to 1878. The close coincidence of the sun spots and the depressions convinced him that there was a casual relationship between the two. Thus the sun spot cycle of 10.45 years was almost identical with the 10.466 year period of the commercial cycle. The sun spots were held responsible for causing stronger sun's rays and more plentiful rainfall, thus producing abundant crops. This surplus of agricultural products upset the distribution of income, setting in motion the business cycle. Neither Jevons' son, nor Professor H. T. MOORE of Columbia agreed with the elder Jevons on the length of the sun spot cycle. They accepted periods of 3.5 years, 8 years, and 10 years respectively. Later authorities while rejecting the relationship to sun spots have emphasized the effect of fluctuations in agriculture in causing business cycles, recognizing the importance of good harvests and bad harvests upon demand for capital, the interest rate, and the mental outlook of the population.

Business Cycles and Psychology

There has been great popular interest in the psychological basis for business cycles from very early times. Daniel Defoe spoke of the over-optimism of business men when business was good causing them to expand their capital equipment beyond the point of safety. The first modern statement of this conception came from JOHN STUART MILL in his *On Credit Cycles and the Origin of Commercial Panics*. He said that economic practices were less responsible for crises than emotional factors which influenced business policy. The cycle might be expressed in psychological terms in this way: Fair trade leads to optimism, optimism leads to recklessness, recklessness to disaster, disaster brings pessimism, and pessimism inhibits action and fosters stagnation. It is perhaps unnecessary to point out that the psychological explanations of the business cycle do not eliminate the economic explanations. As a matter of fact the psychological theory might easily be associated with any one of the economic analyses, because the former merely shifts to the mind of the business man the real cause of the economic action. This situation is well illustrated in the way that Professor Pigou links the psychological together with the economic influences in order to present a complete analysis of the causes of the business cycle. From the psychological point of view, there is an overly optimistic attitude toward business conditions and the prospect for future profits. Professor Pigou calls this the "error of optimism." When the investor or the business man awakens to the fact that his expectations will not be justified, he reacts as strongly in the reverse, producing an "error of pessimism." The pessimistic reaction is about equal to the extent of the original optimism; it may be increased by the number of bankruptcies and other obvious evidences of the depressed state of business conditions.

Keynes and the Business Cycle

One of the most thought-provoking theories of the business cycle proposed in recent years is that of JOHN MAYNARD KEYNES (1883–), one of the foremost contemporary English economists. In his book *The General Theory of Employment Interest and Money* (1936), he goes far beyond the bounds of the classical ideas of the business cycle, and frequently offers unorthodox explanations and proposals. He challenges the generally accepted view that the way to end depressions is to cut expenses, especially wages, and by so doing encourage full employment and revival. In individual plants a reduction of wages may make it possible to expand production and increase employment. A general wage cut, however, would simply reduce consumption and accentuate the depression. In Mr. Keynes' opinion, satisfactory business conditions depend upon maintaining full employment. His argument, therefore, attempts to show why full employment is not achieved and why declining business activity appears as a consequence. The goal of the business man is profit. He operates his business at a level which will yield in his opinion the maximum return. In making his decision on this point he considers three variable factors: (1) the "propensity" of the population to consume; (2) the prospective return of new capital investment; and (3) the rate of interest.

In discussing the "propensity to consume," Keynes shows that as income increases, expenditures also increase, but not as fast as income. Hence there is always a surplus available as saving. But income and employment cannot rise except as a result of investment. Here arises the paradox. Investment cannot rise unless there is an increase in consumption, otherwise there is no demand for increased production. Nor is it possible to consume all that is produced if saving is to be accomplished.

However, business men will be inclined to invest in new productive enterprise if the returns to be expected are larger than the current rate of interest. A rise in the interest rate, he says, reduces productive investment and curtails employment. A reduction in the interest rate tends to have the reverse effect. Contrary to other economists, therefore, Keynes does not believe that a raising of the interest rate encourages saving and promotes investment. Furthermore, the interest rate is not determined by the increases or decreases in demands for money, but is a matter of tradition. If it is to be helpful in controlling business activity, it must be controlled by public authority in the opposite direction to the suggestion of older economic theory. Rather than raising the interest rate to prevent over-investment, it is necessary to keep the interest rate low in order to encourage investment as a means of maintaining full employment. A high interest rate, Keynes believes, would postpone investment and encourage hoarding. To cut wages would be to produce the most disastrous results, for income would be redistributed in favor of property owners who save more than they consume. It is obvious that Mr. Keynes favors any plan which encourages both investment and consumption. For that reason he was one of the most ardent advocates of large-scale public works, and the manipulation of interest rate and money policies as a road out of the recent depression. It is safe to say that the government programs adopted in England and America show definite evidence of Keynes' ideas. The complexity of economic life prevents any conclusive statement as to the effectiveness of these programs. That both England and America have left the depression far behind is certain. Whether war, public works, managed currency, or some other plan was responsible, it is impossible at the present to say. We are still too close to the picture to see it in its entirety.

No one theory or explanation of business cycles meets with the general approval of a sufficient number of well-known economists to make it possible to identify it as the right or the correct explanation. Each economist, therefore, constructs his own theory, introducing various points of emphasis which suit his own peculiar tastes. There is no alternative, therefore, but to canvass each idea, compare it with other ideas on the same subject, and draw as reasonable a conclusion as possible. More definite judgments must wait for more careful analyses of the economic processes involved in the operation of the business cycle.

CHAPTER X

Theories of Taxation

PETTY   THE KAMERALISTS   THE PHYSIOCRATS
MONTESQUIEU   SMITH   PAINE   BENTHAM   RICARDO
MILL   SAINT-SIMON   MARX   HENRY GEORGE

*What is a fair or a just tax? Should taxes be levied accord-
ing to ability to pay or the benefit received? Should one
class in society be taxed for the benefit of another class?
From what taxes does the government derive the most income? Is it better policy to tax through direct or through
indirect and hidden taxes? Is a single tax on land just? Is
such a tax possible? Should the power to tax be used for
regulatory purposes as well as for revenue?*

THE HISTORY OF ECONOMIC THOUGHT might well be described
as the record of the ebb and flow of government influence in economic life. Indeed, the close parallel between economic and political thought and institutions throughout the course of history
has led more than one great student of society to contend that the
character of economic life at any given time determines the form
of the political institutions. Lincoln Steffens, the eminent American journalist of the early days of the present century, after his
extensive investigations of existing political organization, said
that politics and economics were merely the opposing sides of

the same coin. One might draw far-reaching conclusions on this subject from the course of economic thought. Economics had its origins in a period when the state was all powerful and economic activity was conducted ultimately in the interests of the state. It reached the full stature of an independent social science with laws of its own during the two centuries between 1750 and 1930. In recent years when economic controls have begun to shift from the forces of the market place back to the power of the state, the circle seems to be drawing to a close. Moreover, the very idea of economic activity carried on in isolation without regard for the government on the one hand and only incidentally related to other social institutions on the other, somehow seems absurd, or at least unrealistic. Many aspects of the modern relationship of government to economics will be clarified if we begin at the origin of ideas on this subject.

The earliest and most prevalent form of government interference with the economic life of individuals and business enterprises is *taxation*. The right of the chief authority to collect taxes, and the general policy which determines who is to be taxed, how much the tax shall be, and for what purposes it shall be levied has always been a controversial issue. The tremendous increases in public spending accompanying recent depressions and war periods have brought the question of taxation to the mind of each and every citizen. In the twelfth and thirteenth centuries the revenues of rulers came from their own estates; there was no system of general taxation for the support of a public office. But the extension of the power of the monarch and the creation of the great states was expensive. One might say that the financial difficulties of governments was one of the chief causes of Mercantilism. The extravagance and waste of luxurious courts and the increased needs of government could not be met by the revenues from the monarchs' estates. The development of general taxation was inevitable.

Taxes under Mercantilism

Generally speaking, the mercantilists believed that taxes should be paid according to the benefits received from the state. SIR WILLIAM PETTY (1623–1687) wrote the first systematic treatise on this subject. He believed in the sovereignty of the government and he realized that to carry on the necessary functions included not only the traditional patterns such as defense, maintenance of rulers, administration of justice, and the care of men's souls. Three additional functions were added: support of schools and colleges, so that the ablest students might attend rather than those who had money enough but little ability; support of orphanages and care for the dependents; and finally the maintenance of highways, navigable streams, bridges and harbors.

As the basic formula for taxation, Petty stated that men should contribute to the state according to the share and interest they have in the "public peace," that is, "according to their Estates or Riches." In spite of the justice of the formula, Petty found that people were reluctant to pay their taxes. The cause of this might be ascribed to the inconvenience of the time of payment, the scarcity of money, the fact that people thought the sovereign was asking for more than he needed, more of it than necessary was going for unnecessary splendor, and taxes were not levied equitably on all. He attempted to give an economic justification of taxation by saying that taxes did not change the economic position of the nation in the slightest. Money taken in taxation is returned directly to the people. However, taxes ought not to be levied in such a way as to reduce the funds necessary to support the trade of the nation. Therefore, taxes are not harmful as long as they are spent for domestic products. One of the major difficulties, he believed, in making taxes equitable and proportional, however, was the lack of knowledge concerning the number of people and their wealth.

Upon two methods of taxation current in his day, Petty had

decided views. These were debasement of currency and excise taxes. He claimed that debasement was really a very inequitable system of taxation, falling most heavily upon the creditors of the state and the holders of fixed incomes. The normal uses of debasement, such as the attraction of foreign money and lowering of wages, Petty found to be unsuccessful. Consequently he warned that debasement was as "a sign that the state sinketh." He was more charitable to taxes upon domestic consumption, or excises. That each person should be taxed in proportion to his enjoyment or expenditure seemed to him essentially just. Moreover, by encouraging thrift the wealth of the nation would be increased. Duties upon imports and exports were approved if they were levied within reason and somewhat selectively. An import duty should be levied on goods manufactured in England. It should be just high enough to keep the foreign product from domestic consumption. For raw materials necessary for England's industry, no duty at all or only a very light one should be levied. With luxury goods from abroad the interests of the nation would be well served if the duty were excessive. The nation would by such measures be made frugal. Export duties should never exceed a point where they would raise the cost of the product beyond the price asked by competitors in other nations.

To other minor types of taxation Petty stood in opposition. Poll taxes, if levied on all alike, were unfair. He condemned taxes on lotteries because a lottery operated by private interests profited by the gullibility of men. This attribute, if exploited at all, should be done by the state, not private interests. Taxes on monopolies were sound originally because a monopoly right was the reward of an able public benefactor. That was no longer true, and monopolies were rapidly increasing in number. He felt, therefore, that the presence of a monopoly tax encouraged the creation of monopolies, an unwise practice as judged by the present holders of monopolies.

Petty's work stands alone as the first systematic treatment of the problem of taxation. Each tax, however, is an invitation to a discourse upon related economic factors. Thus the statement of critics that Petty's work is not a systematic treatment of economics is completely justified. However, his scattered observations on general economic subjects were vital and enduring. Much of what he said has a distinctly modern flavor.

DAVID HUME (1711–1776) was the next of the English economists to deal at length with the problem of taxation. He contended that both a monetary economy and a relative equality in the distribution of wealth contributed to a strong state, since the sources of revenue were more numerous and the ease with which revenue could be secured from the people was greater. Hume like Petty stood in opposition to all arbitrary taxes because they were unequal and they were costly to collect. On the other hand, he held that the laying of a tax might have good results, especially among laborers who because of the tax might be encouraged to work more efficiently. However, if industry was too heavily taxed, the result would be the death of industry rather than its growth in earning power. Hume believed levies upon luxury to be wise taxation. It taxed those who were wealthy enough to pay for luxuries; the tax was paid in small amounts entering into final price almost as a cost of production; and a person had an element of choice—he could either pay the tax or do without the unnecessary luxury.

In regard to the other relationships of the state to economics, Hume represented a compromise. He believed that commerce thrived in a state where freedom was allowed, and perished where restrictions were too numerous. It was the state's function to insure liberty and at the same time to protect business interests. Yet Hume never indicated that he considered individual welfare superior to that of the state. For the greatness of the nation it was necessary for the state to foster those conditions which cause foreign trade to prosper; at the same time, he denied the basic mercantilist thesis that a nation prospered only through a favorable balance of foreign trade.

Hume, like Mill nearly a century later, lived in a period when economic ideas were in a state of flux. New ideas were developing but they had not crystallized; old ideas hung on as a matter of tradition. Hume brought together the old and the new, but he could never quite eliminate the contradiction which an association of the old and the new made inevitable.

The Kameralists

Although a discussion of the canons of taxation laid down by Adam Smith follows logically after the views of David Hume, we must turn first to a description of the ideas of the Kameralists in Germany. In the work of JOHANN HEINRICH VON JUSTI (1720–1771) the emphasis upon the function of the state reaches its maximum. He not only adopts the central ideas of the Mercantilists as to how the riches of the state may be increased, he inquires into the uses to which the state may put them.

Justi's views on taxation were expressed in detail in his work *Political Economy, or a Systematic Treatise on All Economic and Kameral Sciences* (1755). In a very real sense his ideas antedate similar ideas expressed by Adam Smith. The chief points emphasized by Justi were: Taxes should be such as to be paid willingly; they should not restrict industry and commerce; the tax should fall relatively equally; taxes should be levied only on persons or objects which made collection possible; taxes should be levied in such a way that collection would not require many officials; the time of payment and amount of taxes should meet the convenience of the tax-payer.

Justi continues with a discussion of the regalian and dominal rights of the monarchs. These rights were privileges exercised by the monarch as a source of revenue when the returns from his own estates no longer sufficed to maintain the kind of establishment he felt necessary. The regalian rights seem to lie on a middle ground between income from the domain and revenue from formal taxes. Justi classifies these rights as those pertaining to highways, water, forests, and minerals. WILHELM ROSCHER (1817–1894), German authority in the history of economic thought, gives a more informative classification. There is the exploitation of feudal obligations and duties which the monarch permitted a subject to evade by the payment of money. The king also exercised the right to live off his people, especially when travelling. Property without an owner became the king's as did newly discovered treasure or the property of aliens. Further, the monarch sold offices and protection, received fines and shared in booty. Finally, compensation from trades, especially those requiring service or authorization from the state, was paid to the king. It is obvious that the sources of the state's revenue were complex and undependable. The regalian rights and the revenue derived therefrom tended to disappear as the king was forced to restrict his powers, and as more systematic taxation was introduced as a means of providing financial support for a public office.

The Physiocrats and the Impôt Unique

About the same time as the German Kameralists, perhaps a little before, the reaction against Mercantilism had swung into full force in the Physiocratic doctrines in France. The Physiocrats' principal objection to Mercantilism was to the Mercantilist insistence that foreign trade alone could bring a nation wealth and power. The Physiocrats thought differently and proceeded to show why. This part of their discussion we have already reviewed.

Much of the Physiocratic system is concerned with theories of taxation. In a sense this aspect of their work remains their most significant contribution to economic thought. In spite of the large-scale reduction in the functions of the state which they advocated, the remaining duties of the state—secondary legislation, defense of rights, education, and public works—required revenues. The method of securing them was woven closely into the general pattern of Physiocratic economic theory. They held that agriculture was the only source of wealth. When all expenses are paid for agricultural enterprise, and funds are available for the next season, and capital equipment is reconditioned, the surplus or *produit net* represents the only and the true increase in wealth. This is the source of state revenue and since the entire surplus is taken over by the proprietor he must bear the entire tax. As calculated from the figures given in QUESNAY's *Tableau économique,* the amount of the tax should be approximately 30% of the total income from agriculture.

Objections by the landed proprietors to such a system of taxation were naturally expected, especially since under the old conditions landlords paid but a small proportion of the tax burden. The Physiocrats contended that the landlord did not really pay the tax; therefore, he should not feel the burden of the tax. Land would now be sold at 30% less than its former value, so no one would lose. To the objection that it was unreasonable to ask one class in the population to bear the total burden of taxation, the Physiocrats replied that in taxing the *produit net* they were really taxing the annual surplus. It was true that the landlord received this surplus as income, but if the tax were to be shifted to any other class it would reduce the working capital of farm or industry which would reduce the income of the nation. Wages were irreducible at the subsistence level anyway and consequently could not support the tax. Therefore, the income of the landlords was the only source of revenue which did not affect future production or natural law.

A further advantage of a single tax on the surplus income from agriculture was that it set a natural value upon the tax and prevented arbitrary levies—a barrier against the autocracy of the sovereign. Taxes were definite as to incidence (the landlord) and amount (the *produit net*). The writings of Dupont de Nemours, Baudeau, Turgot, and Quesnay are filled with statements of their distrust of indirect taxes and their implicit faith that the *impôt unique,* that is, the single tax upon the surplus earned by land, provided an ample source of direct taxation that would injure no one.

The idea of a single tax upon land had extensive popularity among the French public until Voltaire held the idea up to scorn and ridicule in his famous literary caricature called *L'homme à quarante écus* (The Man of Forty Crowns). The chief character in the story is a peasant who by dint of strenuous toil forces from his land produce equivalent to forty crowns. The tax gatherer appears, and finding that existence is possible for the peasant on twenty crowns, taxes him the remaining twenty. An old acquaintance of the peasant, originally poor, who received an inheritance worth 400,000 crowns a year in money and securities drives by in a handsome coach with six coachmen each receiving double the peasant's income. "You pay, of course, half your income, 200,000 crowns, to the state?" asks the peasant. "You are joking, my friend," answers the rich acquaintance, "I am no landed proprietor like you. The tax-gatherer would be an imbecile to assess me; for everything I have comes ultimately from the land, and somebody has paid the tax already. To make me pay would be intolerable double taxation. Ta-ta, my friend; you just pay your single tax, enjoy in peace your clear income of twenty crowns, serve your country well, and come once in a while to take dinner with my coachman. Yes, yes, the single tax it is a glorious thing." The story emphasizes well the practical difficulties which have so beset the followers of Henry George, the modern exponent of the single tax. How can the earnings of land be separated from the earnings of the labor expended upon it? Should a tax be levied upon land cultivated by the owner or only on land for which rent is paid?

The Physiocrats proclaimed a conception of the state in relation to economic life which is unique even today. They believed first of all that human society was governed by natural law

which needed no improvement or elaboration by earthly legislators. It was natural that they should seek to reduce legislation
to a minimum, confining its scope to a restatement or specific
application of natural law. In spite of the contempt in which
they held man-made law they nevertheless placed great emphasis
upon centralized authority. Dupont de Nemours felt that only
through the hereditary monarchy could all interests of the state,
present and future, be safeguarded—in fact, he carried his ideas
to the extreme of advocating a despotism. However, the function
of the despot was to guarantee rights and enforce those laws
which were decreed by nature. Thus neither the king's law nor
the people's will was important since the welfare of the state
was dependent upon the obedience to natural law.

The relation of the state to economic life was simply that of
giving free play to natural laws. Violators of such laws of course
should be punished and obstructions should be removed. The
character of these natural laws as related to economic life has
already been reviewed. Private property in land, freedom of
exchange in foreign and domestic commerce, concentration upon
agriculture as the source of all wealth, taxation of the natural
surplus produced by the land (*impôt unique*) as found in the
produit net, were the most important aspects of a natural economic order.

Progressive Taxation

MONTESQUIEU (who lived at the same time as the Physiocrats
but was not one of their number), in his *De l'esprit des lois* (The
Spirit of the Law), is the first to stress the importance of progressive taxation. This idea is one of the cardinal features of all modern systems of taxation. In Montesquieu's opinion the necessities
of life should not be taxed, but a graduated scale of taxation
should be set for consumption above necessities. Useful things
should bear some tax, and luxuries or superfluous things should

be taxed most heavily. We shall see how Adam Smith and others incorporated this idea in their general systems of taxation.

Adam Smith and the Canons of Taxation

The ideas of ADAM SMITH upon the questions of taxation and the function of the state were a natural outgrowth of the doctrines advanced by the Kameralists on the one hand and the Physiocrats on the other. Smith contended that revenue to support the functions of the state could be secured from two sources: revenues from property or other interests owned by the state, or from taxation. He advocated and ardently supported the second. The canons of taxation which he proposed emphasize much the same ideas as appeared in Justi's discussion of taxation, but they are usually credited to Adam Smith. They often appear as quotations in any discussion of taxes, and even in the light of changed conditions they appear practical and reasonable. The canons follow.

"(i) The subjects of every state ought to contribute towards the support of the government, as nearly as possible, in proportion to their respective abilities; that is in proportion to the revenue which they respectively enjoy under the protection of the state. (ii) The tax which the individual is bound to pay ought to be certain and not arbitrary. The time of payment, the manner of payment, the quantity to be paid, ought all to be clear and plain to the contributor and to every other person. (iii) Every tax ought to be levied at the time, or in the manner, in which it is most likely to be convenient for the contributor to pay it. (iv) Every tax ought to be so contrived as to take out of the pockets as little as possible, over and above that which it brings into the public treasury of the state." Briefly stated, any tax should conform to the standards of justice, certainty, convenience, and economy. However, Smith did not follow through consistently. In discussing the sources of the taxation he acknowledged the fact that all taxes must be derived from income, that is, from rent, profits, or wages; but he pointed out that collections from wages and profits were difficult, or could be shifted to the consumer, or adversely affected industry and trade, the source of wealth. Consequently, he adopted the Physiocratic idea that taxes upon rent satisfied his criteria of a good tax better than taxes upon other sources. Even in the land tax, Smith modified his principles, for he contended that taxes on lands cultivated by their owners should be lower than taxes on land owned by absentee landlords. This discrimination may be quite justified as a matter of social policy but it hardly fits well with Smith's defense of the principles of *laissez-faire*.

Just as popular, and perhaps more influential in determining the economic thought of his successors, was Smith's discussion of the functions of the state. Living at a time when the growth of trade was beginning to press upon the arbitrary regulations introduced in an age of Mercantilism, Smith led the revolt against these restrictions. Here again there is ample evidence of Smith's partial dependence upon Physiocratic ideas, for his concepts of free trade and natural law are very similar to those of the French school. If trade could be left to follow its own direction, freed from government regulation and motivated by the self-interest of individual business men, the natural laws of business enterprise would exercise proper control, steer it into the most productive channels, and result in the welfare of all individuals. Since national wealth was simply the sum of all individual wealth, the state needed to take no special measures in its own behalf. What then were the functions of the state under this system of *laissez-faire* or natural liberty? First, there was the duty to protect society from the violence and invasion of other states. Second, the state should protect "every member of society from the injustice or oppression of every other member of it," and to establish an exact administration of justice. Third, it should assume responsibility for "erecting and maintaining certain public works and certain public institutions, which it can never be for the interest of any

individual, or small number of individuals, to erect and maintain." Such public works and institutions, Smith believed, involved three different classifications: public works assisting trade
and commerce such as canals, harbors, and defenses in unsettled
countries, and embassies in foreign countries; schools for the
education of youth; and support for the church. The school and
the church should be self-supporting in so far as possible; if
private interest could not keep these alive then public action
should not be forbidden. As was indicated before, Smith did not
believe in *laissez-faire* in an absolute sense. There were grounds
for government intervention in regulating foreign commerce to
protect certain home industries and as retaliation on countries
which insisted on high protective tariffs on English goods. Banking might be regulated to insure safety of deposits, and interest
rates might well be determined by law. Except for these minor
considerations, the role of the state was confined to non-economic
matters on the assumption that the dabbling of legislators in
affairs of business was unnecessary and dangerous.

Thomas Paine and Income Taxes

A far more powerful attack upon systems of taxation in England during the 18th century was delivered by THOMAS PAINE
(1737–1809). Paine has never been identified as political scientist, philosopher, or economist. For the most part he is recognized
as a pamphleteer; but his work in the American and French
revolutions will be cherished forever. His basic contention was
that the enormous increase in taxation suffered by the people
of England in the past few centuries was due to "extravagance,
corruption, and intrigue." Maintaining that of the total annual
tax bill of 17 million pounds, only one million and a half was
necessary, he proceeded to show how the remaining taxes should
be disposed of. First of all his plan provided subsidies for children
so they might be sent to school, provision for aged persons, pay-

ment to families for childbirths and marriages, funeral payments, and accident benefits.

Paine said that the tax on houses and windows should be abolished, and also the commutation tax because these placed heavy burdens upon persons least able to bear them. Instead of the small indirect taxes which lay so heavily on the poor, he thought the principle of the luxury tax should be applied to incomes. He said, "Admitting that any annual sum, say, for instance, a thousand pounds, is necessary to support a family, consequently the second thousand is in the nature of a luxury, the third still more so, and by proceeding on we shall arrive at a sum that may not improperly be called a prohibitable luxury. It would be impolitic to set bounds to property acquired by industry, and therefore it is right to place the prohibition beyond the probable acquisition to which industry can extend; but there ought to be a limit to property or the accumulation of it by bequest." He then proposed a system of graduated taxes upon incomes. The object of such a tax in Paine's mind was twofold: It would first of all eliminate those arduous duties imposed on the poor by the rich which has been screened too much, and secondly it would break up the large estates and return their substance to all the heirs and heiresses which "hitherto the Aristocracy have quartered . . . upon the public in useless posts, places and offices."

Ricardo on Taxation

The question of taxation continued to occupy a prominent place in the writings of the classical economists. Their contribution, however, was not in a modification or challenge to the basic principles, as was Thomas Paine's, for example, but rather a more elaborate attempt to answer the important question of who ultimately pays the taxes which are levied upon the various sources of income. "Taxes," says RICARDO, "are a portion of the produce of the land and labour of a country, placed at the disposal of the government; and are always ultimately paid, either from the capital, or from the revenue of the country." He then proceeded to show that taxes paid from revenue were satisfactory in the main, but that taxes paid by capital destroyed the productive efficiency of the nation and led, if continued, to economic ruin. But he added that taxes were not necessarily paid by the person nor the source of income on which they were levied. It was important, therefore, to determine in which cases taxes were and in which they were not shifted to other persons or other revenues. Adam Smith dealt at length with this topic, and Ricardo in most instances does little more than restate Smith's viewpoint, with a critical comment from time to time. Briefly summarized, Ricardo's conclusions as to the incidence of taxation were: a tax on raw materials falls on the consumer but will also diminish profits; a rent or land tax falls on the landlord; taxes on houses are paid in part by the occupier and part by the landlord; taxes on profits will be paid by the consumer, and those on wages by the capitalists. Ricardo added little that was new either as to the general theory of taxation or to the understanding of the relationship of the state to economic life. His opposition to the Corn Laws was a dramatic intervention into public affairs but it followed naturally from his general ideas on trade and wages. One must admit, however, that his explanation of rent became in later years the basis for a revival of the single tax and for proposals to nationalize land. His whole theory was based upon an assumption of freedom of economic activity from state intervention.

Whatever may have been the outlook of Smith and Ricardo, taxation was beginning to be viewed in relation to humanitarian philosophy. In the first place, all forms of indirect taxes were being called into question, because, as some claimed, it was through indirect taxes that the rich and powerful pushed the burden of supporting the state off on the poor. In the second place, taxation was seen as a tool with which social ends would be achieved or social programs enforced. Both of these issues resolve themselves into a single basic concept, that a more equal distribution of wealth should be achieved in society.

Land Taxes and John Stuart Mill

Of the great economists in the English tradition JOHN STUART MILL was perhaps the first to advocate a distinct change in the system of taxation with the intention of bringing about social reform. Mill considered rent an economic charge which was detrimental both to his philosophy of individualism and to the economic process of distribution, for it secured to individuals a return for which they had performed no labor. The main contention of individualism was that each man should enjoy the benefits of his own production. Rent nullified this aim. Mill held that this extra payment for the use of land was the result of the increasing density of population and should be returned to the state, through a tax upon rent, which would increase as the increase in population further raised the level of rent. Furthermore, Mill took exception to inheritance because it allowed persons to possess wealth which they had not produced. Mill defended the right of an owner to dispose of his property as he wished. This was merely the right of free people under a rule of individualism. Nevertheless, he held that this right no longer existed at death. He therefore suggested a limitation upon the amount which anyone might inherit. Instead of the state's curtailing the right of a person to dispose of his property as he saw fit, the state merely restricted the right of one to receive as a free gift more than a certain sum.

Although the original idea was suggested by his father (James Mill), John Stuart Mill actively supported a program of land reform based upon confiscation by the state of the unearned increases in land values. In his *Principles of Political Economy,* Mill expounded the theory which subsequently became the stated purpose of the Land Tenure Reform Association founded in

1870. The proposal called for the gradual nationalization of land through a tax upon increases in valuation. A practical beginning was to be made by evaluating the whole of the land on a given date. Subsequent evaluations would be made periodically, and the assessors would estimate how much of the increase in value was due to individual improvements and how much due to community activity such as increases in population and general improvements. A general tax would then be levied transferring this gain to the state.

Mill was not the first to suggest the use of an inheritance tax. As we have noted, Thomas Paine had already mentioned it as a possibility. But the first formal mention of inheritance taxes was made by JEREMY BENTHAM in a brief essay published in 1795, in which he dealt with the problem of disposing of inheritances when no will existed. Inheritance taxes are distinctly modern. Their appearance corresponds clearly with the growth of democracy. Why this association should exist leads of course to a great amount of speculation. Are inheritance taxes clear evidence that the democratic ideal requires economic as well as political equality, or are they merely the logical application of principles established by Adam Smith that taxes should be equal and levied upon those best able to pay? The answer to that question cannot be given definitely. Bentham claimed that the state could receive a revenue without reducing the legitimate income of anyone simply by preventing inheritance from going to any except immediate descendants in the case of persons who died without leaving a will. But Bentham went even farther. He claimed that the state should have an equal share in sums received with or without will by such close relatives as grandparents, uncles and aunts, and perhaps nephews and nieces. This source of revenue Bentham did not consider as a tax, and its chief advantage was its "unburthensomeness." "For hardship depends on disappointment; disappointment upon expectation, and if the law of succession leaves him nothing, he will not expect anything." It was further argued that whatever may have been the original family basis of inheritance, the dispersal of the patriarchal family has reduced family consciousness to the immediate relatives. Later writers have developed the principle of *state co-heirship*—that is, the state a partner to every inheritance—but there is no evidence to show that Bentham had considered this idea. Nor did Bentham think of the state as having a responsibility for preventing the growth of large fortunes and bringing about a more equal distribution of wealth. Later socialistic writers were the first to offer this argument in defense of inheritance taxes.

The Socialists

The program of social reform advocated by the followers of SAINT-SIMON attempted to use inheritance as a means of transferring ownership from individuals to the state. Their argument was clear. Through individual ownership of capital only the needs of the individual and his immediate dependents were taken into account. No general view was possible. But since capital is so important to society as a whole as the means of production, the chaos which existed in the uses to which capital was put should be eliminated. Crises, poverty, and economic anarchy, the Saint-Simonians believed, could be traced to this condition in which capital was not put in use according to any effective plan. The only means of escape was through collectivism, that is, community ownership of capital. To accomplish this end they believed the state should become the inheritor of all forms of wealth; private inheritance would no longer exist. "The law of progress as we have outlined it would tend to establish an order of things in which the State, and not the family, would inherit all accumulated wealth and every other form of what economists call the funds of production." The government once in possession of all capital could then distribute it in the way best suited to community needs. In other words, the government would become the source of capital; lending it, as it were, to those best able to use it. Each man would be assigned work for which he was best fitted, and each would be paid according to his labor. The formula is stated briefly, "Each one ought to be endowed [with capital or land] according to his merits, and rewarded according to his work."

The contribution of KARL MARX to the general thought on taxation is not at all original. The ultimate goal of history is to Marx the establishment of the communistic state where private property has completely disappeared. In the process of advancing toward that goal, however, certain practical measures are necessary. Therefore in the political program for immediate action which he and Engels incorporated in the *Communist Manifesto* several types of taxation are suggested. First, there should be the abolition of all private property in land and the application of rents to public purposes. Second, a heavy progressive or graduated income tax should be introduced. Third, all inheritance should be abolished. This, of course, is the unquestioned use of taxation to accomplish a social purpose. Revenue is not even a minor consideration. There is no doubt that under the influence of Marx, every socialist program from that time forward has incorporated similar tax provisions, in some cases less confiscatory, but certainly aiming at state ownership of the means of production and the levelling of incomes within certain limits.

The Single Tax

In America the idea of a single tax upon land was revived by HENRY GEORGE. The Physiocrats, as we have seen, were the first to suggest and explain such a tax. Of course, the economic basis upon which they justified the single tax differed greatly from that of Henry George. The motives which prompted its use were likewise different. With the Physiocrats a single tax was the logical consequence of a belief that the earnings of land were the only true source of wealth and that this *produit net* was secured by the landlords. Such a tax, therefore, levied upon a surplus interfered neither with capital expenditure nor wages. Private property in land they believed was the cornerstone of national economic life. Henry George, however, was impressed first of all with the unearned character of the return on land; a return made possible by social processes rather than individual labor, and by the harmful economic effects of private ownership of land. The single tax therefore was a means of taxing a return for which no one had worked, and eventually, George believed, it would transfer all land from private to public ownership.

Between the 18th century when the Physiocrats gave their theories to the world, and the latter part of the 19th century when Henry George took up his pen to advocate the single tax, a number of economists and philosophers suggested similar ideas. There was a professor at the University of Aberdeen named Ogilvie, who published an anonymous pamphlet in which a plan was outlined for confiscating the entire value of the soil not due to improvements. Tom Paine also advised a similar procedure. John Stuart Mill offered an extensive program for reclaiming land values through taxation; and Herbert Spencer made a similar proposal, only to recant in a later essay. But it was Henry George who appeared at a time when the common man would be receptive to such ideas. Perhaps it was because Henry George held out such extravagant hopes for the benefits of the single tax that he received greater public acclaim than his predecessors. No doubt his belief that poverty could be abolished by the relatively simple means of a tax on land had something to do with his popularity. Moreover none of the previous sponsors of this idea save the Physiocrats used political means to popularize the tax.

George, as a result of his own experience, became aware of the great extremes of wealth and poverty which seemed to him to increase as civilization advanced. He refused to accept the ideas of Malthus and Ricardo that this was the natural consequence of population outrunning the means of subsistence. Neither did he hold much respect for the Marxian explanation that the increasing poverty of the working classes was due to the exploitation of the wage-earner by the capitalist, for both the worker and the capitalist seemed to George to be the victims of the landlord. He believed that labor and capital were merely different forms of the same thing—human effort. Wages and the return on capital, therefore, tend to be equal, he said, rising and falling together. Furthermore the advance of civilization is marked by the increase in society's ability to produce the substance of human welfare, but the wage-earner does not share in this increase proportionally, for the increased production is taken by the landlord in the form of rent. Without work landowners reap the benefits of the contributions of civilization and the labor of man. Therefore, it is imperative, said George, that private property in land should be taxed out of existence. The *single tax* would not only accomplish this end but it would also help defray the expenses of the state and other forms of taxation would become unnecessary. How is this to be done? The government needs only to levy a tax upon land sufficiently high to confiscate all rent. Ownership might continue undisturbed, but the owner would secure no benefit and land might just as well belong to the state.

Critics of Henry George's plan of reform are numerous, and many of the criticisms are hard to answer satisfactorily in spite of the plausibility of his plan. Land today is acquired mainly through purchase, and ownership of land is really no different from the ownership of capital. To confiscate the one and not the other would be quite unjust. Then what of decreases in land value? Will the owner be reimbursed for any loss he suffers? Rent is no doubt due to the increase in population and other social processes, but the value of other things—labor and capital for example—is increased by similar social activity. If justice were applied, these increases would likewise be taxed. With land, however, the increases in value and the action of society in producing those increases, and the obvious absence of labor, single out rent and increases in land value as special and particularly dangerous instances of "unearned increment." They provide a most prominent and vulnerable point for anyone bent upon attacking the present economic system.

Although no outstanding economist has constructed a general theory of taxation which has found its way into general practice, the problems of taxation and incidentally of government finance continue to mount. The most extensive work in analyzing the principles and practices of contemporary taxation is that done by Professor E. R. A. Seligman of Columbia University. His significant suggestions for reform of the tax structure have not, however, been widely followed in actual taxation practice.

Under the staggering burden of billions of dollars in debt, and the necessity of spending added billions, the search for new sources of taxation goes on apace. But why should it be so difficult to establish sufficient taxes to pay the expenses of government? Explanations are not far to seek. During recent years the use of taxation to equalize wealth in addition to providing revenue for government expenditure has increased taxes far beyond the amount necessary to run the government. Payroll taxes, processing taxes, surplus profits taxes, undivided profits taxes, and a host of others are quite obviously means of taking money from one group of society in order to give added benefits to another. Underlying this system of taxation as well as the creation of public debt in the past decade is the economic belief that business can be improved and prosperity restored by providing people in the low income groups with ample purchasing power to buy the products which industry is able to produce. Consequently, surpluses which might have been available to pay added government expense have already been eliminated by previous taxation. Furthermore, the old doctrine that only those best able to pay should be taxed has served to free the lower income group until recently from income taxes. But this group has been excessively burdened by a host of indirect taxes, sometimes known as "hidden" taxes. It has been estimated that more than 30 cents out of every consumer's dollar goes to pay indirect taxes. With old sources of taxation resentful and impoverished and new sources either already claimed by hidden taxes or protected by social philosophy, it is difficult to raise necessary revenue. Finally, it must be acknowledged that taxation in a democratic nation is always difficult. Public approval is earned by appropriations, not by taxation, therefore legislators refuse to vote taxes on the interests they represent, but are always willing to spend money in their behalf.

The American System of Taxation

In concluding this chapter on taxation we shall review briefly the present tax structure in the United States. There was a time in American history when taxes were levied only by the state and local governments. At that time the federal government received money only by assessments upon each state. This federal dependence upon the states was one of the weaknesses of the *Articles of Confederation* and resulted directly in the framing of the *Constitution*. While federal taxation is usually the most controversial, state and local governments still remain the primary taxing agencies. To a large extent local governments depend upon the property tax for their revenues. This tax is levied at a uniform rate upon the assessed value of real and personal property. Except for the rather feeble gestures in some states the difficulties of assessment of personal property have led to its abandonment. The general property tax arose when land and buildings were virtually the only kind of property a man could possess, and his ownership was therefore a real criterion of his ability to pay.

Now that intangible property in the form of stocks, bonds, and mortgages is such an important part of total wealth, a tax upon real property alone represents an excessive tax upon one portion of the population. With the rapid rise in state and local functions, an increase in revenue became essential, but the sources of property taxes were drying up, so a search for new tax sources was in order. First came *inheritance* taxes. They are usually doubly progressive, that is, they get heavier the larger the inheritance and the greater the distance from the deceased in kinship. The yield on inheritance taxes is unpredictable. Who knows what persons will die in a given year and how much of an estate they will leave? Consequently inheritance taxes do not constitute a stable source of revenue. Then came taxes upon personal and corporate *incomes*. Each year the person or the corporation taxed must file a true statement of his earnings and pay according to an established rate. Income taxes are progressive, a higher rate applying to higher incomes. Interesting political problems have arisen over the question of taxes upon persons and corporations living or chartered in one state and carrying on business in another. In general the policy has been to tax in the state where the income is earned. The newest types of state and local taxes were added during the depression of 1930–1940, although they originated long before that time. Important among these were the *sales* taxes. Beginning with a tax upon the sale of each gallon of gasoline, the tax was extended by some states to cover most if not all commodities. Excise taxes on tobacco, alcohol, and amusements were also introduced. A few states retained the poll tax, that is, a specific charge upon every adult individual as a condition of his voting. This tax was developed in the early part of the 19th century as a more liberal voting requirement than the discriminatory property qualification which had restricted the franchise previously. The few remaining states using this tax have been inspired to abandon its use by the threat of federal legislation on the subject.

It is obvious that even without considering federal taxes a great deal of duplication, or double taxation, is bound to occur, and the dependence of both state and local governments upon the same tax sources has led to endless confusion and needless administrative expense.

In the national government the scramble for sources of taxes is even more pronounced than in the states. Barred by the Constitution from taxing property directly, the federal government relied for more than a century upon customs duties. When the United States began its industrial development and experienced keen competition from abroad, the use of protective tariffs became commonplace. There was one difficulty that was not foreseen: As a tariff becomes completely protective, by its very nature it ceases to produce revenue. Therefore at a time when more revenue was needed, its source was curtailed. The framers of the American Constitution were intent upon creating a federal government of limited powers. It is natural that they should have laid severe restrictions upon such an important power as the tax power. "The power to tax is the power to destroy," said Chief Justice Marshall of the Supreme Court. The Constitution says that Congress may not levy any tax except "to pay the debts and provide for the common defense and general welfare of the United States." Great legal battles have been fought over the question of what constitutes general welfare. The meaning fortunately has been interpreted liberally, so that the functions of the federal government have been kept abreast of the times. In addition to the restrictions upon the use of taxes, the Constitution requires that federal taxes be uniform. This means that taxes must bear with equal weight upon all persons subject to the tax; but this does not prevent progressive taxes upon incomes and inheritances. No tax may be levied upon exports. The reason for such a prohibition was the necessity of protecting the southern states, which at that time were the largest exporting states. With careful use, such a tax might have been a useful tool in protecting natural resources. Finally, the Constitution states that direct taxes must be apportioned among the several states according to population. This clause has prevented the federal government's use of the property tax, and for years was an obstacle to the levying of a federal income tax. A constitutional amendment was finally passed to overcome the constitutional objections to the income tax raised by the Supreme Court. Federal taxation today includes customs duties; excise taxes upon luxury items such as gasoline, cigarettes, playing cards, alcoholic beverages, and amusement tickets; personal and corporate income taxes, inheritance taxes, and payroll taxes. The rapid changes in the amount and kind of taxes levied by the federal government in recent years make it quite impossible to give enlightening figures on per capita taxes. The problem of taxation continues to call for careful study.

CHAPTER XI

Economic Planning

PLATO   MORE   BACON   UTOPIAN SOCIALISTS
TECHNOCRACY   THE NEW DEAL
GOVERNMENT REGULATION   SOVIET COMMUNISM
FASCISM   CONSUMERS' CO-OPERATIVES
OTHER PLANNING AGENCIES

Can competition and private initiative be depended upon to regulate economic activity in the public interest? Can economic planning be carried on in a democratic society? In what areas of economic activity has government regulation and control been most prevalent in the United States? Without government regulation does the consumer have any protection against advertising and price fixing? What planning measures have been proposed, tried, found successful? What is the outlook for economic planning?

THE ECONOMIC SOCIETY of the nineteenth century rested upon assumptions which were accepted without question by most economists. One of these assumptions was that the wealth of the community was equal to the sum total of individual material possessions, and therefore as each individual sought to improve his own economic position he would automatically contribute to the wealth of the community. Another of these assumptions was that economic activity was self-regulating; that is, through the

beneficial power of competition the pursuit of self-interest by
one individual would be automatically checked by the self-interest of others. Consequently there appeared no need for external
control; indeed, as Adam Smith contended, the dabbling of legislators in the problems of business did more harm than good.
Events of recent years have called these assumptions into question. The cut-over forests, the exhausted soil, dust storms and
floods are mute but dramatic testimony that the search for private
profit does not inevitably lead to greater social wealth. Recurring
depressions and the continuing paradox of poverty in the midst
of plenty are further evidence that economic activity cannot regulate itself, that there is no automatic force organizing and directing business interests for the common good. Yet, while individual
business enterprises spent ever larger sums on research, planning,
and administrative organization, the economic aspects of community life as a whole were permitted to drift without purpose or
plan.

Modern Economic Planning

Reaction to these conditions was inevitable. Governments in
Europe and America of necessity began to intervene in the economic life of their people. Not all of these adventures in state controlled economy follow the same pattern, or interfere with
private enterprise in the same degree. The social and economic
planning of the Soviet Union, known as the Five Year Plan, was
comprehensive and detailed. It stated the amount of a particular
commodity needed, and determined the quota of each factory
and field and mine in production. The American "New Deal"
developed its plans more gradually, with a minimum of governmental interference and regulation.

There are two things which all attempts at economic planning
share in common. Each plan must have a socially defined objective. The essence of planning is the recognition that there is a
desirable end to be achieved. This must be followed by a con-

scious effort to organize the available economic resources to accomplish that end. The instruments of direction and control to bring about the necessary integration of elements of production and distribution are also an important part of planning.

Earlier Planning and the Utopias

Although economic planning, in the modern sense, waited until the second decade of the twentieth century to make its appearance as a fixture of economic organization, ideas on the subject were propounded and actual experiments took place in previous centuries. PLATO in his *Republic* presented the blueprint of an ideal state in which planning extended far beyond economic matters. Plato believed first of all that a society was possible in which the good life of the individual could be expressed. He then described how the application of the principles of reason to social organization would produce the good society. Society would be directed by the wise men (philosophers) of the community, who of all men were best able to determine the goals for which society should strive. Each person would be given employment according to his abilities. Children, produced by those especially qualified, would be trained by the community. Property ownership and the amount of goods consumed by any individual would be determined in accordance with that individual's needs. The character of Plato's society may be quite impractical, but he unquestionably believed in the necessity of planning in order to achieve the most desirable form of human living.

The centuries from Plato to the present have not lacked proposals for utopian communities planned and regulated so as to increase human well-being. There was SIR THOMAS MORE, who in 1516 wrote *Utopia*. More was Lord Chancellor of England, but he was extremely critical of the inequalities in wealth and the political autocracy which was characteristic of the England of his time. Consequently his Utopia portrays a society in which property was held in common, everyone had a voice in the government, work was assigned according to ability, education was free to all, and the most able were freed from other work in order to pursue specialized study.

A century later FRANCIS BACON set forth his ideas of a planned society in a book entitled *The New Atlantis*. He laid down certain very definite plans for his community: "First I will set forth unto you the end of our foundation. Secondly, the preparations and instruments we have for our works; Thirdly, the several employments and functions whereto our fellows are assigned. And fourthly, the ordinances and rites which we observe." No clearer statement of the characteristics of economic planning could be given even today. But in addition Bacon's catalogue of resources, his disposition of skills, and finally the emphasis upon invention further emphasize the planned nature of his ideal community.

One and all, these men and the later men who wrote about ideal societies expressed the belief that economic and social well-being cannot be achieved without conscious plan or purpose. Many of the authors were protesting against the poverty and oppression that accompanied the industrial revolution, consequently it was natural for them to advocate principles of economics which they discovered to be absent or neglected in current economic doctrine. They subordinated private property to social use, emphasized the need for state control and direction, lifted the scientist and scholar to superior positions in the social hierarchy, made education free to all, and promised to each man employment in line with his capacity. The policy of drift and the superficial optimism that some beneficent principle was guiding society toward more desirable goals found no place in their writing.

In addition to sponsoring ideas for utopian societies, a considerable number of these writers tried to turn their dreams into reality by founding communities organized on the utopian principles they formulated. We have already discussed the efforts of Robert Owen (at New Harmony) in this respect, but there were others; Etienne Cabet in France and America (at Icaria); John Humphrey Noyes in America (at Oneida); Fourier and Brisbane (at Brook Farm), to mention a few. That most of these experiments ended in dismal failure after a very short life is not so much evidence of the impossibility of planning as it is testimony to the difficulty of creating an oasis of collectivism amidst the plains of individualism. As the negative results of too much individualism have become apparent on a large scale, societies have more or less grudgingly accepted the principle of planned economy as the only adjustment to modern economic difficulties.

Planning appears in many different phases of modern economy, and is operated in the interests of a number of different social groups. For example, in the United States the protective tariff has for decades been an instrument of planning, used primarily to foster the growth of large-scale industry. The regulation of monopolies—to turn to another problem—has been a modified form of planning which has sought to encourage and maintain competition between business units in the interests of the consumer. Labor legislation has attempted to bring about security in the life of the wage-earner. Pure food and drug legislation has been designed to protect the consumer against fraudulent and dangerous articles. Along more positive lines the government has sought to restrict the use of natural resources by conservation programs, and it has tried to offer economic services that private enterprise could not perform because profitable returns were not forthcoming. This catalogue of government activity in America is but a general appraisal of the economic endeavors carried on by the government of the United States; there are, of course, scores of others. Nevertheless, except for the extraordinary program for the War, economic planning in the United States is less far-reaching than the planning in the Soviet Union under the various Five Year Plans or in the early days of Fascism in Italy and Germany, when regimentation permitted strict regulation. The type of planning in a democracy necessarily commences with general standards, principles, or rules which serve to set the outside limits within which private initiative must operate and beyond which public welfare is likely to be impaired.

Technocracy

The most forceful and dramatic proposal for economic planning ever to arise in the United States came in the depression years of 1932 and 1933 as a result of the work of a research organization known as *Technocracy*.

Under the direction of Howard Scott a group of economists, architects, and industrial engineers were organized for the purpose of investigating the physical resources of the United States made available in the past quarter century through the development of modern machine methods or technology. The survey was known publicly as the *Energy Survey of North America*. No plan of economic reorganization was specifically recommended by the "Technocrats"—as members of the organization were called—but they believed that the facts presented made certain conclusions inevitable, for example, that the price system alone stood in the way of our utilizing for everyone's benefit the tremendous productive power which modern invention and discovery had made available. One basic fact brought out by Technocracy's investigations was that by the use of machines and non-human sources of power we were increasing production at a rapid rate but at the same time utilizing the services of fewer and fewer men. The Technocrats also showed that the volume of debt had been increasing faster than either the rate of production or the rate of population increase. This latter fact was due entirely to the constant process of borrowing and reinvestment necessary to sustain and improve the mechanical equipment of the nation's business enterprises. They argued that the pressure upon business men to increase the efficiency of their plants and equipment accelerated artificially the rate of obsolescence and led to the scrapping of machines long before their period of usefulness was ended.

Through current methods of financing, new loans were secured to purchase new machinery long before the old loans had been met. Thus business enterprise, although far more efficient than ever before, could never make savings available to consumers because all additional earnings were gobbled up by creditors and investors. Sooner or later, the Technocrats believed, the gravitation of business incomes into the hands of owners and lenders would result in the accumulation of unsaleable surpluses of goods, for neither the working man nor the consumer were benefiting by the increased efficiency of business since the depression. The fundamental conclusion of Technocracy was that bankers, merchants, and industrialists in pursuit of profit were no longer capable of managing the economic system. This function, the Technocrats believed, should be delegated to those whose technical knowledge and professional attitude would qualify them to direct economic activity in the interest of society—namely, the industrial engineers.

Technocracy appeared at the time of greatest pessimism in the economic outlook of the American people. The time was ripe for a simple formula to guide the people back to the prosperous years of the late 1920's. For a brief time Technocracy seemed to fill this need. But closer examination of the facts showed that the Technocrats had been a bit careless with figures and too sweeping in their generalizations. Reputable economists deprecated their efforts and the radical implications of their conclusions did much to destroy their popularity.

It should be clearly understood that economic planning is primarily a matter of practice rather than ideas. Whereas in previous chapters our main concern was with what men thought about certain economic matters, in this chapter we must deal with what is being done. There is room for a difference of viewpoint on only two issues in economic planning; the goals to be achieved and the extent of planning—the rest is a matter of acquiring knowledge and choosing the most effective means to achieve the ends in view. Once having accepted a planned economy as an alternative to *laissez-faire* capitalism, techniques and procedures become paramount and relegate theories to a very minor role. Planning represents a pragmatic approach to economics: whatever works is valid. To a large extent, then, this chapter will deal with the practical measures taken by government to control economic enterprise.

Planning for the Use of Land and Natural Resources

Public interest in land is as old as the first American colonists. When the settlers landed on the shores of the New World their chief concern was to parcel out the land in an equitable fashion. In some cases land was awarded on the basis of the amount each colonist had contributed to the enterprise. Regardless of the method, the land policy of the colonies and later of the United States was to place land at the disposal of individuals. The Homestead Act of 1862 merely confirmed this policy. Any citizen could receive from the government a plot of 160 acres to which he secured title either by paying $1.25 an acre at the end of six months or by continued residence thereon for five years and the paying of small administrative expenses. The near exhaustion of public lands put an end to public disposal of land in 1891. The underlying assumptions of this policy were those of the 19th century classical economists: individualism, private property, *laissez-faire*.

During the first decade of the 20th century, largely under the direction of Theodore Roosevelt, the federal government turned its attention to the conservation of non-agricultural lands. One hundred sixty million acres of public lands were set aside for forests and game preserves and for scenic, scientific, and historical purposes. Although the authority was rather ineffectively exercised, the federal government was also granted power to acquire lands to protect the head waters of navigable streams and to engage in timber production.

Foundations for more comprehensive planning of natural resources were laid in 1931 when the Secretary of Agriculture under President Hoover called a National Conference on Land Utilization. In addition to recommending several items of policy for land use, the conference also recommended the creation of a National Land Use Planning Committee. After two years of operation this Committee was superseded by the National Planning Board of the Public Works Administration, which in turn became the National Resources Board and then the National Resources Committee headed by one of the President's executive assistants. The National Resources Committee has no authority in itself; it collects data, and suggests programs to the President who then submits certain of these recommendations to Congress for enactment. In general the conservation program of the federal government has numerous phases. We shall survey two of these phases—the Soil Conservation Program and the Tennessee Valley Authority.

The depressed condition of agriculture throughout the United States began in the days immediately following World War I. Overexpansion of farms to meet the tremendous wartime demand brought temporary prosperity to American farmers. But when European countries returned to normal peacetime production and the various governments were no longer responsible for feeding huge armies, the boom market collapsed. Farmers were left with burdensome debts, with abundant harvests and no markets. Prices of farm commodities declined steadily from year to year, checked occasionally by artificial price pegging policies instigated by the government. Little of a permanent nature was done until the Agricultural Adjustment Act was passed in President Roosevelt's first term. The Act inaugurated a program of crop production control based upon contracts between the government and individual farmers. The contracts required the farmer to limit production in return for compensating payments from the government. In the case of cotton, for example, a national quota was set; allotments were then made to each state, and these in turn served as the basis of quotas for individual farmers. Each crop was controlled by a variation of this general principle applicable to the peculiar circumstances of each crop.

To secure the money with which to pay these subsidies to farmers, the government levied "processing taxes." These taxes were paid by those industries which "processed" or prepared the farm product for the market, such as cotton and flour mills, tobacco factories, and packing houses. However, the processor was expected to "pass on" the tax to the ultimate consumer.

After nearly three years of operation and some very obvious gains to agriculture, the Agricultural Adjustment Act was declared unconstitutional by the United States Supreme Court. The advantages of such regulation not only to agriculture but to the economic community as a whole were so great that the principal features of the AAA were incorporated into another act. In the Soil Conservation Act of 1935 Congress opened up a new approach to this program. This Act declared it to be "the policy of Congress to provide permanently for the control and prevention of soil erosion and thereby to preserve natural. resources, control floods, prevent impairment of reservoirs, maintain the navigation of rivers and harbors, protect public health and public lands, and to relieve unemployment." In order to secure the cooperation of farmers in soil conservation they were a year later subsidized for shifting their acreage from crops in which there is an oversupply into a soil-building crop such as alfalfa and clover. According to Henry A. Wallace, at that time Secretary of Agriculture, the soil conservation program alone did not provide sufficient control over agriculture to eliminate the tremendous surpluses that were building up year after year. In 1938 a revived AAA program was introduced in which the states shared with the federal government the work of stabilizing agriculture. Limitation of acreage, and quotas set upon the sale of produce featured the program. It was financed out of general taxation.

The keystone of the New Deal power arch is the Tennessee Valley Authority. Becoming owner of over 2000 acres on the Tennessee River at Muscle Shoals used primarily as a site for nitrate manufacture during World War I, the government was at a loss to know how to use the property when the war was over. No solution to the controversy which raged over this issue was found until 1933 when Congress passed the Tennessee Valley Authority Act. This legislation was designed to improve the navigability and control floods on the Tennessee River to provide for reforestation, reclamation, and profitable use of the land in the Valley, and to operate the nitrate plants in the interest of national defense. The program was financed by a $50,000,000 appropriation from Congress and the sale of bonds up to a similar amount to the general public. The generation of electric power as incidental to building the dams for flood control has been one of the most significant phases of the program. Power thus developed is sold to public and private organizations at rates which presumably act as a yardstick for the production and sale of electric power by privately owned public utilities. Taken all together the T.V.A. program represents the most spectacular effort in America to plan the economic and social relationships of 2,000,000 Americans and 40,000 square miles of land.

A great variety of minor programs have been established in recent years to plan the use and conservation of natural resources and the stabilization of agriculture. There is the Farm Security Administration which is responsible for taking out of use about 10,000,000 acres of marginal land, and for resettling the owners or tenants of such land on good land. It also is responsible for assisting farm tenants to become owners and alleviating the distress of those caught by natural or economic catastrophes. Then there is the Civilian Conservation Corps which consists of young men between the ages of 18 and 25 whose parents are unemployed or otherwise in need of public assistance. Designed partly as a means of combating unemployment among young men, the program contributed largely to the conservation and beautification of public and private farm and forest land.

The Soviet Union has worked out planned control of Russian agriculture and natural resources. The socialistic ideal, expressed in the *Communist Manifesto* of 1848, is complete ownership by the State of all land and natural resources. The road of the Russian leaders has not been easy in this respect. Farming has been for centuries Russia's chief industry. It was also the stronghold of individualism. The chief aim of every peasant in the days of the Czar was to acquire a small strip of land for himself. Consequently when Lenin first attempted collectivization of farm land during the period of war communism, he met with strong opposition in the form of destruction of herds and seed grain. He was forced to accept a partial return to private ownership and private enterprise. Under his new Economic Policy, the kulak (private farmer) thrived and grew wealthy. Several years later under the Five Year Plan, Stalin attempted to collectivize the farms. Again sabotage and non-cooperation greeted his efforts, but the farms were collectivized. Conflicting reports made it difficult to describe accurately the success or failure of the general principle of State ownership and management of mass production farms. The kulak has been eliminated and private hoarding condemned. Agriculture, mining, and other industries concerned primarily with the production of raw materials are now assigned quotas under the successive Five Year Plans just as industry has been.

Government Regulation of Labor Relations

Traditionally the function of government in labor relations has been that of umpire, empowered in a vague way to see that the general social rules were observed by employer and employee alike. Since most of our laws, particularly common law, arose when individual employers dealt with individual employees, it is no easy task to adjust them to the problems of organized employers and organized workers. Until 1842 in the United States labor unions could be declared illegal by law. In that year a Massachusetts court declared trade unions legal. Ever since that time courts and laws have been trying to determine which actions of trade unions are legal and which are illegal, and what responsibility an employer has toward a trade union.

The first law dealing directly with this issue was the Clayton Act of 1914. Specifically designed to strengthen existing legislation regarding trusts, the Act included several notations of importance to labor. One declared that labor was not a commodity, therefore trade unions should be exempt under the anti-trust laws. Another stated that injunctions should not prohibit strikes, boycotts, or picketing. And it also stated that trade unions should not be restrained in pursuing legitimate objectives. Subsequent court action failed to justify the belief that the Clayton Act was Labor's Magna Charta. A series of damaging injunctions against trade unions in the 1920–30 decade forced labor to seek new safeguards.

In 1932 the attitude of the government toward labor changed sharply from mere toleration to one of positive encouragement. Evidence of the change appeared first in the Norris-LaGuardia Act. This Act made two important improvements in labor's position. The injunction procedure was restricted by the introduction of a number of safeguards such as requiring both parties affected by an injunction to appear in court to testify before the injunction is issued; and requiring violations of the injunction (contempt proceedings) to be tried before a different judge and a jury if the defending party desired. The other improvement was that contracts signed by the employee stating that so long as he worked for this employer he would not join a union or engage in trade union activities were outlawed. The fact that this Act as federal legislation applied only to interstate commerce was a momentary drawback; but since then most industrialized states have passed similar laws.

The next bit of evidence indicating the government's policy of encouragement was Section 7a of the National Industrial Recovery Act. By this section employers were required to recognize trade union organizations and to bargain collectively with them, and they were prohibited from engaging in any practice which would obstruct collective bargaining and prevent the organization and growth of the union, such as dismissal for union activity and blacklisting.

When the National Industrial Recovery Act was declared unconstitutional by the United States Supreme Court, Section 7a was incorporated into the National Labor Relations Act which became law in 1936. The N.L.R.A. advocated trade union organization and collective bargaining as essential to economic stability and recovery. The Act provides that employees shall have the right to organize into unions and to bargain collectively with the employer through representatives of their own choosing. Employers are forbidden to interfere with the organization of a trade union or to seek to dominate it once it has been formed. They must not discriminate among employees because of union activity. To see that these provisions are carried out the National Labor Relations Board was established with full powers of investigation and decision. Their decisions, however, are subject to review by the Circuit Court of Appeals of the United States.

It is often asked, "But how does the employer figure in these laws?" Many people feel that the employee gets everything, the employer nothing. By common law and statute the employer has until recently been absolute dictator of his own business and his right to carry on business has been protected by the courts. Until recently he opened and closed when he wished, started or stopped his business when he chose, hired and dismissed freely, secured his material, and sold his goods subject only to economic competition. The organization of a trade union is a distinct encroachment on these rights. When the government says to the employer you must discuss conditions of employment with the union, and you cannot dismiss a man for trade union activity, the government is definitely protecting the workman by removing certain rights from the employer. The answer to the original question is that the employer already has the protection he needs except at those points where the government has consciously granted rights to employees and taken them from the employer to equalize the bargaining position of labor and management.

This process is economic planning, for it substitutes the conscious power of the government for economic forces in order to achieve an accepted goal. In England the right of workers to organize and bargain collectively was established by tradition decades ago. Unions are a recognized part of English economy. In Fascist countries membership in trade unions was more numerous than in either England or America because such membership was well-nigh compulsory. A union in Germany and Italy was a semi-public body acting as a complement to an organized group of employers in the same industry.

At this point we shall summarize the economic aspects of Fascist doctrine in order to show how these applied in Italy and Germany.

The basis of economic life under Fascism is syndicalism, but it is syndicalism subordinated to the needs of the nation. A. Pennachio, in his book *The Corporative State,* has described clearly this aspect of Fascism. He states that whenever a person opposes his own individual interest to that of the nation, he is exhibiting a narrow, selfish, immediate, and material attitude—an attitude contrary to the principles of Fascism. He proceeds to point out that Fascism denies that the workers can usurp the place of the entrepreneur or the well-trained administrator. Each must perform the function for which he is best fitted; therefore a division of labor must be preserved and the interests of the resulting classes harmonized, none favored at the expense of the others. To bring about collaboration and to subordinate rival interests, Fascism organizes both employers and employees in the same manner and puts them on an equal footing in a given industry. Harmony is secured by an agency of the state which stands above and supervises the organization of employers and employees. These ideas were first formulated in the Labor Charter promulgated by the Italian government in April of 1927.

The planning unit under Italian Fascism is the National Council of Corporations. With its almost unlimited powers of intervention, reorganization, and control the national council has complete authority over economic activity. Mussolini has acted from time to time as Minister of Corporations, dictating general economic policy. To provide for carrying out the details of any plan which might be developed, the government has fostered the growth of corporations. Composed of representatives of employees and employers in a given industry, the corporation is responsible for the overall management of the industry. In order to integrate the economic life of the nation more closely with political life, it was decreed that the lower house of the Italian Parliament was to be elected directly by the corporations and federations rather than by geographical areas.

Security for the Worker

It is no longer possible for families to be economically self-sufficient. The wage-earner in mine or factory produces little or nothing that he can directly consume; for the most part the necessities of life are produced by others. Even the farmer produces only a small part of what his family consumes. For him an adequate standard of living can be procured only by the exchange of some of his crops for other needed articles. This mutual interdependence makes the process of exchange of fundamental importance in the wellbeing of all the people in modern society. To facilitate the process of exchange we use money. The wage-earner sells his labor for money, just as the farmer sells his crops for money; they then use the money to buy the commodities they need. The wellbeing of the wage-earner and the farmers is obviously dependent upon their ability to sell their services or goods for money; if there is no one willing or able to buy, their condition is desperate. From time to time in our society there have been great numbers of wage-earners and farmers ready to sell their goods and services but unable to find buyers; at other times because of illness or accident they have been unable to offer goods and services for sale. These times have been so prevalent and have recurred so frequently that they constitute one of the major problems of contemporary civilization. For want of a better term we call this condition social insecurity.

Concern with this problem began in the early part of the 19th century when the industrial revolution changed the character of English civilization. The financial distress of many English families combined with the need for unskilled work in the cotton mills led to the employment of very young children and women. The policy of individualism and *laissez-faire* left each manufacturer free to pay the lowest wage the women and children would accept, and to provide the poorest working conditions these people would agree to. Consequently poverty and unsanitary working and living conditions were rampant. It was against such situations that Robert Owen, Sismondi, Thompson, and others protested so vigorously. These protests and the growing organization of workmen brought about the first intervention of the government to protect the interests of working persons.

The first of the so-called labor legislation consisted of a series of acts of the English Parliament designated to protect young children and women from long hours, night work, and unsanitary working conditions. These acts, covering the period from 1802 to 1840, were known as the Factory Acts. Some years later, as the industrial revolution fell with full force upon them, the United States and other countries passed similar laws. Gradually these laws in modified form were extended to apply to men as well as women and children. Factory laws require safety precautions, regulate lighting, and set minimum standards for health and sanitation. These matters are considered as a public interest, since society is naturally interested in the health and safety of the working population. Conditions which impair the welfare of the working men or women are and ought to be subject to public control.

In the last half century social insurance has been one of the most important means of promoting social and economic security among wage-earners. Briefly defined, social insurance is a system of insurance established by law to guarantee benefit payments and services as a right to all wage-earners incurring some disaster which causes loss of income. Nineteenth Century Germany was the pioneer in systems of social insurance. In order to combat the poverty resulting from sickness and industrial accidents, and to forestall the growth of socialism, Bismarck introduced in 1881–83 both industrial accident and health insurance. Later, old-age insurance was established. Great Britain was the next large nation to feel the necessity of protecting workmen against the hazards of modern industry. In 1911, under the leadership of Lloyd George the English Parliament set up a comprehensive plan of social insurance including health insurance, old age pensions, and unemployment insurance. Workmen's compensation had been established some years earlier. In the United States state governments, one by one, introduced workmen's compensation. Beginning with New York State in 1910, all states in the nation have now adopted a workmen's compensation law.

The basic cause of workmen's compensation legislation was that as a result of industrial accident the income of a family was temporarily or permanently curtailed either wholly or in part. The family consequently was forced to seek assistance through public or private charity. Where the employer was at fault it was difficult for the workman to secure damages in the courts; even if the worker was himself at fault the community had to bear the expense of his injury. In theory a responsible workman would save himself the embarrassment of appealing for charity by providing for just such emergencies. In practice it was found that very few wage-earners could or did make such provision. To most people the community could best deal with this problem by preparing for it in advance through some kind of social insurance. Much the same line of reasoning supports unemployment insurance, old age pensions, and health insurance. The fact that workmen are not directly responsible for many of these hazards lends force to the argument that a community-wide program should be· established to meet emergencies efficiently, systematically, and without stigma to the wage-earners.

With the passage of the Social Security Act in 1935, the United States accepted the principle of social insurance as the basis for measures combating the most disastrous types of insecurity. Because of the federal nature of the American government the Social Security Act encourages the passage of State legislation rather than the establishment of comprehensive federal programs. This encouragement is achieved through extensive grants-in-aid, the grant being conditioned upon the acceptance by the State of certain minimum standards for each of the various programs. The Act includes provisions for unemployment insurance, old age pension, care of dependent children, maternal and child health, pensions for the blind, vocational rehabilitation of physically handicapped and blind persons, and the federal old age insurance which is an exception to the general pattern established by the Act in that it is wholly federal in its administration.

The unemployment provisions of the Act cover all employees of a business employing eight or more workers. Workers in non-profit educational, philanthropic, and religious enterprises are excluded as are marine workers, agricultural workers, domestic servants, and casual laborers. When a man becomes unemployed he registers with the United States Employment Service and after a waiting period of three weeks he will receive a benefit equivalent to approximately ½ his weekly wage. The minimum is $7.00 a week and the maximum is $20.00. States of course vary in the amount of minimum and maximum payable. Benefits are paid for a total period of 16–32 weeks, but benefits for only half the number of weeks can be received in any given year. Some states have introduced the merit-rating principle, which allows the state to reduce the taxes on any employer who maintains full employment for his workers.

The old-age pension (or assistance) program is also a state program. Any person 65 years of age without visible means of support may receive a pension up to $40.00 (this varies greatly for different states) per month depending upon his need. Most states require that the person be a citizen of the United States and a resident of the state for at least 5 years in order to qualify. The federal government will pay half the cost of each pension granted by the state up to a maximum payment of $20.00 for each person. This is the real reason why the maximum pension tends to be $40.00.

The old-age insurance features of the Social Security Act are federal in scope. All workers working in establishments employing one or more workmen are eligible for benefits when they reach the age of 65 if they are no longer employed. In addition, dependents' benefits are paid, the amount paid being a portion of the total benefit calculated above for each dependent. The total benefit, however, cannot exceed $85.00. To finance this program the federal government levies a tax upon every employer and employee. The excluded occupations are the same as in unemployment insurance.

The United States did not include health insurance in the Social Security program although this has long been a fixture in foreign systems of social insurance. Under the direction of the Social Security Board extensive investigation has been under·

taken to ascertain how such a system might best be introduced. Suggestions for health insurance have already been made in the form of proposed legislation in state and federal legislatures.

One other aspect of the government's attempt to provide security for workers must be mentioned. This is the minimum wage law. Under classical economic theory it was assumed that wages, like the price of any other commodity, would be set by the economic forces of the market place. Government interference was unjustified and would do more harm than good. In spite of this attitude, and the firm resistance of employers, minimum wages have been legislated in every industrialized nation. The first laws on this subject were passed in New Zealand and Australia in the 1890's, and in England in 1908. Massachusetts in 1912 became the first state in the United States to adopt such legislation; many other states followed. However, reaction of the American courts to minimum wages was unsympathetic. The laws were upheld by a tie vote of the Supreme Court in 1916, declared unconstitutional in 1923 and again in 1936 only to be declared constitutional in 1937 and 1940.

American minimum wage laws are of two types. There is first the federal law (Fair Labor Standards Act of 1938) which sets a minimum of 40 cents an hour applicable in 1945, and a 40-hour week. Any person working above 40 hours is entitled to time and a half-time for the extra labor. This law covers all workers employed in industries engaged in interstate commerce. Whereas the federal law determines wages and hours by statute, state laws require that industrial committees be appointed in each industry. These industrial committees, representing the employer, the employee, and the public, investigate the economic condition of the industry and the needs of the employees and arrive at a minimum wage which is reasonable for both. The latter method is the one applied generally in other countries with minimum wage laws, especially Great Britain.

Planning for Business Activity

The first business enterprises to come under governmental direction and control were the railroads. The period of expansion following the Civil War placed tremendous economic power in the hands of the railroads. Abuses in the operation of railroads could not be curbed by state action. Consequently in 1887 the federal government took the first step in that direction. The Interstate Commerce Act prohibited discrimination in rates and service, rebating and pooling. The Act was to be enforced by the Interstate Commerce Commission. Since that time the number of regulations and the power of the Commission have grown tremendously. The Commission must approve rail rates, schedules must be adequate for public service, accounts must be open to the public, and the Commission is empowered to investigate and recommend consolidation of railroads. Mergers or changes in the capital structure of a railroad must be approved by the Commission. In addition to railroads, the Interstate Commerce Commission also has general supervision over bus and truck lines, water transport and interstate pipe lines. Its original control over electric light and power, telephone and telegraph and radio has been given to two other federal Commissions, the Federal Power Commission and the Federal Communications Commission.

In addition to the railroads, other types of public utilities fell under government regulation. Street railways, electric, gas, and water companies were made subject to both the state and local governments because of the character of the business and the dependence of the public upon their services. The state governments through the granting of franchises and the appointment of commissions have sought to guarantee the public adequate service at reasonable rates and at the same time see that the private owners of these utilities receive a fair return on their investment. To accomplish these aims has not been easy. Endless hearings, investigations, and legal disputes have arisen over questions of property evaluation, rate making formulae, and the rights of owners and consumers. Throughout, however, the ideal of the government has been to retain as much of private ownership and private initiative as the public welfare would stand.

The growing importance of the interstate business of public utilities, especially electric light and power companies, and the power and complexity of holding companies in this field led to federal regulation. The public utility holding company is a device for consolidating the operation and enlarging the area of control of public utilities by means of a central company which owns a controlling interest in a number of operating companies. Undoubtedly economies of operation can be achieved by this centralized direction. Nevertheless, the abuses to which the holding company easily lent itself were pernicious. It will be sufficient to cite two. Holding companies own no assets save the stock of operating companies. On the basis of such ownership, shares of holding company stock were sold to the public in order to increase the holdings of the holding company. This resulted not only in an overabundance of new stock issues without a corresponding increase in the capital equipment of the company, but it also made possible fraudulent manipulation of stock. Furthermore, the holding company having a controlling interest in the operating company could force the latter to purchase goods and services from the holding company or from its affiliated companies at exorbitant rates, thus transferring the legitimate earnings of the operating company into fraudulent gains for "insiders" of the holding company. Recognizing the legitimate place that some holding companies held, the Public Utility Holding Company Act of 1935 outlawed all holding companies except those confined to single integrated utility systems, *i.e.* holding companies just once removed from operating companies. All holding companies are registered with the Securities and Exchange Commission which exercises control over the financial organization of the companies.

The traditional policy of the American government has assumed that consumer interest is best served by small competitive business units. Consequently the most striking characteristic of business regulation has been the regulation of trusts and monopolies. Although the evils of combination among large-scale industry were recognized in the decades of industrial expansion following the Civil War, no action was taken until 1890. Sporadic efforts at regulation under common law by the states proved wholly inadequate. The Sherman Act, passed in 1890, was the Congressional answer to the problem. The first provision of the Act states: "Every contract, or combination in the form of trust or otherwise, or conspiracy in restraint of trade or commerce among the several states or with foreign nations, is hereby declared illegal." Furthermore criminal prosecution of violators of the Act was provided.

Enforcement of the Sherman Act was in the hands of the Attorney General. Pressure of other work, however, and the unsympathetic attitude of the courts, prevented adequate enforcement of the law. Prosecution of the trusts was almost a dead issue until the accession of Theodore Roosevelt to the presidency in 1901.

In making its decisions the Supreme Court gradually modified the original meaning of the Act; whereas the Act declared any combination in restraint of trade illegal, the Court said that dissolution would be ordered only where the restraint of trade was unreasonable. This dictum has since become known popularly as "the rule of reason." Certain justification exists for this attitude on the part of the Court. All trusts are not harmful, or—as Theodore Roosevelt once said—there are "good trusts and bad trusts." Competition among industrial enterprises frequently leads to waste, destructive price wars, cheapening of products, and reduction of wages. Certain industries cannot operate except as semi-monopolies. Therefore to enforce the law literally would have brought real hardship. On the other hand, "the rule of reason" opened numerous loopholes through which combinations could escape prosecution.

Agitation for a stiffening in the anti-trust policy resulted in the passage of the Clayton Act and the creation of the Federal Trade Commission. By these acts the scope of federal regulation was expanded to include a number of unfair economic practices in addition to combination in restraint of trade, and the method of enforcement was simplified and made more direct by charging the Federal Trade Commission with investigation and prosecution. The Commission, either on its own initiative or as a result of a protest by businesses or individuals, can summon individuals and records for purposes of investigation. It can issue orders to cease and desist if its investigation indicates that the concern in question has been engaging in a practice of unfair competition.

In spite of the modifications of the Sherman Act, serious question as to the basic philosophy of competition by small business units did not arise until the national government was forced to devise a program for economic recovery in 1933. It appeared that competitive rivalry only made the depression more serious. Under the National Industrial Recovery program combinations, price fixing, and market allocations, which had been only recently condemned were encouraged as means of securing economic benefits for workers and consumers and stability for producers. Specifically the aims of the N.R.A. were to spread the work among the unemployed by the elimination of child labor and the reduction of working hours; to increase the purchasing power of the masses by setting minimum wages; to stimulate the organization of labor and collective bargaining; to stabilize industrial relations; and to abolish unfair competition among business men, and to introduce some planning into industry.

It is not necessary to describe in detail the administrative organization of the National Recovery Administration. The codes of fair competition were the core of the program. In accordance with the ideal of self government each industry through its trade association or special conference was responsible for formulating a code embodying the principles of the N.I.R.A. When accepted by the National Recovery Administrator and signed by the President of the United States these codes became law. Various advisory boards were available to assist the industries in framing their codes and to protect the interests of labor and consumers. The use of codes to govern their activities was common practice in monopolistic industries long before the N.R.A. The procedure now was different only in the fact that the practice was now legal and the rights of workers and consumers were incorporated into the codes. In spite of the optimism with which it was launched, the N.R.A. was not a success. It was already unpopular when it was declared unconstitutional by the Supreme Court. The idea on which the program was founded was apparently sound, however, and almost surely will be revived in the future as a means of industrial regulation and planning. But the enforcement machinery was inadequate, various factions within each industry were not willing to accept new relationships in good faith or to accept fixed relationships to rival groups.

With the passing of the N.R.A. the United States returned temporarily to a policy of "trust busting," but the menace of war quickly forced upon the government a more rigid program of regulation than even the wildest dreams had contemplated. Industry during the war period made what the government asked for, in the quantities which the government determined, and sold the product to the government or to the public at prices which the government prescribed. Only in the Soviet Union has government control of industry surpassed that of the United States in World War II.

Let us now review the development of economic planning in the Soviet Union. The goal of the Communist Party in Russia has been the erection of the economic structure of the Soviet Union upon the theoretical foundations laid by Karl Marx. In the *Communist Manifesto,* published in 1848, Marx and Engels described the general structure of a socialistic society, not the final form perhaps, but Socialism in its initial stages. The chief characteristics were specifically stated: abolition of all property in land and the application of all rents to public uses; a heavy progressive income tax; abolition of all rights of inheritance; centralization of credit in the hands of the state through the creation of a central national bank with state capital and exclusive monopoly; state ownership of means of communication and transport; extension of factories and means of production owned by the state; employment of all persons so that none should be voluntarily or involuntarily idle; creation of agricultural labor corps; planned relationship of agriculture to industry so as to remove inequalities and secure balanced production; free education for all children in public schools.

Ever since the Russian Revolution of 1918 when the Communists (Bolsheviki) under NICOLAI LENIN (Vladimir Ilich Ulianoff, 1871–1924) came to power, the economic system has been in a constant process of adjustment. Lenin believed implicitly in communistic ideals, hence he lost no time in introducing various elements of the communistic state. Money was eliminated; all means of production, transportation, and communication were confiscated by the state; food and clothing were given by the state according to need; and each person was expected to work in any occupation to which he was assigned without pay. Through rigid dictatorial control Lenin expected to force the acceptance of these procedures until they became habitual. Opposition by individualistic elements among the population, especially among the farmers, led to open sabotage. Severe shortages of food resulted, ultimately forcing Lenin in 1921 to accept a limited amount of private production and exchange and, of course, the revival of the use of money. This was known as Lenin's New Economic Policy, a temporary expedient to get the forces of production running once again. The immediate goal was achieved; and after two disastrous years marked by widespread famine, food became plentiful once more. But the policy also effected the rise of a class of private landowners and traders known as kulaks and nepmen who were responsible for a considerable part of the domestic economic activity.

To Lenin goes the credit for the establishment of the political dictatorship of the Communist Party in Russia. It was JOSEPH STALIN (Yosif Dzhugashvili, 1879–   ), however, who really fostered economic communism and large-scale economic planning. Defeating Leon Trotsky, Lenin's first associate, for control of the Communist Party on the death of Lenin, Stalin turned the interest of his followers from international affairs to the development of Russian economic resources. In spite of much opposition, he held unswervingly to his idea that it was possible to build a socialist state, strong economically and politically, in the midst of a capitalistic world order.

Under Stalin industry was organized into a group of trusts comprising a large number of productive units in a given industry. In some cases there were several trusts in one industry; in oil, for example, there was a trust for each of the major oil fields. These trusts were controlled in matters of general policy, prices, and capitalization by the Supreme Economic Council, a division such as a government department in the United States Government. Each trust had its own managing board, appointed by the Supreme Economic Council, which assumed responsibility for operating the trust within the broad lines laid down by the Council. From this point on the various businesses comprising the trust were operated as independent business enterprises, seeking a profit which, of course, could only arise through efficiency in production. The "profit," however, went to the government, for workers' insurance and for expansion. Frequently the earnings of one trust were applied by the Council to cover the deficit in another, if the deficit arose from experimentation, newness of the industry, or other legitimate cause. Transportation and communication systems were not incorporated in the trust system, since they were already managed as separate departments of the government.

In matters of distribution the system was more flexible. In addition to state trusts there were co-operatives and private merchants. The Supreme Economic Council exercised control over prices and quantities provided to these agencies through wholesale trusts. Over a period of years the policy of the Council favored the state trusts and gradually forced the co-operatives and the private dealers out of business.

The principal planning operation in the Soviet Union was the co-ordination of the forces of production and distribution. The goal was the greatest production of material goods consistent with the health, safety, leisure, and education of the masses. With limited capital, a tremendous population to feed and clothe, and the necessity of building basic industries, only comprehensive planning could prevent complete chaos. Thus in 1923 the State Planning Commission was created. For years this planning commission did little but collect data and offer rough experimental plans such as the 1926 plan. The fruition of the preparatory work appeared in the latter months of 1927 when the Five Year Plan was published. Designed to cover the years between 1928 and 1933, the plan had two main goals: to increase the general economic productivity of Russian industry, and develop those resources and industries necessary to make Russia self-supporting. The plan was carried through in four years, but not without seriously endangering the production of consumers' goods industries which were at times drastically curtailed to provide men and material for the basic industries. The work of the planning commission was highly centralized, but less powerful commissions were organized in provinces and districts. Their chief work was to gather statistics and plan for the needs of the local areas, subject to review by the State Planning Commission at Moscow. There was unquestionably a vast scope in the planning in the Soviet Union.

Planned Banking and Credit

Because of the importance of banking and credit to economic enterprise, the banks were among the first businesses to fall under governmental supervision and regulation. We have already noted in earlier chapters how in the United States the Federal Reserve System was established by the government in order to provide an elastic currency, credit facilities operated for the public interest, and an integrated banking system. But the government has not stopped at this point. As a result of the need for agricultural credit, a system of federal land banks was established in 1916 to enable farmers to secure credit for the purchase of land and the planting or marketing of crops. Capital for these credit functions was obtained in part from federal appropriations and the sale of tax exempt bonds backed by the government.

This pattern of government credit was put to further use in the depression of the 1930's. The Reconstruction Finance Corporation was created to extend government credit to municipalities, banks, and industrial enterprises whose financial position was sound, but which for one reason or another were unable to secure credit through private sources. In this way the government became creditor to banks, railroads, insurance companies, building and loan associations, and manufacturing companies. The original endowment of $500,000,000 by the federal government grew into several billions, and the R.F.C. became a super-credit agency. The functions of the R.F.C. were greatly expanded in the period of the war when it lent money to private industry for wartime expansion, and to foreign countries to provide funds for their purchase of American-made goods.

Further extensions of government credit were in the field of housing. One part of the government program involved the Federal Housing Administration which guaranteed mortgages made by local banks for purposes of home construction and renovation. The local bank made the loan; by meeting certain requirements, however, the person securing the mortgage loan could have the mortgage guaranteed by the federal government up to 90% of its face value. In case of default, the government paid the bank and assumed title to the mortgage. The government might then work out a program of payments more suitable to the home owner. If that measure should fail the government might assume full title to the property and endeavor to dispose of it through a sale on the open market. The Home Owners Loan Corporation, a temporary semi-public corporation set up by the government during the depression, followed the above procedure in an effort to stave off the mass foreclosures of mortgages against home owners and the consequent insolvency of banks.

The second part of the federal government's housing program involved both the extension of credit and outright subsidization to local communities which wanted to develop a publicly owned and operated low-rent housing project. The United States Housing Authority, beginning as a division of the Public Works Administration in the early days of the depression of the 1930's, soon achieved independent status. The authority was empowered to advance as much as 90% of the cost of a public housing project to be repaid over a period of sixty years. In addition it paid small annual subsidies to pay for the interest on government loans and use of public utilities in the community.

The role of planning in the field of housing includes far more than mere granting of subsidies and extension of credit. All of the larger cities in the United States have established community plans, to be carried out through application of zoning ordinances, the demolition of slum areas, and the construction of express highways, parks, and playgrounds. This type of planning goes considerably beyond the original ideas of economic planning.

Planning for the Protection of the Consumer

Interest in the consumer as a factor in economic activity is of recent origin. Adam Smith and his followers assumed that the consumer would be the final arbiter of economic activity, for by his power to buy or withhold his patronage he could determine what was produced, how much was offered for sale, and the price at which goods were sold. No one really believed this; and virtual control over economic life gravitated into the hands of the producers. Through advertising and monopoly, producers controlled consumers' desires and prices. The consumer soon became the "forgotten man" of economics. Resentment against this condition has found an outlet in two directions: through legislation and through consumer organizations. Through the former the consumer has secured protection against the most dangerous and fraudulent practices of producers; through the latter consumers have been using their power to bargain and demand fair treatment, on the threat of withholding patronage and establishing a consumer controlled system of production and distribution.

Protection is after all a negative process. The government does not assist the consumer in getting the best values for his money. Although the Bureau of Standards does in fact make tests of food and drug products, it is not at liberty to publicize its findings as comparisons of various products, and much of its information is available only on specific request. Government publications dealing with topics of interest to consumers cannot name products by name. Cases brought by the government against producers of illegal products are seldom, if ever, reported in the nation's newspapers or magazines. If the consumer wants positive assistance, he must secure it through organizations initiated and supported by himself.

The most extensive of all consumers' organizations consists of the thousands of societies in the Consumers' Co-operative Movement. As we noted in a previous chapter, consumers' co-operation was a product of the pioneering genius of Robert Owen, but it got its official start in England in 1844 with the organization of the Rochdale weavers. Since then consumers' co-operatives have grown rapidly in the Scandinavian countries, less spectacularly in England, and somewhat slowly as yet in the United States. In Germany, Italy, and Russia the rather extensive co-operative movements were subordinated to the totalitarian and socialistic regimes. The goal of the consumers' co-operative is to increase the members' real income by securing commodities of high quality at reasonable prices, mainly through the direct purchase of specified products, thus eliminating the costs of advertising and the middle man's charges. The co-operative organization consists of unlimited voluntary members, each of whom has one vote regardless of the amount of money invested. Borrowed capital is paid for at no more than the legal rate of interest. Commodities and services are sold at the current retail market price; and the difference between cost price and sale price (after deduction of expenses) is returned to purchasers in proportion to their purchases. Thus the co-operative society is controlled democratically by consumers, and is run for the service of members rather than for profit. Beginning with retail outlets, the co-operative movement has developed its own wholesale distributors, and in certain instances its own productive enterprises. In America the strongest part of the co-operative movement was originally the farm population. Pressed on the one side by strongly organized buyers of farm products and on the other side by monopolistic sellers of essential farm materials, the farmer found his only salvation in organized buying groups, formed frequently in connection with the local grange. The movement has spread, however, among all consumers, especially throughout the Middle West—where one finds gas and oil co-operatives with their own distribution service and refinery, credit unions, insurance, creameries, bakeries, and grocery stores. A co-operative grocery store today is stocked largely by co-operative trade-marked articles secured through a co-operative wholesale owned by the stores which it serves. The wholesale secures products of its own specifications directly from the producer—which may be a private concern or a producers' co-operative organization such as a co-operative dairy or flour mill.

Although not nearly as strong as in Great Britain, where approximately two families out of every three belong to a co-operative society, the consumers' co-operatives in the United States are increasingly important. There are over five thousand non-farm consumer co-operative societies, and their business amounts to several hundred million dollars annually. However, this represents only about 1% to 2% of the total business of the country. Farmers do a much larger share of their buying through co-operatives than do city folks. When one considers that in a country like Sweden nearly one-fourth of the nation's retail trade is carried on through co-operative societies, it is obvious that the co-operative movement in America has not achieved anything like its potential strength.

Only the most fanatical supporters of co-operation, however, look upon it as an eventual substitute for the present economic system. More conservative persons recognize that the great value of the co-operative movement lies in offering competition and a "yard stick" for private business enterprise. Co-operative business activity will probably never be able to enter the field of large-scale industry where heavy overhead requires a type of financing not open to co-operative groups. Furthermore, the co-operative undertakings are subject to the fluctuations in business activity which undermine the stability of the economy as a whole. The consumer co-operative movement is not yet in a position to act as a stabilizing factor, albeit there are some who claim that the co-operatives were responsible for the ease with which the storm of depression was weathered in Scandinavian countries. In recent years the organized consumers speaking through their co-operative societies have been notably instrumental in forcing consideration for the consumers' problems into the forefront of government economic activity.

Just what form economic planning should take in a democracy

is still a very open question. To a certain extent any individual with initiative resents all-inclusive planning. On the other hand, the steadily increasing complexity of modern life seems to make considerable planning necessary in order to provide any opportunity for individual accomplishment or individual security.

In our survey of the basic teachings of the great economists, we have considered their views on each of the major fields of economic activity. Few of them would have thought comprehensive planning possible; fewer still would have considered it desirable. But time and events change men's ideas no less than their actions. The economic ideas of the past supported *laissez-faire;* it seems probable that the ideas of the future will emphasize economic planning.

Biographical Notes

AQUINAS, THOMAS (1227?–1274). Famous scholastic philosopher, born of noble parents in southern Italy. He was educated first in a monastery, then at the University of Naples, at Cologne where he studied under Albertus Magnus, and at Paris where he received his degree. He assumed the orders of St. Dominic and spent the rest of his life lecturing in the leading universities of Europe. Just before his death he was called by the Pope to aid in finding a basis for co-operation between the Greek and the Latin Churches. He was an extensive writer; his best known work is the *Summa Theologiae*.

ARISTOTLE (384–322 B.C.). Great Greek philosopher. He was the tutor of Alexander the Great and student of Plato. During the later years of his life he founded a school in the Lyceum at Athens. Aristotle and his followers were known as the Peripatetics because of their custom of carrying on conversation and discussions while walking.

BACON, FRANCIS (1561–1626). English philosopher, statesman, and essayist, noted as the joint founder along with Descartes of modern scientific methods. His *Novum Organum* marks a turning point in human thought; and his *New Atlantis* stands in the forefront of Utopian literature. His life was bound up with the court intrigue prevailing during the reigns of Elizabeth and James I.

BAKUNIN, MICHAEL ALEXANDROVITCH (1814–1876). Born of Russian parents of wealth and liberal thought, he became the center of a young philosophical group in Moscow after failing to achieve success in a military career. Fleeing Russia because of the opposition to his political views, he spent his life as a roving revolutionist, inciting organized labor to revolt and establish an anarchist social order. His name is always associated with the philosophy of anarchism.

BARBON, NICHOLAS (1640–1698). English economist trained as a physician in the universities of the Netherlands. He took part in rebuilding London after the great fire of 1680, and it is said that he was the first to develop the idea of fire insurance. He founded a land bank and wrote extensively on economic subjects, expressing extremely modern ideas on such subjects as value, rent, and foreign trade.

BASTIAT, FRÉDÉRIC (1801–1850). The French representative of the Optimistic School of economists. He secured a good education in French universities and entered the business of his uncle. Finding business distasteful, he retired to a small estate inherited from his grandfather. He showed great interest in local politics and economics, but the importance of his writings brought him into national prominence. He became the leader of the free trade group in France and many of his most witty writings were on this topic. Overwork in connection with this cause and its final defeat in the Revolution of 1848 brought declining health, and although he succeeded in completing his most extensive work *Les harmonies économiques* in the spring of 1850, he died in the fall of that year.

BENTHAM, JEREMY (1748–1832). English philosopher and essayist. He was the son of a prominent attorney and was himself trained for the profession of law. From the age of three he gave evidence of unusual mental capacity. At thirteen he entered Queens College, Oxford, and after receiving his degree he studied law in London. When called to the bar he found various excuses for not entering practice. His essays upon law, legislation, and government secured for him an international reputation. An ample inheritance made it possible for him to spend his life in study, writing, and developing plans for model prisons, canals through Suez and Panama, and codes of laws. In economics his importance rests upon his proposal for inheritance taxes, his development of utilitarianism which provided the philosophical basis for much of the economic theory of his time, and especially his theory of diminishing utility.

BLANC, LOUIS (1811–1882). French historian, political figure, and economist with distinct socialistic ideas. He was the son of a French statesman, but differences in opinion within the family group forced him to secure his education without family assistance. His famous work *L'Organisation du travail* set forth his socialist views. History, however, was his chief interest and although he left his historical researches from time to time, as for instance in the Revolution of 1848, he ultimately published an outstanding work on the French Revolution. He became a member of the Constituent Assembly in 1849 and was a strong advocate of Workers' interests. His activities ultimately brought such opposition that he was forced to flee to England where he continued to advocate socialistic doctrine through a newspaper published in Paris.

BODIN, JEAN (1530–1596). French political philosopher. He was trained for the law at the University of Toulouse and for a time lectured there. Later he became an advocate in Paris but abandoned this profession for the work of scholar and author. He wrote several important economic treatises on money and government regulation of trade. His chief work *Six livres de la République* included several excellent sections on economics.

BÖHM-BAWERK, EUGEN VON (1851–1914). Austrian economist who served as Minister of Finance for the Austrian government on three occasions. He was professor of economics at the University of Vienna. His chief contribution to economic thought is his analysis of capital and interest.

BRAY, JOHN F. (1809–1895). An American who went to England at an early age and joined the agitation for social reforms which marked the period between 1832 and 1845. His work *Labour's Wrongs and Labour's Remedies,* published in 1839, expressed socialistic views.

CAIRNES, JOHN ELLIOT (1823–1875). Irish political economist. He was the son of a brewer and began his career by entering his father's business, only to find that his interests lay in scholarship. He entered Trinity College, Dublin, and after receiving his degree studied law. However, he devoted most of his time to the study of economic problems. When the chair of political economy became vacant at the University of Dublin he was appointed to the post through the influence of Bishop Wheatley. In later years he held the chair of political economy at Queens College, Galway, and then at the University of London.

CALVIN, JOHN (1509–1564). Swiss theologian and political reformer known as the founder of the evangelical faith at Geneva.

CANTILLON, RICHARD (1680–1734). French banker and economist. His *Essai sur la nature du commerce en général* was not published until several years after his death. His work was rediscovered in the 19th century by W. S. Jevons. Many of Cantillon's ideas were seen to be the basis for the Physiocratic protest against Mercantilism and were extremely modern even in Jevons' time.

CAREY, HENRY C. (1793–1879). American economist born in Philadelphia, the son of a well-known economist, political reformer, editor and publisher. He inherited his father's publishing business at the age of 28 and having acquired a fortune he retired early and devoted his life to writing on economic matters. He is best known for his refutation of Ricardo's theory that land becomes less productive as civilization increases, and for his defense of the protective tariff. The similarity between his optimistic theories and those of Frédéric Bastiat in France led to charges and counter charges of plagiarism. Evidence seems to support Carey's claims to priority, but it is quite likely that Bastiat was unaware of Carey's writings.

CARVER, THOMAS NIXON (1865–   ). Distinguished American economist, Professor Emeritus of Economics at Harvard University.

CASSEL, GUSTAV (1866–1945). Swedish economist prominent as an advocate of the quantity theory of money and its application to the economic condition of nations during the period following World War I.

CHILD, SIR JOSIAH (1630–1699). English merchant, economist, and governor of the East India Company. He entered business as a merchant of naval supplies and acquired a comfortable fortune most of which was invested in the East India Company. His articles supporting the political and economic practices of the Company brought him to the attention of the share holders and he was elected a member of the board of directors. In later years he was the most dominant figure in the management of the Company. He held economic views that supported Mercantilism but which were considered quite far advanced for his time.

CLARK, JOHN BATES (1847–1938). Outstanding American economist representing the ideas of the classical school. His college education, secured at Brown University and Amherst College, was interrupted by the necessity of earning a living. After graduation from Amherst he studied under Professor Karl Knies at Heidelberg. His life was spent as a university teacher holding positions successively at Carleton College, Smith College, Amherst College, and Columbia University. His most important work is *The Distribution of Wealth* published in 1899.

COLE, GEORGE DOUGLAS HOWARD (1889–   ). English economist, one of the leaders of the movement known as Guild Socialism which was particularly active just before the First World War. Among Mr. Cole's more recent books are *Gold, Credit, and Unemployment* (1930) and *Guide Through World Chaos* (1932).

COURNOT, ANTOINE AUGUSTIN (1801–1877). French economist and mathematician. During his lifetime he held many important academic posts at important French universities. His fame rests upon the fact that he was the first to apply mathematics to economics, but his work was so far in advance of his time that it received little recognition. Although he restated his theory many times, it remained unnoticed until rediscovered by later economists.

DAVENANT, CHARLES (1656–1714). English economist, son of Sir William Davenant, the poet. He was educated at Balliol College, Oxford, but left without taking a degree. Much of his life was spent in various posts connected with taxes and imports and exports and as a member of Parliament. In economic thought he must be classed as a mercantilist but showed a willingness to adapt his ideas to the practical needs of the offices he held.

DEFOE, DANIEL (1660–1731). English essayist and novelist best known as the author of *Robinson Crusoe*. Although a mercantilist he contributed many suggestive ideas in his *A Plan of English Commerce*. He is recognized as one of the first to attempt a description of business cycles.

DUPONT DE NEMOURS, PIERRE S. (1739–1817). The originator of the term *Physiocratie* from which the group of French economists, of which he was a member, took their name. Born in Paris, he was educated to be a physician, but under the influence of Quesnay and Turgot he turned to problems of economics. He contributed greatly to the clarification of the physiocrat's economic theories through his numerous essays. A large part of his life was spent in public service, first in the employ of the King of Poland, then as assistant to Turgot during the latter's brief period of office as minister of finance. His fortunes during the French Revolution fluctuated violently. He was at one time President of the Constituent Assembly; on at least two other occasions he was forced to flee for his life. Once he was imprisoned and only narrowly missed the guillotine. On another occasion he fled to America, only to return to France to take an active part in politics until the restoration of the emperor in 1815. He finally left France for good and joined his brother who had set up a powder plant in the State of Delaware.

ENGELS, FRIEDERICH (1820–1895). The associate of Karl Marx in the intellectual leadership of the socialist movement of the 19th century. He was the son of a German merchant who insisted that his son also follow a business career. Although employed in a Bremen business house, Engels published some pamphlets on economic and political matters under an assumed name that made a striking impression upon the general public. Later as an agent of his father's business he lived in Manchester, England, and found time for research and writing and participation in the social movements that marked England at the time. He wrote *The Condition of the Working Classes in England,* collaborated with Marx on the *Communist Manifesto,* and edited much of Marx's *Das Kapital.* His later years were spent in research and organizational activities. His influence in the socialist movement is not sufficiently recognized.

FISHER, IRVING (1867–1947). Professor of Economics at Yale University and best known for his exposition of the quantity theory of money and the application of mathematical principles to economics.

FOURIER, CHARLES (1772–1837). French economist who sponsored numerous socialistic experiments. The son of a wealthy merchant, he received a good education and a sizeable inheritance, the latter being lost in the Revolution. After a brief career in the army he entered business. Having established a small enterprise of his own, he devoted most of his time to the elaboration of a socialistic theory of society. He wrote several books but none attracted attention until the publication of *Le nouveau monde industriel.* The ideas of Fourier were Utopian; with the advent of scientific socialism they ceased to have much influence.

GEORGE, HENRY (1839–1897). American publisher and journalist who startled the world with his proposal to abolish poverty by instituting the single tax. His father was a publisher of religious books in Philadelphia. Henry George left school at 13 and went to sea when but 16 years of age. For six years he followed this calling, visiting Australia and India. Returning to Philadelphia, he got a job as a printer's helper, but he soon went to sea again. In 1861, he reached San Francisco, where he again secured work in a newspaper office as a compositor. He married, and there followed years of a pitiful struggle to make a living for himself and family. The rapid increase in land values, the ease with which some persons acquired great wealth, and the presence of extreme poverty in this boom city influenced his thinking. He began the development of his theory in 1868, but spent an additional ten years in study trying to clarify his basic ideas. In 1879 he published *Progress and Poverty.* The remainder of his life he spent in writing, lecturing, founding Land and Labor Clubs, and in running for minor political offices. He died while campaigning for the office of Mayor in New York City in 1897. Strangely enough Henry George and his work seem to have made a greater impression in England than in the United States.

GODWIN, WILLIAM (1756–1836). The son of an austere English minister with dissenting views. The son's early education was secured under the direction of stern religious leaders and he eventually started his career as a clergyman, but this soon ended with his growing disbelief in the principles of religion. He then turned to writing and immediately became successful. The French Revolution stimulated Godwin to formulate his own ideas of political philosophy, which he did in *An Inquiry Concerning Political Justice.* The popularity of this work was tremendous. The anarchistic character of the philosophy brought an attempted suppression but without success. Unfortunate marriages brought a burden of debts, and the spirit of Godwin's writing disappeared with the advent of the necessity of writing for a living.

GOSSEN, HERMANN HEINRICH (1810–1858). German economist whose work anticipated the marginal theories of W. S. Jevons. His work was too advanced for his time, and the lack of interest in it caused him great disappointment and led him to withdraw his work from publication.

GRAY, JOHN (1799–1850?). English reformer and the author of a number of books and pamphlets with distinct socialistic leanings. He was a leader of the social agitation which characterized England between 1830 and 1845.

GRESHAM, SIR THOMAS (1519?–1579). English merchant and financier and member of the famous Mercer's company, who was appointed the personal foreign financial agent of King Henry VIII. In order to offset an unfavorable foreign balance of payments he required the Merchant Adventurers to pay the King's creditors in Antwerp out of the income earned from the sale of English cloth in that city. This debt the King agreed to repay in English currency. Later he advocated that Queen Elizabeth restore the original gold value of English currency, showing that debasement under Henry VIII had driven fine gold out of the country. The "law" which states that bad money will drive good money out of circulation has been known as Gresham's Law since H. D. MacLeod ascribed it to him in 1858, but the "law" was known and accepted long before Gresham's time.

GROTIUS, HUGO (1583–1645). Dutch legal authority, whose great work *De jure belli et pacis* (Concerning the Laws of War and Peace) is the most famous and influential of all treatises on international law.

HALES, JOHN (died 1571). English statesman and scholar. He secured a practical knowledge of economic problems while serving as a member of a commission on enclosures. In his work *A Discourse of the Common Weal of This Realm of England,* he supported Mercantilism but was extremely practical about application of its principles. He was forced to flee from England because of his opposition to mass enclosures.

HAMILTON, ALEXANDER (1757–1804). American patriot and early political leader who exerted great influence upon the economic policies of the United States, serving in Washington's cabinet as the first Secretary of the Treasury.

HAWTREY, R. G. (1879–   ). English economist connected with the Treasury of Great Britain. He is an authority on currency and credit.

HAYEK, FRIEDRICH A. VON (1899–   ). Austrian authority on money. He was formerly Professor of Economics at the University of Vienna but has for some time held the same post at the University of London.

HERMANN, F. B. W. VON (1795–1868). German economist and public administrator and professor of economics at several well-known German and Austrian institutions of higher learning.

HOBBES, THOMAS (1588–1679). Early English philosopher and one of the first and ablest exponents of the social contract theory. His contribution to economics lies more in his emphasis upon the philosophic necessity for freedom than in any specific economic principle he formulated. He was the son of a poor and uncultured vicar. Hobbes because of his aptitude was educated by relatives, attending Magdalen College, Oxford, and coming under the influences of the times.

HOBSON, JOHN A. (1858–1940). English economist and social reformer. He was educated at Oxford where he was influenced by the social philosophy of Toynbee and other liberal thinkers. The education of workers through university extension service was one of his chief interests.

HORNICK, PHILIPP WILHELM VON (1638–1713). Austrian advocate of the mercantilist economic philosophy. He was German born but spent most of his life in Vienna. His chief work *Oesterreich über alles wann es nur will* set forth a program of industrial self-development which he believed would make Austria the foremost nation of Europe.

HUME, DAVID (1711–1776). Better known as a philosopher than economist he exerted great influence upon Adam Smith and later members of the classical school. Born of moderately wealthy parents, he secured his education at the University of Edinburgh, entering at the age of twelve. His early interests were in the fields of philosophy and literature. After trying law and business in the hope of finding a career he turned to study and writing. His first works upon metaphysical subjects were poorly received. Consequently he turned to the writing of essays on more practical problems. These met with immediate success. He died in 1776. His place in philosophy and economics is secure because of his analytical powers, his ability to bring diverse ideas into harmony, and his clearness of expression. His influence upon later economists is incalculable.

HUTCHESON, FRANCIS (1694–1746). Professor of Moral Philosophy at the University of Glasgow when Adam Smith was a student there. It was his breadth of interest in economic matters that first excited Adam Smith to their importance. He was the son of Scottish parents who had migrated to Ireland. After a university education he was about to begin a career as a clergyman among dissenting groups in north Ireland, but he was persuaded to open a small academy. While in this post he wrote his best known works although at the time they were published anonymously. A little later he was called to the chair of moral philosophy at the University of Glasgow. His fame as a teacher attracted to him some of the most brilliant men of his time. The remainder of his life was devoted to teaching.

JEVONS, WILLIAM STANLEY (1835–1882). English economist. The son of an educated iron merchant, he was sent to University College, London, where he studied chemistry and botany. The failure of his father's business led him to accept appointment as assayer of the mint in Sydney, Australia, a post which he held for five years, returning to complete his college education at London. He became tutor at Owens College and later professor. During this time his interest had shifted from the natural sciences, through morals and philosophy to economics so that he was glad to accept appointment as professor of economics at University College, London. Failing health led him to resign his post in order to devote more attention to writing, but before he had finished what was to be his principal contribution to economic thought he was drowned while swimming.

JUSTI, J. H. G. VON (1720–1771). One of the early German mercantilists. Because of his career in public service he was interested primarily in the role of the state in business. He anticipated Adam Smith in his careful analysis of the problem of taxation.

KEYNES, JOHN MAYNARD (1883–1946). One of the outstanding English critics of contemporary economic practice and theory. He distinguished himself primarily by his opposition to the economic aspects of the Treaty of Versailles the failure of which he predicted in 1919. In recent years he has caused heated controversy among economists by the radical nature of his monetary theories. He is Fellow at Kings College, Cambridge.

LASSALLE, FERDINAND (1825–1864). One of the early leaders of the German socialist movement. He was the son of a German-Jewish merchant who intended that the boy should follow a business career and for that reason sent him to a commercial school in his home city. He left this school however and took up the study of philology and philosophy at the University of Berlin. Here he met a young countess who was having legal difficulty with her husband. Lassalle took up her case, studied law, and after 15 years of litigation finally saw the case through to a successful conclusion. In the meantime he had identified himself with the cause of the German working men and when Bismarck became leader of the German government Lassalle decided to counteract the influence of the middle-class liberals by the creation of a strong political movement among the working-class. Between 1860 and 1865 he devoted his life entirely to writing and speaking for the cause of the working-class. In 1864 however he fell in love with a young noblewoman. Because of Lassalle's socialistic ideas her hand was refused him and she was betrothed to another. Lassalle challenged her father and his rival to duels and was mortally wounded.

LAUDERDALE, JAMES MAITLAND, 8th Earl of (1759–1839). Scottish statesman and economist. He was a member of Parliament and challenged the policies of the Tory party. In addition he wrote *The Inquiry into the Nature and Origin of Public Wealth*, a book which refuted the contentions of Adam Smith in *The Wealth of Nations*. However, before his death he became a reactionary and voted against the Reform Act of 1832.

LAW, JOHN (1671–1729). Scottish economist best known as the originator of the "Mississippi Scheme," a banking and speculative venture in France. The son of a goldsmith and banker, he lived at home on the family estate until he was twenty, at which time he went to London to learn modern business. A dissolute life culminating in a love affair and a duel in which he killed his antagonist forced him to flee to Holland. Here he seriously investigated the business practices of the Dutch, and returned later to Scotland with a plan to revive the financial position of his country. Very little attention was paid to him or his plan. His disappointment was so great that he went to France, where his acquaintance with the Duke of Orléans gave him the opportunity to put his plan to work. His plan called for the extensive use of paper money. To his credit it must be said that he succeeded in stabilizing the financial situation in France but his attempt to incorporate a number of overseas trading companies into the national banking system caused tremendous speculation and then a terrible panic. Law escaped to Belgium and died almost unknown in Venice in 1729.

LIST, FRIEDRICH (1789-1846). German economist acknowledged as the leader of the romantic school of economic thought. He was the son of a tanner but, unwilling to follow his father's occupation, he became a clerk in the public service and rose to be ministerial secretary. He was appointed professor of administration and politics at the University of Tübingen but a change in government forced him to resign. A brief political career ended when he was imprisoned for advocating administrative reforms. He was released when he signified his intention of emigrating to America. Settling in Pennsylvania, he worked as a farmer and as a journalist until coal was discovered on his land, making him independently wealthy. He became acquainted with the writings of Alexander Hamilton and a friend of the Careys, noted American economists. An appointment as American consul at Leipzig took him back to Germany where he suggested many of the economic reforms introduced years after his death, such as the nationalization of the railways and a Zollverein (custom's union). He also finished his great economic work *A National System of Political Economy*. The loss of his fortune and the despondency over ill health and social ostracism caused him to commit suicide.

LOCKE, JOHN (1632-1704). Great English philosopher. The son of a small land owner and attorney of puritanical leanings, he was educated in the liberal tradition by his father. Concluding an unsatisfactory public school education, he matriculated at Christ Church, Oxford, and later served there as tutor. Although he originally intended taking orders in the church he lost interest and turned to medicine as a career. Accidentally becoming acquainted with 1st Earl of Shaftesbury, he became his secretary and advisor and for years followed a hectic political career which ended with the death of Shaftesbury. The opposition to the policies of his leader fell upon Locke and he fled to Holland, spending years of uninterrupted study in exile. When the government again changed in the Revolution of 1688 he returned and accepted a minor post in the government although he had been offered a superior one. Meanwhile his writings had earned him an international reputation. The Revolution falling short of his ideals, Locke retired to a country estate and continued his studies until his death.

LONGFIELD, MOUNTIFORD (1802-1884). Irish economist and jurist noted for his anticipation of the principle of diminishing utility.

MALTHUS, THOMAS R. (1766-1834). Famous English economist. He was the son of a wealthy gentleman of some means who was a friend of Rousseau. Educated by private tutors until old enough to enter Cambridge, he quickly distinguished himself as a scholar and became a Fellow of Jesus College. Not long after his appointment he took holy orders and undertook the charge of a small parish in Surrey. The following year he published the first edition of his great work *An Essay on the Principle of Population*. The public interest in his book aroused in him a desire for more thorough research on the subject, so he left the pastorate and spent considerable time abroad gathering information for the second edition of the *Essay*. He received an appointment as professor of modern history and political economy at the East India Company's training college which he retained until his death. He was intensely interested in contemporary social and economic problems and from time to time carried on controversies with the leading economists of his time on public issues.

MALYNES, GERARD DE (about 1586–1641). English merchant. He was the son of an English merchant who had settled in Antwerp acting principally as an agent for the sale of raw wool. The son returned to England and became a member of the Mercers company and assayer at the London mint. He carried on a bitter controversy with Misselden who wished to restrict the exportation of raw wool from England, hoping to finish the cloth in England and thus break the monopoly of the Hanseatic League in European cities.

MARSHALL, ALFRED (1842–1924). The recognized leader of the neo-classical school of economic thought in England. He is perhaps the best known and the most widely read of the recent economists. Educated at the Merchant Taylor's School and at St. John's College, Cambridge, he held teaching posts at University College, Bristol, and at Balliol College, Oxford. From 1885 until his retirement he was Professor of Political Economy at Cambridge. The publication of his *Principles of Economics* in 1890 placed him in the front rank of modern economists. From time to time he served on various commissions studying economic trends and conditions. His interest in economics developed slowly. Coming from a middle class English family, he was awarded scholarships for further study because of demonstrated mental ability. At the Merchant Taylor's School he followed the classics but his interest turned toward mathematics. His original intention, however, had been to take orders in the Church and become a foreign missionary. Confusion of mind led him into the fields of philosophy, history, and theology. Not until he had been teaching for some time did he introduce a great amount of economics in his lectures on moral philosophy. With his appointment at Cambridge his interest remained humanitarian but never swerved from the economic emphasis. His work made Cambridge the leading university in the English speaking countries for the study of economics.

MARX, HEINRICH KARL (1818–1883), always known as Karl Marx. The recognized founder and leader of the socialist movement during the latter part of the 19th century. He was the son of a German-Jewish lawyer who became a Christian convert. The father's interest in philosophy and history was passed on to the son. The latter received a university education in preparation for a career as a university teacher. His radical views forced him to abandon all hopes of teaching and he became a journalist, editing the *Rhenische Zeitung,* but the direction he gave the paper was opposed by the authorities of state. He fled to France. His exile there ended when the Prussian Government made complaints to France about the character of publications which Marx was issuing from Paris. After a brief stay in Belgium, he returned to Germany. Several years of political activity followed ending with Marx's final exile to London where he spent the remainder of his days in research and writing done largely in the British Museum.

MENGER, KARL (1840–1921). Austrian economist who was the first critic of the German historical school of economic thought. To replace the historical view, Menger himself originated another line of thought emphasizing the importance of utility. This school is sometimes called the Austrian school, and more recently the Psychological school.

MILL, JOHN STUART (1806–1873). English philosopher and economist. He was the son of James Mill, who was in his own right a famous economist. His father was his tutor. Few persons in the world have shown the mental ability exhibited by John Stuart Mill. At the age of three he was taught the Greek language so that when he was eight he could read the great literature of ancient Greece. He had also read the great English works of philosophy and history. At thirteen he was an accomplished scholar in the economic literature of his day. He was able to spend nearly a year in France as the guest of the Bentham family when he was sixteen. At seventeen he was hired for a post with the East India Company where he hoped to train himself as an executive. For over thirty years he held an administrative office in the Company. Aside from his business interests, Mill devoted his entire life to study, writing, and practical social reform. Much of the writing was in the nature of newspaper editorials, articles in journals, and essays. Events abroad, especially in France, held his attention, many of his articles were concerned with the political struggle which engaged that great nation. His most extensive writing was delayed until the later years of his life, his *Political Economy* appearing in 1848. According to his own account, his marriage in 1851 began a period in his life which was marked by maturity of thought and sincere humanitarian interests. To the end of his life, especially after his retirement from the East India Company when it was dissolved in 1856 and his wife's death in the same year, he maintained his interest in economic and political affairs and in writing. His latter efforts, it is true, became more philosophical rather than specific or practical. The death of his wife occurred at Avignon in France, and until his own death nearly 20 years later Mill made this French community his home.

MISSELDEN, EDWARD (about 1608–1654). Early English writer on economic matters. He was associated with the efforts of a group of wool merchants to break the monopoly of the Merchant Adventurers, a favored group of traders, in the wool industry. The attempt ended in a depression of English industry and trade. His analysis of the subject and the controversy he aroused constitute some of the best economic writing of the time. He was one of the strongest advocates of Mercantilism.

MITCHELL, WESLEY C. (1874–1948). Noted American economist whose analysis of business cycles was the first comprehensive work in the field. He has held positions as Professor of Economics at the University of California and more recently as Director of the National Bureau of Economic Research. Much of the interest in the institutional approach to economics is due to Mitchell's influence.

MONTCHRETIEN, ANTOINE DE (1576?–1621). French dramatist and economist. The son of an apothecary, he became famous as a swordsman. Having killed a man in a duel, he fled to England but subsequently returned to open an iron foundry. This he cast aside to engage in the Huguenot wars. His economic writing is largely a résumé of the views of Jean Bodin but he emphasizes the mercantilist views more than his predecessor.

MONTESQUIEU, CHARLES LOUIS DE SECONDAT (1689–1755). Great French philosopher and historian. He was born of well-to-do parents, followed the profession of law, and became a noted political figure of his time. He is known primarily for his advanced social ideas expressed in *De l'esprit de lois*.

MOORE, HENRY L. (1869–   ). Professor of Economics at Columbia University, known especially as an authority on business cycles advocating a modern version of the sun spot explanation of business cycles.

MORE, SIR THOMAS (1478–1535). English Lord Chancellor in the reign of Henry VIII, and author of the famous book *Utopia*. He was the son of a prominent family and received his education first with the family of the Archbishop of Canterbury and then at Oxford. Trained as a lawyer, he found the profession distasteful and consequently revolted from it and became a humanist philosopher and political leader.

MÜLLER, ADAM (1779–1829). The originator of the Romantic school of economic thought. He was a German who served as tutor to a German prince and later became a member of the Austrian Government, acting as Councillor in the State Chancellory at Vienna.

MUN, THOMAS (1571–1641). An English merchant and economist. He was the son of a London mercer but at an early age set out to establish his own business in Mediterranean trade. He acquired a large fortune. Having invested it in the East India Company, he became a prominent figure in its councils. His economic works were written largely to justify the current practices of the East India Company in shipping metal out of the country for trading purposes but they subsequently became the clearest criticism of the mercantilist policies written in his time, although Mun himself generally must be classed as a Mercantilist.

NORTH, SIR DUDLEY (1641–1691). Early English economist. He built up a very successful trade with Turkey and the Levant and acquired a considerable fortune. His ability was recognized by the appointment to several important financial posts in the government. However, during the Tory reaction under Charles II he became a sheriff-inquisitor for London. With the success of the Revolution of 1688 he was brought to trial for the conduct of his office. He died three years later.

OWEN, ROBERT (1771–1858). English economist and social reformer usually recognized as the father of the co-operative movement. He was the son of a Welsh artisan and after apprenticeship became a master spinner with capital borrowed from his father. Making rapid progress he became proprietor and director of the New Lanark Mills, where he introduced a number of reforms in the technical and social aspects of mill operation. The financial success of the mills excited great interest in Owen's reforms, but the slowness with which these reforms were adopted led him to experiment with model communities emphasizing public education, labor exchanges, and co-operative principles. Although his experiments proved failures he never lost confidence in his ideas and proceeded to propagate them until his death.

PAINE, THOMAS (1737–1809). The son of English peasant folk who became one of the most famous pamphleteers of all time. He was poorly educated and seemed unfitted for any type of useful work until he came to America, where, with a recommendation from Benjamin Franklin he obtained work as a journalist. Within a year Paine was known in America and in Europe as a great advocate of economic and political freedom. He took an active part in both the American and French Revolutions but lost much of his popularity before his death, and only achieved his present fame long afterward.

PARETO, VILFREDO (1848–1923). Noted Italian sociologist and economist, who was Professor of Economics at the University of Lausanne, Switzerland, where he succeeded the famed mathematical economist, Léon Walras. Although his chief contribution to economics was the application of mathematical methodology to the analysis of utility, he was far more than an economist. His later works emphasize the unity of society. He was an early teacher of the Italian dictator, Mussolini. Presumably many of Pareto's ideas found partial application in Italian fascism.

PATTEN, SIMON N. (1852–1922). American economist. He was professor of economics at the University of Pennsylvania and one of the few advocates of protectionism in a time when free trade was popular among economists. In many other things he showed himself to be quite unorthodox, and always expressed a keen interest in the social aspects of economics.

PETTY, SIR WILLIAM (1623–1687). English statistician and economist. Born in Hampshire, England, he acquired most of his education in France and the Netherlands. However, he secured his degree at Oxford and became a Fellow of Brasenose College. He gained notoriety by restoring to life a woman who had been hanged. While physician of the army in Ireland he complained so bitterly about the distribution of land that he was asked to make a new survey. The data included in the survey was the first social and economic work using comparative statistics. He was able to make himself independently wealthy as a result of his Irish surveys. In his later years he continued to write on various economic matters closely associated with the problems of government such as taxation and trade.

PIGOU, A. C. (1877–   ). Professor of Economics at Cambridge University, England, the successor to Alfred Marshall. His interest in business cycles and the economics of welfare have given him an independent position.

PLATO (428?–348? B.C.). Great Greek philosopher, student of Socrates in Athens, and founder of the first great school of philosophers known as the Academy. His economic teachings are incidental to his theories of politics and ethics. The communism espoused in his earlier writings was abandoned for a realistic approach to economic life in later works.

PROUDHON, PIERRE JOSEPH (1809–1865). One of the most colorful and original of the early socialist leaders in France and frequently classed as an anarchist because of his antagonism to the state. He was the son of a poor brewer's cooper and at an early age was required to herd cattle and do other miscellaneous work to secure an income. His mental alertness earned him the opportunity to study at the university in his native city of Besangon. Upon leaving college he became a compositor in a print shop but used his spare time to write essays. His work showed promise and he was awarded a stipend good for three years. The essays which he wrote challenging the right of private property displeased the academy awarding him the stipend and gained him a reputation as a radical. He finally settled in Paris, editing journals supporting the cause of the workingmen and socialists. In the Revolution of 1848 he was the people's representative in the assembly and brought forth many socialistic proposals such as an extremely heavy tax upon interest and rent. His attempt to found a people's bank failed and he was later imprisoned for the radical nature of his ideas. However, his life thereafter was comparatively quiet until he wrote a book attacking the reactionary position of the Church. He was forced to flee to Belgium. On his return his health broke down and he died a few months afterwards.

QUESNAY, FRANÇOIS (1694–1774). The son of a French advocate and small land holder. He was given a medical education, and later he was appointed physician to Louis XV and Mme. de Pompadour, but he never succumbed to the luxury and reactionary influence of the court. He had already published numerous works on medical matters when the leisure of his court appointment gave him the opportunity for studies in economics. His first works on *Les Grains and Les Fermiers,* published as articles in the "Grande Encyclopédie" in 1756–57, were followed by his famous *Tableau économique* in 1758. His last publication in 1860 was merely an elaboration of his former ideas. Although his writings were not numerous he was the recognized head of the Physiocratic school of thought and influenced his followers greatly.

RAE, JOHN (1796–1872). A Scotsman who migrated to North America and led a rather obscure life in Canada. He was one of the earliest critics of the theories set forth by Adam Smith. His ideas have been revived in recent years, and show great similarity to those of Thorstein Veblen.

RICARDO, DAVID (1772–1823). English economist and outstanding exponent of the classical ideas of economic activity. He was born in London, the son of a wealthy Jewish-Dutch stockbroker. He went to work in his father's brokerage office at the age of fifteen and although he had little formal education he became extremely well read in the economic literature of the time. His marriage to a Christian woman was the occasion for his adoption of the Christian faith. This act brought a strong family rebuke and his withdrawal from the family group. The great ability he had already demonstrated in economic matters was now put to use in his own behalf and he is reputed to have acquired an independent fortune at the age of 25. Financially independent, he gave himself to diligent study of economics. From the start his interests were practical, his first public works being an attack upon the government's monetary policies especially as they concerned the dispute over the relationship of bullion to bank notes. Public and parliamentary interest was the result of Ricardo's writings. Next Ricardo turned his attention to the corn law controversy. His *Essay on the Influence of a Low Price of Corn on the Profits of Stock* embodied most of his later theoretical work, including his theory of rent. Ricardo advocated abolition of the corn laws as a means of reducing the cost of labor and hence increasing the return on capital. In 1819 having fully retired from business, Ricardo lived in the country and became a member of Parliament. He served with energy and enthusiasm both through his formal speeches and his diligent committee service until his death in 1823.

RODBERTUS, JOHANN KARL (1805–1875). German socialist whose ideas had a significant influence upon Karl Marx. He was the son of a university professor and was educated for the law at the Universities of Göttingen and Berlin. After a few years of travel he bought a country estate and settled down to a life of study with occasional ventures into politics. After the Revolution of 1848 he was elected to the Prussian National Assembly but resigned in protest against a classification of Prussian voters on a discriminatory basis. From that time on he had little to do with public life. His ideas were those of state socialism. He opposed the internationalism of the prevailing socialistic theory.

ROSCHER, WILHELM GEORG FRIEDRICH (1817–1894). The originator of the historical school of economic thought. A German economist, he studied at Göttingen and Berlin and became professor of political economy at Göttingen and then at Leipzig.

ROUSSEAU, JEAN JACQUES (1712–1778). French political philosopher whose theories contributed largely to the intellectual ferment which preceded the American and French revolutions.

SAINT-SIMON, CLAUDE HENRI DE ROUVROY, COMTE DE (1760–1825). The founder of French socialism. A member of a very famous French family, he alienated his family by his radical ideas and actions. He indirectly assisted the American colonies in their fight for freedom. Although imprisoned as a nobleman during part of the French Revolution he had no part in it save to win a small fortune through land speculation which he claimed would be used only for human betterment. In pursuing many of his rather wild schemes he lost his fortune and was reduced to utmost poverty before he died. His literary efforts in behalf of socialism began late in life and attracted little attention until just before he died. At one time poverty and discouragement led him to attempt suicide. In spite of the lack of appreciation during his life time his influence through men like Auguste Comte, founder of scientific sociology, cannot be denied.

SAY, JEAN BAPTISTE (1767–1832). French economist and famous as the chief Continental exponent of the ideas of Adam Smith. He was born of French Huguenot parents who were forced to live in Geneva. He and a brother were sent as commercial apprentices to business houses in England. Upon his return to France he was employed in the insurance office of one Clavière who later became an important political figure and brought Say into a government post. Although accepting a post under Napoleon's government he soon resigned because he held certain principles which were not attuned to the desires of Napoleon. With the fall of the Napoleonic regime he was commissioned to study industrial conditions in England. During the interim he had made a comfortable living as a manufacturer. The successful conclusion of this mission ended with his appointment to a teaching post first in a small conservatory and then at the *Collège de France* where he remained as professor of political economy until he died. He wrote extensively but the publication of his important works was withheld until after the defeat of Napoleon.

SENIOR, NASSAU WILLIAM (1790–1864). Famous English economist. He was the son of a clergyman and received an excellent education at Eton and at Oxford. When the chair of political economy was founded at Oxford he was appointed to fill it, holding it between 1825 and 1832 when he resigned to conduct a poor law investigation for Parliament. Further government appointments, mainly for the purpose of research into contemporary economic conditions, kept him occupied until 1847 when he returned to teach at Oxford. He continued his investigations privately and for the government. His last work being a study of popular education in England.

SISMONDI, JEAN CHARLES LEONARD DE (1773–1842). Historian and economist of first rank whose family connections remain somewhat obscure. He was born of an upper middle class family in Geneva, Switzerland, whose name was Simonde and who were known to have migrated from France to escape the Protestant persecutions. He claimed without much basis they were connected with the noble Italian family of de Sismondi. The son was educated and took a post as banker's clerk in France but the Revolution with its repercussions in Geneva forced the family to flee to England. They returned later only to find their fortune confiscated. Selling what little was left, they bought a farm in Italy. Sismondi's first book on economics followed closely the ideas of Adam Smith. This was merely incidental to his great historical work on the history of Italian cities. However, the stay in England and his historical research convinced him that the *laissez-faire* system did not produce the favorable results its sponsors claimed for it. Consequently when asked by a friend to write a brief article on economics for the Edinburgh Encyclopaedia he found his ideas so changed that he required an entire book to describe them and substantiate them. This was his *Nouveaux principes d'économie politique* which advocated government intervention in the interest of social welfare. He was a prolific writer on historical subjects but his fame as an economist rests on his early statement of the basic theories of socialism. He retired to Geneva and engaged in local politics. His discouragement with social reform led him to become a reactionary.

SMITH, ADAM (1723–1790). Adam Smith is commonly known as the father of political economy, which is misleading in the light of the systematic treatment of economic ideas advanced by Turgot and the others of the Physiocratic school. He is assuredly the originator of the classical doctrines which for over one hundred years dominated English and American economic thought. He was the son of a comptroller of customs at Kirkcaldy, Scotland. Educated in a private school in his home community, he subsequently attended the University of Glasgow where he attended the lectures of Dr. Hutcheson. Later he studied at Balliol College, Oxford. After a brief lectureship at Edinburgh he returned in 1752 to Glasgow first as Professor of Logic and then as Professor of Moral Philosophy, a chair once held by Dr. Hutcheson. Here he remained for twelve years, publishing in 1759 his *Theory of Moral Sentiments*. He resigned his post to become tutor to the young Duke of Buccleuch with whom he lived and travelled in France for several years. It was on these excursions that Smith met Quesnay, Turgot, Dupont de Nemours, and others of the Physiocrats. The years following his return to England were spent in research and writing for the preparation of his great work *An Inquiry into the Nature and Causes of the Wealth of Nations,* which appeared in 1776. With the aid of the Duke of Buccleuch he was appointed in 1778 a Commissioner of Customs in Scotland. This, of course, necessitated his taking up residence in Edinburgh where he lived until his death in 1790. Through numerous visits to London, however, he made the acquaintance of such prominent political figures as Edmund Burke, William Pitt, and Edward Gibbon.

SOREL, GEORGES (1847–1922). French syndicalist who advocated the violent overthrow of the existing economic leaders in favor of a worker-controlled economy. He was born of good family, well educated, and filled a governmental engineering post with credit. His radical ideas led him to resign his position in favor of a career as writer and organizer in the workers' movement.

STEUART, SIR JAMES (1712–1780). English economist who had the misfortune to write the ablest exposition of economic doctrine from a Mercantilist viewpoint just before Adam Smith revised the thinking on that subject by the publication of *The Wealth of Nations.*

TAWNEY, R. H. (1880–   ). English economist and sociologist, born at Calcutta, India. Educated at Rugby, and at Balliol College, Oxford; taught at Oxford 1908–1914; served in the First World War; Fellow at Balliol College 1918–1921. Mr. Tawney's first book to arouse wide interest among ℩conomists was *The Acquisitive Society,* an original and critical approach to ℩conomic life. Later books are *Religion and the Rise of Capitalism* (1926), ⅃nd *Equality* (1931).

TAYLOR, FREDERICK W. (1856–1915). Member of the American Academy of Mechanical Engineers and known as the "father of scientific management," because he originated many of the systems of industrial engineering.

THOMPSON, WILLIAM (1783–1833). Irish landowner and economist whose book *An Inquiry into the Principles of the Distribution of Wealth* set forth many of the doctrines popularized by later socialists.

THORNTON, HENRY (1760–1815). English economist. He was throughout his lifetime a prominent banker. His chief contribution to economic thought lies in his discussions of the paper money problem while a member of Parliament in the later part of the 18th century. He was one of the directors of the Sierra Leone Company.

THORNTON, WILLIAM THOMAS (1813–1880). A clerk in the East India Company becoming a civil servant after the dissolution of the Company, holding the post of secretary for public works for India until his death. He was a diligent student of economics and wrote at length on current economic problems. His most important contribution was his refutation of the wages-fund theory.

THÜNEN, JOHANN HEINRICH VON (1783–1850). German economist of the classical school. He was the son of a landed proprietor. At an early age he bought an estate and spent the rest of his life in agricultural experimentation. His chief economic work *The Isolated State* is a masterpiece of deductive logic backed by the vast experience of owning and operating an agricultural enterprise. He was one of the first to notice the importance of transportation in economic activity.

TURGOT, ANNE ROBERT JACQUES (1727–1781). French statesman and economist. Probably the best known of all the French economists known as the Physiocrats. Born the son of a Norman merchant, he was educated for the priesthood and took advanced work at the Sorbonne. His early writings were on religious subjects and literary criticism. After his decision in 1750 not to take holy orders he entered upon a political career. As a companion of Gournay, who at the time was an official in government bureaus attending to matters of commerce, he travelled widely throughout France and became acquainted with Voltaire and members of the Physiocratic school—Quesnay and Dupont de Nemours. He continued his study and writing, but in addition accepted appointment as intendant for Limoges, in the poorest and most overtaxed part of France. Here he attempted to introduce the economic theories of the Physiocrats especially those concerning taxation. As a result of his practical efforts there were obvious improvements in the economic condition of the people. Turgot's best known work *Réflexions sur la formation et la distribution des richesses* was written during his intendancy, for the benefit of two Chinese students.

Turgot's successes as a local administrator brought him an appointment in the royal government first as a minister of marine and then as comptroller-general. He came into office at a time when the financial affairs of the French nation were desperate. By reorganization of the tax structure, development of a state budget, economies in administration, and a drastic reduction in the privileges granted to the favorites of the court, he stabilized finances to a marked degree. However, his efforts earned for him the enmity of powerful classes—land holders, nobility, and speculators in grain who refused to support his ministry. Consequently he was forced from office in 1776. He retired to a country estate and spent the remainder of his life in scientific and literary studies.

VANDERLINT, JACOB (? –1740). Early English economist of Dutch extraction, who was especially concerned with the relationship between the money in circulation, the price level, and general prosperity.

VEBLEN, THORSTEIN (1857–1929). American economist and one of the severest critics of classical economic doctrine. The son of Scandinavian immigrants, he spent his early life in the pioneer communities of Minnesota. He received his degree from Yale University although he had studied at several colleges prior to that time. He showed himself to be a man of brilliant mind but unstable personality. He moved from university to university, first as a graduate student and then as instructor. His unwillingness to support the conventional morality of his time was in part responsible for his inability to hold a teaching post. His greatest contribution to economic thought is his clear challenge to the basic assumptions upon which classical economy rested. It is still too early to estimate the full force of his influence upon American economic and social thought, but present indications show it to be considerable even now. Among his most important works are: *The Theory of the Leisure Class* (1899), *The Theory of Business Enterprise* (1904), *The In-*

stinct of Workmanship (1914), *The Place of Science in Modern Civilization* (1920).

WALKER, FRANCIS A. (1840–1897). American soldier and economist. He was the son of a very famous economist who, following a very successful commercial career, taught at Oberlin, Harvard, and Amherst in addition to attending various international peace conferences. The son was educated at Amherst, entering the Union Army on his graduation and serving with distinction throughout the war. When the war was over he was appointed to a post on a Massachusetts newspaper and then became statistician for the United States Government directing the censuses of 1870 and 1880. He was professor of economics at Yale University and then President of Massachusetts Institute of Technology. Under his leadership the latter institution grew to be a technical school of first rank. In spite of his many public interests he found time to write important works on economic subjects. His most important contribution was a devastating attack upon the wages-fund theory.

WALRAS, LÉON (1834–1910). French economist who lived most of his life in Switzerland. He was professor of political economy at the University of Lausanne. His chief contribution to economics was the application of mathematical principles to utility.

WARBASSE, DR. JAMES P. (1866–   ). An outstanding American surgeon who became a leader of the movement for economic reform through consumers' co-operation was the first president of the Co-operative League of America.

WEBB, SIDNEY (Lord Passfield) (1859–1947). One of the leaders of the Fabian Socialist group in England. He wrote most of the material setting forth in systematic form the ideas of this group. A staunch supporter of the Labour Party, he is presumed to have written the Party platform advocating a minimum living standard for all. He was made Lord Passfield as a means of giving the Labour Party representation in the House of Lords.

WEBB, BEATRICE (1858–1943). Before her marriage to Sidney Webb she was Beatrice Potter, an able social worker and investigator into economic and social conditions in England. She was an early advocate of minimum wage laws and took a large part in the investigation of English local government leading up to a revision of English poor laws. She has collaborated with her husband on many economic works.

WICKSELL, KNUT (1851–1926). Swedish economist whose main contribution is an explanation of the influence of money upon economic matters such as interest, rent, and investment.

WIESER, FRIEDRICH VON (1851–1926). Austrian economist and one of the leaders of the Austrian or Psychological school of economic thought.

XENOPHON (403? B.C.–355 B.C.). Greek historian and philosopher who came under the influence of Socrates but found military life more to his liking than the quiet of scholarly pursuits. In spite of his participation in numerous campaigns Xenophon found time for extensive literary work

Index